Lecture Notes in Computer Science   14063

Founding Editors

Gerhard Goos
Juris Hartmanis

The series Lecture Notes in Computer Science (LNCS), including its subseries Lecture Notes in Artificial Intelligence (LNAI) and Lecture Notes in Bioinformatics (LNBI), has established itself as a medium for the publication of new developments in computer science and information technology research, teaching, and education.

LNCS enjoys close cooperation with the computer science R & D community, the series counts many renowned academics among its volume editors and paper authors, and collaborates with prestigious societies. Its mission is to serve this international community by providing an invaluable service, mainly focused on the publication of conference and workshop proceedings and postproceedings. LNCS commenced publication in 1973.

Dangxiao Wang · Aiguo Song · Qian Liu ·
Ki-Uk Kyung · Masashi Konyo ·
Hiroyuki Kajimoto · Lihan Chen · Jee-Hwan Ryu
Editors

Haptic Interaction

5th International Conference, AsiaHaptics 2022
Beijing, China, November 12–14, 2022
Proceedings

Springer

Editors
Dangxiao Wang
Beihang University
Beijing, China

Qian Liu
Dalian University of Technology
Dalian, China

Masashi Konyo
Tohoku University
Sendai, Japan

Lihan Chen
Peking University
Beijing, China

Aiguo Song
Southeast University
Nanjing, China

Ki-Uk Kyung
Korea Advanced Institute of Science
and Technology (KAIST)
Daejeon, Korea (Republic of)

Hiroyuki Kajimoto
The University of Electro-Communications
Tokyo, Japan

Jee-Hwan Ryu
Korea Advanced Institute of Science
and Technology (KAIST)
Daejeon, Korea (Republic of)

ISSN 0302-9743   ISSN 1611-3349 (electronic)
Lecture Notes in Computer Science
ISBN 978-3-031-46838-4   ISBN 978-3-031-46839-1 (eBook)
https://doi.org/10.1007/978-3-031-46839-1

This Springer imprint is published by the registered company Springer Nature Switzerland AG
The registered company address is: Gewerbestrasse 11, 6330 Cham, Switzerland

Paper in this product is recyclable.

Preface

AsiaHaptics is one of the four major international conferences in the field of haptics. It is an international academic conference featuring interactive demonstrations. In 2022, AsiaHaptics was held in China for the first time since its establishment. The conference was jointly organized by Beihang University, Beijing Society for Image and Graphics, IEEE Technical Committee on Haptics, IEEE Computer Society, and the Virtual Reality Society of Japan. The conference aimed to demonstrate the latest research achievements in the field of haptics and provide an international platform for communication and exchange among haptics professionals.

For the first time in AsiaHaptics' history, we held the conference in 4 venues due to the Covid situation, including the main venue in Beijing, and 3 satellite venues in Nanjing, Tokyo and Daejeon. AsiaHaptics 2022 provided a wide variety of activities, including plenary sessions (i.e. Haptics in Robotics & HCI, Haptics in Metaverse, and Special Industrial Session), keynote talks provided by world-famous researchers in haptic technology, including Zhonglin Wang from the Beijing Institute of Nanoenergy and Nanosystems, Hong Z. Tan from Purdue University, and Domenico Prattichizzo from the University of Siena, as well as live and video demonstrations. The AsiaHaptics conference series is well known for its interactive demonstration sessions. AsiaHaptics 2022 presented the latest developments of haptic hardware in education, culture, tourism, medicine, elderly care and disability assistance. With the rise of the metaverse, Asia-Haptics 2022 also included showcases of multimodal perception (e.g. vision, hearing and touch) systems in XR environments. We received a total of 46 regular papers and 77 short papers, and finally accepted 17 regular papers and 39 short papers to present at the conference.

On behalf of the organizers and Program Committee of AsiaHaptics 2022, we thank all authors for their submissions and camera-ready copies of papers, and all participants for their thought-provoking ideas and active participation in the conference. We also acknowledge the sponsors, members of the organizing committees, Program Committee members, and other supporting committees and individuals who gave their continuous help and support in making the conference a success. Thank you!

August 2023

Dangxiao Wang
Aiguo Song
Qian Liu
Ki-Uk Kyung
Masashi Konyo
Hiroyuki Kajimoto
Lihan Chen
Jee-Hwan Ryu

Organization

General Chairs

Dangxiao Wang   Beihang University, China
Aiguo Song   Southeast University, China

Program Chairs

Qian Liu   Dalian University of Technology, China
Ki-Uk Kyung   KAIST, South Korea
Masashi Konyo   Tohoku University, Japan

Award Chair

Edward Colgate   Northwestern University, USA

Publication Chairs

Hiroyuki Kajimoto   UEC, Japan
Lihan Chen   Peking University, China
Jee-Hwan Ryu   KAIST, South Korea

Publicity Chairs

Seungmoon Choi   POSTECH, South Korea
Feng Tian   Software Institute of CAS, China
Yon Visell   UC at Santa Barbara, USA
Shoichi Hasegawa   TokyoTech, Japan
Claudio Pacchierotti   IRISA, France
Shana Smith   National Taiwan University, Taiwan
Ingvars Birznieks   University of New South Wales, Australia

Workshop Chairs

Yingqing Xu   Tsinghua University, China
Ildar Farkhatdinov   Queen Mary University of London, UK

Web Chairs

Tao Zeng   Xiamen University, China
Shuai Li   Beihang University, China
Inwook Hwang   ETRI, South Korea

Local Organization Chairs

Yue Liu   Beijing Institute of Technology, China
Guangyang Liu   Beihang University, China
Han Jiang   Beihang University, China

Live Demo Chairs

Xiao Xu   Technical University of Munich, Germany
Minghui Sun   Jilin University, China
Wenzhen Yang   Zhejiang Science and Technology University,
                                 China

Industry Chairs

Hongwei Zhou   Pico Technology Co., Ltd., China
Haoyang Liu   Noitom Ltd., China
Francois Conti   Force Dimension Inc., Switzerland
Munchae Joung   LG Electronics Inc., South Korea

Sponsorship Chairs

Xiaoying Sun   Jilin University, China
Dongdong Weng   Beijing Institute of Tech., China

Contents

Effects of Duration and Envelope of Vibrotactile Alerts on Urgency, Annoyance, and Acceptance

Ahmed Elsaid⬥, Wanjoo Park⬥, Sohmyung Ha⬥, Yong-Ak Song⬥, and Mohamad Eid(✉)⬥

Engineering Division, New York University Abu Dhabi, Saadiyat Island, Abu Dhabi 129188, United Arab Emirates
mohamad.eid@nyu.edu

Abstract. Vibrotactile feedback has been receiving increasing attention as an effective modality to draw the user's attention to an urgent situation. The current study examines the effects of alert duration and envelope on perceived urgency, annoyance, and acceptance using a dual-task condition. Participants are instructed to complete a simple arithmetic task (primary) during which the vibrotactile alert (secondary) is provided via a wristband attached to the non-dominant hand. Experiment 1 investigates the effects of the alert duration and found that an alert duration of 1,950 ms significantly increases the perceived urgency and acceptance, while significantly decreasing annoyance. Experiment 2 compares three vibration envelope patterns (constant, increasing, and decreasing intensity) and found that a constant vibration intensity of 2.25g significantly increases the perceived urgency without significantly changing the perceived annoyance and acceptance. These findings inspire the development of vibrotactile alert systems.

Keywords: Vibrotactile Alerts · Alert Duration · Alert Envelope · Urgency · Annoyance · Acceptance

1 Introduction

In many applications where visual and auditory channels are becoming increasingly loaded, vibrotactile alerts present a viable alternative to elicit a sense of urgency. Vibrotactile feedback does not increase visual and auditory demands [1,2], is robust to audible noise [3], affordable [4], and confidential [5]. On the other hand, given how vibrotactile signals come into physical contact with the skin, they may also be perceived as highly annoying or unacceptable. Therefore, vibrotactile alerts must be designed to provide a desirable level of urgency with minimal effects on annoyance and acceptance.

A number of temporal parameters of the vibrotactile signal are studied in the literature. Key factors, including the pulse rate, inter-pulse duration (IPD), number of pulses, waveform, and the envelop, are known to affect the perceived

Supported by New York University Abu Dhabi.

urgency [6–9]. An early study examined how the pulse duration (PD), IPD, and the number of pulses influence the perceived urgency [10]. The results demonstrate that a short vibration (200 ms) heightens the perceived urgency while a longer one (600 ms) diminishes its strength. Moreover, the largest differences in perceived urgency as a function of IPD occurred at the smallest PD [7]. Other studies demonstrated that the perceived urgency increases with an increase in pulse rate [6,7], however, pulse rate was found to have more impact on urgency than on annoyance [6]. The effects of the vibration waveform on perceived urgency were also studied [8] where a fade-in envelope led to a lower sense of urgency.

It is known that the subjective judgment of perceived urgency can be affected by a primary task [11]. Therefore, in this study, the effects of vibrotactile alert duration and envelope on perceived urgency, annoyance, and acceptance, are studied in a dual-task scenario. In this study, urgency is defined as the quality of being very important and needing immediate attention, annoyance is defined as a mental state that is characterized by irritation and distraction from one's conscious thinking of a primary task, and acceptance represents the general agreement that something is satisfactory. The urgent feedback may affect how quickly the user should recognize and respond to the alert. The annoyance may influence whether the user will ignore the alert, particularly in situations with many false alerts. Finally, the acceptance may influence the user's decision to enable/disable the alert. Experiment 1 examines how the alert duration influences the perceived urgency, annoyance, and acceptance whereas experiment 2 investigates the effects of the signal envelope (constant, increasing, and decreasing intensity) on the perceived urgency, annoyance, and acceptance. The aim is to inspire the design of vibrotactile alerts that significantly enhance the perceived urgency, reduce annoyance, and achieve a higher sense of acceptance.

2   Methodology

2.1   Participants

A total of 30 participants (15 females, 15 males, ages 18–27 years) are recruited for the study. The inclusion criteria are: (1) participants above 18 years old, (2) right-handed, and (3) with no known sensorimotor, developmental, or cognitive disorders. The study is approved by the Institutional Review Board for Protection of Human Subjects at New York University Abu Dhabi (Project #HRPP-2021-64).

2.2   Vibrotactile Alert Parameters.

A vibrotactile alert is defined as an arrangement of repeatable sequences of the vibration motor's "on" and "off" state, with a specific duration assigned to each state. The duration of the "on" state is known as the pulse duration (PD) whereas that of the "off" state is referred to as the inter-pulse duration (IPD).

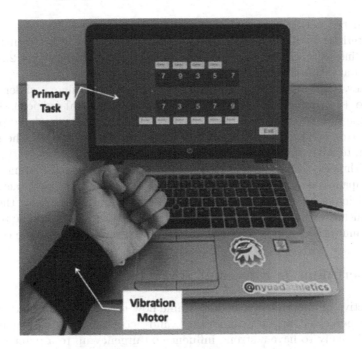

Fig. 1. Experimental setup: wristband with vibration motor and the primary task shown on the screen.

Based on previous research [12], the PD and the IPD are set to 350 ms and 40 ms, respectively, in order to provide a clearly perceptual but non-irritating experience (this is also verified through a pilot study). The total duration for the number of repetitions of the "on" and "off" states is known as the alert duration. On the other hand, the alert envelope is defined by varying the intensity of vibration over time. Three envelopes are considered, increasing, decreasing, and constant intensities.

2.3 Apparatus and Experimental Task

The vibrotactile feedback prototype is in the form of a wristband as shown in Fig. 1. A vibration motor (Pico Vibe 310-177, Precision Microdrives) is attached to the volar wrist (palm side) of the wristband to provide vibrotactile feedback. The vibration motor is attached to the volar wrist due to its ability to affect the sensorimotor cortex of the brain without interfering with the hand movements performing a primary task [13]. The vibration motor is 10 mm in diameter and 2.7 mm in thickness. An ATMEGA328 microcontroller unit is utilized to control the vibration motor and connect through a serial connection over a USB cable to a laptop. The stimulation intensity is controlled by adjusting the duty cycle of the pulse width modulation (PWM) signal that feeds the vibration motor. Increasing the duty cycle of the PWM signal would increase the effective voltage applied to the actuator and thus the vibration intensity. The alert envelope is characterized by a vibration intensity that varies linearly between the least perceived intensity of 0.5g and the maximum vibration intensity of 2.26g. The experimental setup is shown in Fig. 1.

Urgency, annoyance, and acceptance are evaluated using a slider ranging from -1 to +1 (the default value is 0, representing a neutral opinion). The user controls the slider to rate each of the parameters, and once completed press the submit button to save the ratings before moving to the next trial. The user has the option to early quit the application via the exit button.

An arithmetic task is developed in order to simulate a realistic scenario where the participant is engaged in a primary task when receiving the vibrotactile alert. The participant is asked to complete a five-digit addition task on the screen during which the vibrotactile alert is provided, as shown in Fig. 1. The perceived urgency, annoyance, and acceptance are evaluated in a more realistic context.

3   Experiment 1: Effects of Alert Duration

The objective of experiment 1 is to examine how the vibrotactile alert duration influences perceived urgency, annoyance, and acceptance. Increasing the alert duration is likely to have a strong influence on urgency up to a point when the alert becomes too annoying and potentially unacceptable. The vibrotactile alert duration consists of a repetition of the vibration cycle (PD and IPD) ranging from 2 up to 10 repetitions. Additional repetitions beyond 10 were found too annoying and unacceptable during a pilot study.

3.1   Experimental Protocol

After introducing the experiment's purpose and setup, participants were asked to complete the consent form. The wristband was then attached to the non-dominant hand of the participant. The participants were told to not move their hands throughout the experiment. Each participant completed 18 trials of vibrotactile alerts (ranging from two to ten and back to two repetitions). On each trial, the participant felt the vibrotactile alert and then was asked to rate the urgency, annoyance, and acceptance after the stimulation. Once the participant submits their response, the next trial started. The independent variable was the alert duration. The dependent variables were the ratings for urgency, annoyance, and acceptance for each alert duration.

Statistical analysis was performed to confirm whether the participant's response was significantly higher or lower compared to neutral rating. The p-value was corrected for multiple comparisons using the Bonferroni method.

3.2   Results

Figure 2 shows the results for the perceived urgency ratings. Vibrotactile alerts with two and three repetitions were rated as significantly lower than neutral for

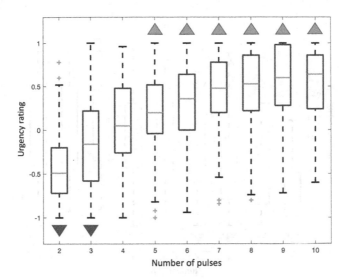

Fig. 2. Perceived urgency ratings. The blue and red triangles indicate significantly lower and higher ratings compared to neutral status, respectively. Wilcoxon signed-rank test or One-sample t-test was utilized depending on the Jarque-Bera test to check if the data follows the normal distribution. p-value is corrected using the Bonferroni method. The triangles indicate $p<0.001$. (Color figure online)

urgency (Wilcoxon signed-rank test, Bonferroni correction method, $p<0.001$). On the other hand, repetitions from five to ten repetitions are significantly higher than neutral (Wilcoxon signed-rank test, Bonferroni correction method, $p<0.001$). It is also noticeable that as the number of repetitions increases, the average rating for the perceived urgency increases. It can be concluded that a minimum of five repetitions is needed to elicit a significant increase in the perceived urgency.

It is also noted that a large number of repetitions may cause annoyance. Figure 3 shows the results for the perceived annoyance. As expected, the perceived annoyance increases as the number of repetitions increases and peaks at and beyond 8 repetitions. Statistical analysis demonstrated that the perceived annoyance is rated as significantly lower than the neutral (Wilcoxon signed-rank test, Bonferroni correction method, $p<0.001$) for repetitions two to five. On the other hand, the annoyance rating is significantly higher than the neutral for repetitions eight and nine (Wilcoxon signed-rank test, Bonferroni correction method, $p<0.001$). Combining the findings with the perceived urgency, it can be concluded that five repetitions produce significantly higher urgency and lower annoyance.

The perceived acceptance is also investigated. As shown in Fig. 4, the general trend for the acceptance rating is that as the number of repetitions increases, the acceptance rating decreases. While examining statistical differences, it is found that repetitions from two to eight are rated significantly higher than the neutral

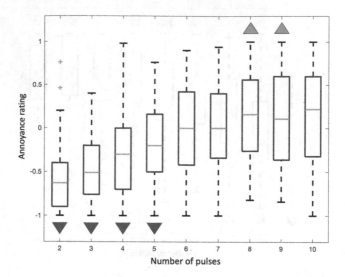

Fig. 3. Perceived annoyance ratings. The blue and red triangles indicate significantly lower and higher compared to neutral, respectively. Wilcoxon signed-rank test or One-sample t-test are utilized depending on the Jarque-Bera test to check if the data distribution follows the normal distribution. p-value is corrected using the Bonferroni method. The triangles indicate $p<0.001$. (Color figure online)

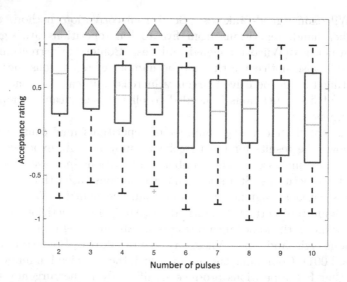

Fig. 4. Perceived acceptance ratings. The red triangles indicate significantly higher ratings compared to neutral. Wilcoxon signed-rank test or One-sample t-test are utilized depending on the Jarque-Bera test to check if the data followed the normal distribution. p-value is corrected using the Bonferroni method. The triangles indicate $p<0.01$. (Color figure online)

(Wilcoxon signed-rank test, Bonferroni correction method, $p<0.01$). Combining the results of the perceived urgency, annoyance, and acceptance, it can be concluded that a vibrotactile alarm with five repetitions (a total of 1,950 ms) elicits a significantly higher sense of urgency, a significantly lower sense of annoyance, and a significantly higher acceptance.

4 Experiment 2: Vibrotactile Alert Envelope

The second experiment explores the effects of the vibration intensity envelope on perceived urgency, annoyance, and acceptance. Three types of intensity envelopes are considered: constant, increasing, and decreasing.

4.1 Experimental Setup

This experiment used the same setup as shown in Fig. 1. Three vibration-intensity envelopes were utilized: constant, increasing, and decreasing. The constant intensity envelope used the same vibration intensity (2.25g) throughout the entire duration of the alert. The increasing intensity envelope started from the least perceivable vibration (0.5g) and increases linearly to reach the maximum intensity (2.25g) by the last repetition. The decreasing intensity envelope followed the reverse direction in vibration intensity (starting from 2.25g at the first repetition to 0.5g for the last one). In order to minimize the variances of parameters, a linear envelope was selected. The alert duration was set to five repetitions (a total of 1,950 ms) based on the findings of Experiment 1.

4.2 Procedure

After completing the consent form, participants were directed to the computer screen and given instructions about the arithmetic task and the experiment. Each participant completed a total of 18 trials, six trials per envelope condition (constant, increasing, and decreasing). The order in which these trials were presented was counterbalanced to avoid any order or memory effects. A trial started by asking the participant to complete the arithmetic task, during which the user feels the vibrotactile alert. The vibrotactile alert was presented randomly for three to six seconds after starting the arithmetic task. Participants were told that they would be evaluating vibrotactile alerts on the basis of their subjective urgency, annoyance, and acceptance.

4.3 Results

The perceived urgency, annoyance, and acceptance are evaluated for the three intensity envelope conditions: constant, increasing, and decreasing. Statistical analysis was performed to confirm significant differences among the three intensity envelope conditions. Results show no significant differences in the ratings of annoyance and acceptance among the three intensity envelope conditions

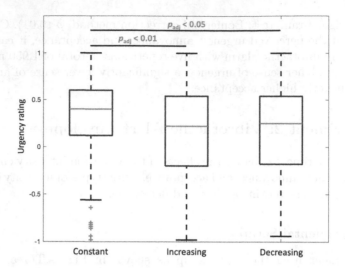

Fig. 5. Perceived urgency ratings for constant, increasing and decreasing vibration envelope. Kruskal-Wallis test, Bonferroni correction.

($p>0.05$). However, when examining the perceived urgency, it is found that alerts with constant vibration intensity are rated significantly higher for perceived urgency than the increasing intensity envelope alerts (Kruskal-Wallis test. Bonferroni correction, $p<0.01$) and the decreasing intensity envelope alerts (Kruskal-Wallis test. Bonferroni correction, $p<0.05$).

Therefore, a vibrotactile alert with constant vibration elicits a significantly higher sense of urgency without significantly influencing annoyance and acceptance. When combining the results of Experiment 1 and Experiment 2, it can be concluded that five repetitions (1,950 ms) with a constant vibration intensity of 2.25g elicit a significant increase in the perceived urgency without significantly degrading annoyance and acceptance.

5   Discussion

The current study shows that the duration and intensity envelope of the vibrotactile alert have significant effects on perceived urgency. The alert duration has a similar effect on urgency and annoyance; increasing the alert duration increases the perceived urgency and annoyance. As expected, acceptance decreases as the alert duration increases. That is probably caused by an increase in perceived annoyance. These results suggest that the vibrotactile alert parameters can be adjusted to increase perceived urgency with relatively little effect on perceived annoyance and acceptance.

It is also found that constant vibration intensity alerts elicit a significant increase in perceived urgency without significantly degrading annoyance and acceptance. Several participants reported that an increase in the vibration intensity is perceived as pleasant and thus not urgent or annoying. Furthermore, some participants indicated that a decrease in the vibration intensity is interpreted as a fading sense of the initially elicited urgency. Therefore, it seems that a constant vibration intensity works best for conveying a sustained sense of urgency.

Although the current study demonstrates that the duration and envelope of the vibrotactile alert have significant effects on perceived urgency, annoyance, and acceptance, a few limitations must be acknowledged. First of all, the context in which the alert is received may influence the relative effects of urgency, annoyance, and acceptance, prompting a consideration of a trade-off between urgency and annoyance in alert design. Examples of context effects include the type of the primary task or the frequency of false alerts. Furthermore, the high variance in participants' responses shows significant individual differences, suggesting that a personalized vibrotactile alert design might be a more effective approach. Finally, there are other characteristics of the vibrotactile alert that can influence perceived urgency, such as the body part where the alert is presented and must be considered in future research.

6   Conclusion

The current study investigates the effects of the duration and intensity envelope of vibrotactile alerts on perceived urgency, annoyance, and acceptance. Experiment 1 demonstrates that an alert duration of 1,950 ms (five repetitions of PD and IPD cycles) elicits a significant increase in perceived urgency, a significant decrease in annoyance, and a significant increase in acceptance. Experiment 2 confirms that a constant vibration intensity envelope of 2.25g elicits a significant increase in the perceived urgency without significantly modulating annoyance and acceptance, as compared to increasing or decreasing vibration intensity envelope.

An important future research direction involves examining the influence of context on perceived urgency, annoyance, and acceptance. For example, involvement in a primary task such as driving or interacting with a smartphone may significantly influence how vibrotactile alerts will be perceived (i.e. the perceived vibration is affected by active hand movement). Furthermore, since false alerts can not be completely avoided, studying the impact of false alert frequency will be another interesting future direction. It will be even more interesting given how touch sensitivity decreases with long-term vibration exposure.

References

1. Poupyrev, I., Maruyama, S.: Tactile interfaces for small touch screens. In: Proceedings of the 16th Annual ACM Symposium on User Interface Software and Technology, pp. 217–220 (2003)
2. Shah, V.A., Risi, N., Ballardini, G., Mrotek, L.A., Casadio, M., Scheidt, R.A.: Effect of dual tasking on vibrotactile feedback guided reaching – a pilot study. In: Prattichizzo, D., Shinoda, H., Tan, H.Z., Ruffaldi, E., Frisoli, A. (eds.) EuroHaptics 2018. LNCS, vol. 10893, pp. 3–14. Springer, Cham (2018). https://doi.org/10.1007/978-3-319-93445-7_1

3. Azenkot, S., Prasain, S., Borning, A., Fortuna, E., Ladner, R.E., Wobbrock, J.O.: Enhancing independence and safety for blind and deaf-blind public transit riders. In: Proceedings of the SIGCHI Conference on Human Factors in Computing Systems, pp. 3247–3256 (2011)
4. Van Erp, J.B.F.: Guidelines for the use of vibro-tactile displays in human computer interaction. In: Proceedings of Eurohaptics, vol. 2002, pp. 18–22. Citeseer (2002)
5. Ferris, T.K.: Informative vibrotactile displays to support attention and task management in anesthesiology. PhD Thesis University of Michigan (2010)
6. Pratt, S.M., Lewis, B.A., Peñaranda, B.N., Roberts, D.M., Gonzalez, C., Baldwin, C.L.: Perceived urgency scaling in tactile alerts. In: Proceedings of the Human Factors and Ergonomics Society Annual Meeting, vol. 56, no. 1, pp. 1303–1306. Sage CA: Los Angeles, CA: Sage Publications (2012). https://doi.org/10.1177/1071181312561378
7. Van Erp, J.B., Toet, A., Janssen, J.B.: Uni-, bi- and tri-modal warning signals: effects of temporal parameters and sensory modality on perceived urgency. Saf. Sci. **72**, 1–8 (2015)
8. Chancey, E.T., Christopher Brill, J., Sitz, A., Schmuntzsch, U., Bliss, J.P.: Vibro-tactile stimuli parameters on detection reaction times. In: Proceedings of the Human Factors and Ergonomics Society Annual Meeting, vol. 58, no. 1, pp. 1701–1705. Sage CA: Los Angeles, CA: SAGE Publications (2014)
9. Omata, M., Kuramoto, M.: Design of syllabic vibration pattern for incoming notification on a smartphone. In: CHIRA, pp. 27–36 (2020)
10. Saket, B., Prasojo, C., Huang, Y., Zhao, S.: Designing an effective vibration-based notification interface for mobile phones. In: Proceedings of the 2013 Conference on Computer Supported Cooperative Work, pp. 149–1504 (2013)
11. Suied, C., Susini, P., McAdams, S.: Evaluating warning sound urgency with reaction times. J. Exp. Psychol. Appl. **14**(3), 201 (2008)
12. Kaaresoja, T., Linjama, J.: Perception of short tactile pulses generated by a vibration motor in a mobile phone. In: First Joint Eurohaptics Conference and Symposium on Haptic Interfaces for Virtual Environment and Teleoperator Systems. World haptics conference, pp. 471–472. IEEE (2005)
13. Seo, N.J., et al.: Use of imperceptible wrist vibration to modulate sensorimotor cortical activity. Exper. Brain Res. **237**(3), 805–816 (2019)

Optimal Design of Braille Display Based on Adaptive-Network-based Fuzzy Inference

Chang Liu[1], Zhongzhen Jin[2], Kaiwen Chen[2], Wentao Tao[1], Hongbo Liang[1], and Wenzhen Yang[1(✉)]

[1] Research Center for Humanoid Sensing, Zhejiang Lab, Hangzhou 311121, China
{liuchang,wentaotao,lianghb,ywz}@zhejianglab.edu.cn
[2] Faculty of Mechanical Engineering and Automation, Zhejiang Sci-Tech University, Hangzhou 310018, China

Abstract. Although electromagnetic braille displays have fast response, reliable performance, and low price, they also have high power consumption and are susceptible to heat generation. For the development of a braille display, in this paper, we propose a solution based on an adaptive network-based fuzzy inference system(ANFIS). First, we analyze and optimize the driving voltage of the electromagnetic driver, the resistance value of the electromagnetic coil, the fingertip touch support force, and the operation temperature of the device, and we describe the development of a prototype of an electromagnetic braille display with a hierarchical structure. We verified experimentally that the device developed in this study can provide a fingertip touch support force of more than 150 mN, with a contact response frequency of 35.8 Hz, while maintaining a temperature of 32°C, which is suitable for fingertip contact after a long operational period. In addition, the correct display rate of the braille characters can reach 100%. All of these specifications meet the design requirements and can provide users with an optimal braille reading.

Keywords: Braille display · Electromagnetic driven · Adaptive network fuzzy inference system

1 Introduction

There are currently 285 million visually impaired people throughout the world, and this number continues to grow [1]. With the development of the Information Age, the visually impaired have a stronger reading demand, and braille is a tactile text specially designed for the visually impaired and is the main means for such readers to acquire knowledge. However, traditional paper braille books

This paper is supported by the National Key Research and Development Program of China (2021YFF0600203); the Key Research Project of the Zhejiang Lab (K2022PG1BB01,2022MG0AC04); the Zhejiang Provincial Natural Science Foundation (LY20F020019, LQ19F020012); the Zhejiang Basic Public Welfare Research Project (LGF19E050005).

D. Wang et al. (Eds.): AsiaHaptics 2022, LNCS 14063, pp. 11–27, 2023.
https://doi.org/10.1007/978-3-031-46839-1_2

are extremely bulky, costly, get easily damaged, and are difficult to store; thus, with the rapid development of an information-based society, such books can no longer meet the needs of most visually impaired people. A braille display is an automated device that can dynamically generate braille, thereby drastically improving the learning and reading efficiency for visually impaired individuals. It is therefore important to study ways to further improve and optimize the design of braille displays and improve their performance.

The mechanical structure of a braille display can control the protrusion and retraction of the braille contacts and form the digital braille characters, which generally consist of a 3 × 2 dot matrix on one braille cell, arranged in the form of three rows and two columns, with each dot matrix corresponding to a driving mechanism. From the 1960 s up to the present, scholars throughout the world have developed various forms of braille display devices, mainly including piezoelectric ceramic drives [2–4], pneumatic drives [5–7] memory alloy drives [8–10], and drives using new material types [11–13]. In 1979, the first piezo-ceramic braille display (Versabraille) was developed in the United States [14]. The piezo-ceramic drive technology is reversible, achieving a stable braille drive performance. This technology remains the dominant solution for braille devices on the market today. However, a piezoelectric ceramic chip has a complex structure, its production and processing are tedious, and its use of an L-shaped structure increases the size of the driver. Most importantly, a piezoelectric ceramic chip is costly, thus limiting the popularity of braille displays. For these reasons, various novel drive technologies have been developed, including pneumatic haptic display devices mainly using a polydimethylsiloxane soft material as the actuator, high-pressure gas in a closed chamber to deform the film projection and generate the haptics, and mechanical contacts pushed in an upward movement for haptic generation. However, a limitation of the film thickness under the maximum atmospheric pressure leads to insufficient contact support, whereas the large size of the closed cavity slows down the refresh rate, making it difficult to provide a better user touch experience. The braille dots developed using memory alloy driven technology cannot easily ensure the long-term stability and reliable operation of braille contacts, owing to the fatigue-prone nature of the shape memory alloy material. A representative study on new material-driven braille displays uses an electroactive polymer, which is a material that can produce a deformation under a high voltage or electric field, is light in weight, and has a broad range of applications. However, the current displays require extremely high driving voltages, and the large size of the module limits their diffusion in practical applications.

There is also an electromagnetically driven braille display [15–17], which is highly valued by researchers. As early as 2000, Schonherr [18] invented the world's first braille display device based on a small electromagnetic drive pin capable of displaying and erasing braille characters. Electromagnetically driven braille displays are much less costly to manufacture than piezo-ceramic displays and have much lower drive voltages, new material drives, and a longer lifetime. However, there is still room for optimization and improvement of electromagnetically driven braille displays in terms of contact support and heat generation.

This study is aimed at the innovative development of a prototype of an electromagnetically driven braille display with a hierarchical structure. It also aims at improving the reliability and practicality of the electromagnetic braille display by learning to train and optimize the main design parameters of the electromagnetic driver based on an adaptive network fuzzy inference system. This paper first introduces the specific design objectives of the braille display, the mechanical ontology structure, and the working principle of the innovative developed braille display. The optimization process of the braille display design parameters is then introduced. Next, an operational test of the prototype is conducted to verify the key indicators of the braille display, i.e., the support force, operating temperature, response speed, and driving accuracy of the braille contacts. Finally, some concluding remarks are provided.

2 Design of an Electromagnetically Driven Braille Display

2.1 Design Goals for Braille Display

To refresh the braille dots of braille characters in real-time, while meeting the required psychological and physiological characteristics of touch for the visually impaired, the braille dots must fulfill the following objectives:

1. **Distribution of Braille Contacts**
   A braille character consists of six braille contacts with a fixed dot spacing, which is referenced on one braille cell. The braille contact size described in this paper according to the national braille standard of the People's Republic of China (GB/T15720-2008) [19]. The dot diameter of each braille contact is $\phi 1.5$ mm, the projection height is 0.7 mm, the dot pitch is 2.5 mm, and the square pitch is 6.0 mm.
2. **Braille Contact Support**
   The design requirements of braille displays for contact support are based on the ability of the visually impaired person to feel and read the braille accurately and comfortably. The human body has a distinct tactile sensation for forces above 40 mN [20,21], and studies have shown that the greater the tactile force is, the more obvious the tactile sensation will be [22]. Therefore, the design goal of this study is to achieve a braille contact support force of greater than 150 mN.
3. **Response Speed of Braille Contacts**
   The response speed refers to the refresh time of the braille contact from a flat state to a completely raised state, or a completely raised state down to a flat state, for which the shorter the refresh time is, the faster the response speed will be. When visually impaired people learn braille characters, their reading speed is extremely high, and to avoid affecting the user's reading experience, the response speed of the braille point display device should be no less than 1 Hz [16].

4. **Operating Temperature of Braille Display**
   The braille display designed in this study uses electromagnetic drive technology, and the solenoid will inevitably generate heat after the power is applied, which will in turn increase the temperature of the device. To ensure that the braille display can work normally while providing user comfort, according to the tolerance of the human finger to temperature [23], the operating temperature of the braille display after a long period of use should be lower than 42°C.

5. **Operating Power Consumption of Braille Display**
   A braille display device should fulfill the above requirements of a contact support force, response speed, and tolerable operating temperature; meet the requirements of energy-saving and environmental protection; and reduce the power consumption of the braille display as much as possible.

2.2   Design of Electromagnetically Driven Braille Display

To achieve the above design objectives, the innovative design of the electromagnetically driven braille display developed in this study is shown in Fig. 1. Each of the six braille contacts is arranged in one braille cell, and a staggered combination of the top, middle, and bottom layers is used, which solves the design problem of a dense braille contact arrangement and achieves the design goal of meeting the braille standards. Taking the six contacts in one braille cell as an example, the driving mechanisms of the six braille contacts are arranged on the three layers of the braille display module, with two driving mechanisms for each layer of the braille display module, i.e., the driving mechanisms for points 1 and 6 are distributed in the lower layer, those for points 2 and 5 are distributed in the middle layer, and those for points 3 and 4 are distributed in the upper layer. Each braille contact is driven by an independent electromagnetic driving mechanism, which includes, in order from top to bottom, the braille

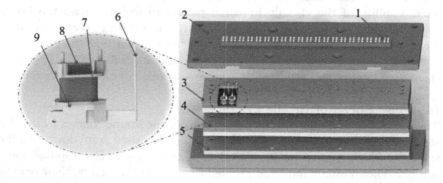

Fig. 1. Overall structure of the braille display.(1: braille dot, 2: touch module, 3: top layers, 4: middle layers, 5: bottom layers, 6: armature pin, 7: solenoid, 8: trapezoidal iron core, 9: return spring.)

dot, touch module, armature pin, and electromagnetic driving mechanism. The electromagnetic driving mechanism consists of a solenoid, trapezoidal iron core, return spring, and armature pin.

When the power is on, the solenoid in the electromagnetic drive mechanism magnetizes the trapezoidal iron core to generate an electromagnetic force, which attracts the armature needle to move upward while simultaneously driving the braille contact to protrude out of the touch panel to form a braille character that can be perceived by touch. When the power is off, the magnetic field disappears and the armature needle moves downward under its own gravity and the thrust of the return spring, at which point the braille contact will lose its support and fall back into the touch plate. Therefore, by independently controlling the on-off power of each electromagnetic drive mechanism, it is possible to achieve independent upward and downward movements of the braille contacts, which in turn form all possible concave and convex contact information, constituting different braille characters for the user to touch and read.

3 Optimization of Design Parameters for Electromagnetic Braille Display

After completing the design of the overall structure of the electromagnetically driven braille display, the test results showed that the contact support force and the operating temperature of the braille display are affected by multiple parameters, each of which has a non-linear relationship. To achieve the design goals of a contact support force and operation temperature of the braille dots, the design parameters of the electromagnetic actuator are optimized using an adaptive network-based fuzzy inference system (ANFIS), with support from MATLAB.

3.1 Components of ANFIS System

The ANFIS system combines the self-learning function of a neural network with the inference function of a fuzzy inference system. Assume that the fuzzy inference system under consideration has two inputs x and y, and a single output f. For a first-order Sugeno fuzzy model, a typical if-then rule with two fuzzy rules is as follows:

Rule 1: if x is A_1 and y is B_1, then $f_1 = p_1 x + q_1 y + r_1$,

Rule 2: if x is A_2 and y is B_2, then $f_2 = p_2 x + q_2 y + r_2$,

where the parameters p_1, p_2, q_1, q_2, r_1, and r_2 are linear, and A_1, A_2, B_1, and B_2 are nonlinear.

The ANFIS structure has five layers, as shown in Fig. 2. In practical fuzzy inference, it is assumed that the two inputs considered, x and y, and the output, f, are known datasets, and that each node in the same layer of the network has a similar function, denoting the output of the ith node in the first layer by $O_{1,i}$, and so on.

Layer 1: Selection and fuzzification of input parameters. This is the first step in the establishment of fuzzy rules. Each node i in this layer is a square node

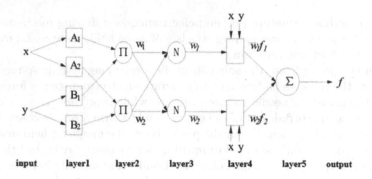

Fig. 2. Typical ANFIS structure.

represented by a node function,

$$O_{1,i} = \mu_{Ai}(x), i = 1, 2 \qquad O_{1,i} = \mu_{B(i-2)}(y), i = 3, 4 \tag{1}$$

where A_i and $B(i-2)$ are the linguistic variables associated with this node function, and $O_{1,i}$ is the affiliation function of the fuzzy set A ($A = A_1$, A_2, B_1, B_2), which is usually available as a bell function.

$$\mu_{Ai}(x) = \frac{1}{1 + [(\frac{x-c_i}{a_i})^2]^{bi}} \tag{2}$$

where $\{a_i, b_i, c_i\}$ is the set of parameters of the affiliation function, i.e., the antecedent parameters. In addition, the trigonometric affiliation function (trimf) and trapezoidal affiliation function (trapmf) are commonly used in fuzzification. The set of parameters of this part is called the set of antecedent parameters.

Layer 2: The fuzzy rule excitation strength is calculated by multiplying the affiliation of the input signal, the output of which is as follows:

$$O_{2,i} = w_i = \mu_{Ai}(x)\mu_{Bi}(y), i = 1, 2 \tag{3}$$

Layer 3: The nodes in this layer conduct a normalized calculation of the applicability of each rule, i.e., the ith node calculates the ratio of w_i of the ith rule to the sum of the w values of all rules:

$$O_{3,i} = \overline{w_i}f_i = \frac{w_i}{w_1 + w_2}, i = 1, 2 \tag{4}$$

Layer 4: Each node i in this layer is an adaptive node, the output of which is as follows:

$$O_{4,i} = \overline{w_i}f_i = \overline{w_i}(p_ix + q_iy + r_i), i = 1, 2 \tag{5}$$

where w is the output of the third layer, and pi, qi, ri are the conclusion parameters.

Layer 5: The single node in this layer is a fixed node, which can be used to calculate the total output of all input signals as follows:

$$O_{5,i} = \sum_i \overline{w_i} f_i = \frac{\sum_i w_i f_i}{\sum_i w_i}, i = 1, 2 \tag{6}$$

The nodes and weights of each layer of ANFIS have a clear physical significance, and their outputs are unique. The first and fourth layers in the ANFIS structure belong to adaptive nodes, and the antecedent parameters in the first layer control the shape of each physical affiliation function, whereas the postcedent parameters in the fourth layer control the output of the corresponding rules. The rules of ANFIS are generated automatically, and the learning algorithm is a hybrid of a gradient descent and least squares applied to adjust the antecedent and conclusion parameters. Afterward, its affiliation function is given an initial value, and the learning process adjusts the antecedent and consequent parameters according to the characteristics of the sample, thereby avoiding the influence of subjective human factors.

3.2   Building an ANFIS Model of the Braille Display

ANFIS is a learning method that provides relevant information (affiliation functions and fuzzy rules) from a dataset for the process of fuzzy modeling through a fitting based on the input-output dataset. Therefore, determining the inputs and outputs of the model is the primary prerequisite for building an ANFIS. In previous experiments, we concluded that the main factors affecting the contact support force and operating temperature of the braille display are the driving voltage and the resistance of the electromagnetic coil. Given the nonlinear relationship among these four aspects, the ANFIS inference system used in this study is as shown in Fig. 3, with the input variables being the contact support force and the resistance of the solenoid coil, and the output variables being the drive voltage of the braille display and the operating temperature of the braille display device. Because ANFIS only supports a single-output system, it can be decoupled into two ANFIS systems, namely, an ANFIS inference system for the input voltage, and such a system for the operating temperature.

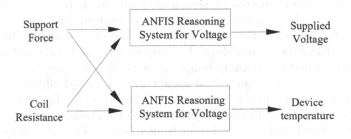

Fig. 3. ANFIS reasoning system for braille display device parameters.

The braille display developed in this study can be driven from 3 to 10V (1V for each gradient, with a total of eight gradients), and the resistance of the solenoid coil ranges from 30 to 51 Ω (3 Ω for each gradient, with a total of eight gradients), forming a total of 64 training datasets. The contact support force of the braille display was measured using a pressure distribution test system developed by Tekscan, USA. The system mainly measures the average value of the contact support force of six random braille contacts of the braille display at different driving voltages corresponding to the resistance value of the solenoid coil used to obtain the data of the contact support force. The operating temperature of the braille display device was measured using a thermocouple sensor, which was applied to measure the temperature of the touch panel surface at 20°C i.e., room temperature, for different driving voltages and different solenoid coil resistances after 120 contacts were raised and operated at the same time for a 30-min period. The contact support force and operating temperature generated when driving the braille display with different driving voltages and coils of different resistance values were experimentally measured to build the training dataset. Next, the above ANFIS system was trained to obtain the relationship between the design parameters and the operating temperature and driving voltage of the device.

3.3   Model Training

The dataset obtained from the experimental measurements was then fed into the ANFIS for training. Before training, a Sugeno-type fuzzy inference structure (FIS) was first generated from the training dataset as the initial conditions used for model training. A dataset consisting of a contact support force and coil resistance as input quantities and the drive voltage as the output quantities was first input into ANFIS for training. The membership function is a bell-shaped function, and the membership function is two. Once the model network structure had been determined, the model was trained, and the parameters of the model were adjusted to optimize the parameters. The training dataset was fed into ANFIS, which determined the network structure, and the system was trained using a hybrid learning algorithm to obtain the required model parameters. Figure 4 shows the affiliation function before and after the drive voltage training. Figure 5 shows the root-mean-square error and training step size for the driving voltage training. From the results shown in the figure, it is clear that after 200 training sessions, the root mean square error is close to zero, and the training step size first increases to the maximum value, and then gradually decreases.

Similarly, the dataset consisting of a support force and coil resistance as the input quantities and the running temperature as the output quantity was then fed into the ANFIS for training, the same two bell-shaped affiliation functions were selected, and the model was trained using a hybrid learning algorithm. After 200 training steps, the mean square error of the training data obtained was close to zero. The training steps began to increase to the maximum value, and then gradually decreased. The affiliation functions before and after temperature

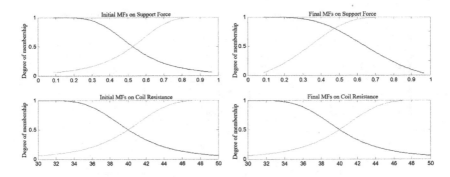

Fig. 4. Before and after the input voltage training membership function.

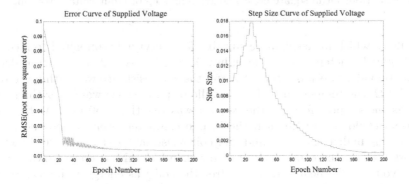

Fig. 5. Root mean square error and training step of input voltage training.

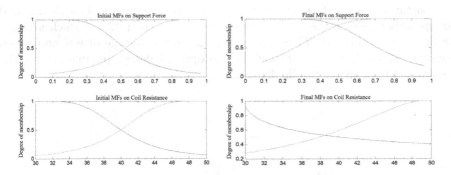

Fig. 6. Before and after the input voltage training membership function.

training are shown in Fig. 6, and the root-mean-square error and step length are shown in Fig. 7.

The results of the analysis of the support force and the temperature of the device after the ANFIS training are shown in Fig. 8. According to the design goal of the braille display, the support force of the braille contact is more than 150 mN, and the operating temperature of the braille display should be lower

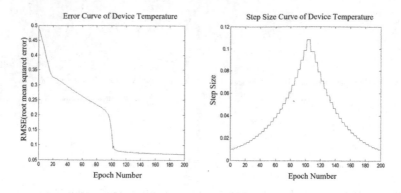

Fig. 7. Root mean square error and training step of input voltage training.

than 42°C, which makes it more suitable for the visually impaired to recognize the braille characters. From the figure, it can be seen that when the driving voltage provided was lower than 4 V and the coil resistance was within the range of 30–50 Ω, the temperature of the braille display device was lower than 42°C, whereas the support force of the contact was less than 150 mN. At this time, the users could not distinguish the braille characters well. When the driving voltage was higher than 7 V and the coil resistance was within 30–50 Ω, the support force of the contact was greater than 150 mN. However, owing to the higher voltage, the heat generated after the coil was energized increased, thus causing the operating temperature of the device to exceed 42°C, which was uncomfortable for the user. When a driving voltage of 6 V was selected and the coil resistance was 39 Ω, the contact support force was greater than 150mN and the operating temperature of the device was lower than 42°C, which satisfies the design requirements. Therefore, a solenoid drive voltage of 6 V and a coil resistance of 39 Ω were confirmed as the optimal design parameters for the solenoid actuator in the braille display.

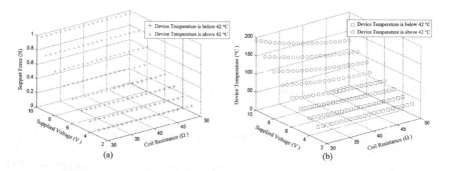

Fig. 8. Root mean square error and training step of input voltage training.

4   Prototype Development of Braille Display

In the present study, according to the mechanical structure design of the braille display and the parameter optimization of the ANFIS system used in a previous study, a prototype of the braille display was created. The braille display consists of 20 braille cells, each with six braille dots according to the Chinese braille standard, with a total of 120 braille contacts driven by an electromagnetic coil. With the coil-energized contacts raised, the presented braille-shaped symbols allow visually impaired people by touching them. The physical prototype is shown in Fig. 9. We also designed a control system for the braille display. The system uses a USB flash drive as the storage medium for reading the text and braille dot sequence. Through the key operation of the visually impaired user, the text and braille dot sequence in the USB flash drive can be presented in a visual, auditory, and tactile manner simultaneously, providing a means for visually impaired persons to read braille digitally. A cooling fan is equipped to further reduce the temperature of the braille display during operation, enabling users to comfortably touch and read the braille when displayed.

The overall control flow of the system is shown in Fig. 10. The braille display control system is powered by a 6 V power adapter, which is passed through a buck circuit module to meet the working voltage of each module. The system uses the STM32F4 series chip as the main control unit and then applies a USB flash drive using the USB-OTG function as a USB host to read the content of the text and braille dot sequence stored on the flash drive. The visually impaired user then interacts with the system through the keypad and realizes the screen display, voice announcement, braille display, and other functions under the operation of the keypad. The system uses an LTDC controller to drive the screen, displays the content of the text on the screen by reading the font data in the flash drive, and draws the braille shape symbols for sighted people to tutor the visually impaired group to touch and read. The system uses UART to control the speech synthesis chip and broadcast the content of the text for the visually impaired group to listen to. The system uses a darlington transistor array to improve the driving

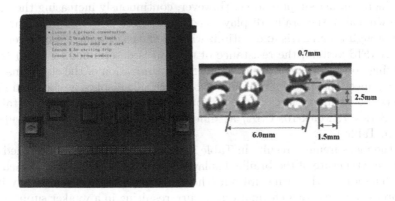

Fig. 9. The prototype of the braille display.

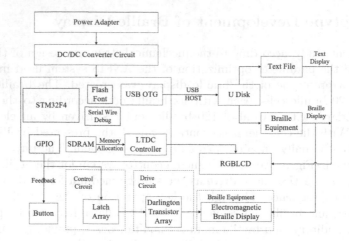

Fig. 10. The overall control flow of the braille display control system.

capability and a latch array to control the serial processing of the braille dot sequence, and finally controls the braille display hardware designed to present the braille dot matrix for the visually impaired person to read.

5   Validation Experiments

5.1   Measurement of Dot Support Force

The contact of the braille display is controlled by the main control chip in the control system for controlling the electromagnetic coil and realizing the projection and retraction. The size of the contact force is determined by the size of the electromagnetic force of the electromagnetic coil. The higher the voltage and current driving the solenoid, the greater the electromagnetic force that the solenoid will be able to provide, thus enabling the contact to provide a sufficiently high contact support force. However, continuously increasing the driving voltage will cause the braille display to consume more power and generate more heat. Through an analysis and optimization of the electromagnetic driver based on the ANFIS system, the resistance of the coil is determined to be 39 Ω, and the driving voltage is 6 V. To verify that the optimization of the electromagnetic driver can meet the design requirements of the braille display, as shown in Fig. 11 for the contact support force of the prototype was measured using a digital force meter (Series 7, Mark-10, USA) at different driving voltages. The results are shown in Table 1.

As the measurement results in Table 1 indicate, owing to the combined staggered layer structure of the braille display, the armature pin length of each layer differs. The longer the armature pin (the third layer) is, the more likely it will be to produce an elastic deformation, in turn resulting in a weaker support force transmitted by the electromagnetic force to the pin cap. However, at a driving

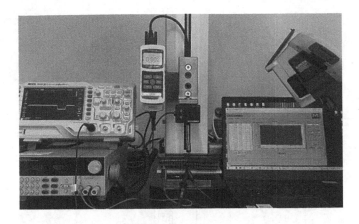

Fig. 11. The experimental test environment.

Table 1. Support force of braille dots.

Driving voltage (V)	Support force (mN)					
	top layer		middle layer		bottom layer	
4	226	150	138	126	105	107
5	322	295	156	166	137	147
6	332	277	220	239	162	169
7	430	321	241	257	195	210

voltage of 6 V, the support force of each contact exceeds 150 mN. These results are in line with the conclusions inferred in this study based on the ANFIS system, while also satisfying the design goal of the braille contact support force.

5.2   Measurement of Dot Response Speed

The response speed of the electromagnetic braille display designed in this study includes the time required for document reading, data sending, and movement of the electromagnetic drive mechanism.

When the USB memory is opened, the program automatically reads the content of the document and saves it in an array waiting for the user's keystroke, and thus the time required for reading the document is negligible. When the user presses a key, the device enters the data sending and distribution phase. Although the speed is related to the main frequency of the master control, data distribution and sending can be completed in an instant, and we add a 10 ms delay in the key scanning program to ensure that the detected key signal has not been caused by interference. After the main control system has completed the above operation, it waits for the electromagnetic drive mechanism to complete the protruding motion of the braille contact, i.e., the braille display completes the entire display process of the braille character.

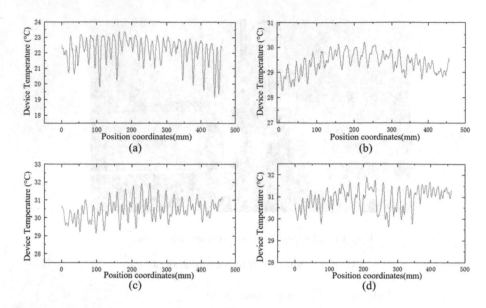

Fig. 12. Operating temperature of the touch panel.

Therefore, we mainly measured the movement time required for the electromagnetic drive mechanism. A high-speed camera (CP70-1-M-1000-RT, Optronis, GER) and an oscilloscope (MSO8064, RIGOL, CHN) were used to capture the time from the moment the electromagnetic driver was powered on until the braille contact completed its motion, which was 9:7 ms, and the time from the moment the power was cut off until the braille contact fell completely, which was 8:2 ms. From this result, we can see that the time required for the braille contact to complete a full refresh movement after the user has given a command by pressing a key is 27:9 ms, i.e., the response frequency of the braille display is 35:8 Hz. This is much higher than the design target of 1 Hz and can thus provide efficient braille reading for visually impaired persons.

5.3 Measurement of Braille Display Operating Temperature

The drive voltage is 6 V, and the resistance of the solenoid coil is 39 Ω. The motion temperature of the braille display designed according to these parameters was examined in this paper using a thermal imager (Ti401, FLUKE, USA) at a room temperature of 20°C.

The test realistically simulates a scenario in which a visually impaired person is touch reading, and the temperature changes of the touch panel from left to right are measured at four time points after 30, 45, 60 and 90 min of continuous braille reading with the braille display. The experimental results are shown in Fig. 12. The four sets of measured data were collated, and the maximum, minimum, and average temperatures of the touch panel were calculated for different operating hours, as shown in Table 2.

Table 2. Touch panel temperature for different working hours.

Machine time (min)	Operating temperature(°C)		
	mean	highest	lowest
30	23.46	23.72	22.57
45	29.36	30.19	28.34
60	31.57	32.11	30.53
90	31.86	32.24	30.64

The experimental results show that the temperature of the touch panel surface tends to stabilize at approximately 32°C after 90 min of continuous operation of the braille display. This result is consistent with the results of the optimization of the electromagnetic driver based on the ANFIS system described in this paper, which achieves the design goal for the motion temperature of a braille display.

5.4 Measurement of Braille Display Accuracy

To confirm the accuracy of the braille display through a braille driver display test, we prepared a section of content from the New Concept English course (53 English words in total, corresponding to 267 braille characters). The test environment is shown in Fig. 13. The LCD screen of the braille display shows the content and corresponding braille characters in a dot sequence, which facilitates identifying and comparing the display of braille graphics and braille characters under the English braille standard. After careful comparison of the 267 braille characters displayed by the braille display, the results show that the braille display developed in this study achieves accurate driving and a stable operation

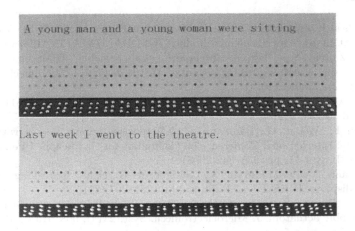

Fig. 13. Braille display based on english braille standard.

and can reach 100% accuracy for a braille character display. For braille touch reading, the real-time braille display function can ensure a positive braille reading experience for visually impaired persons.

6   Conclusion

In this study, we designed and developed a layered structure of an electromagnetic braille display for the visually impaired. We then used an adaptive network fuzzy inference system to analyze and optimize the design parameters of the structure, selected the drive voltage and electromagnetic coil meeting the design criteria of a braille display, and completed the development of the braille display prototype. In the testing of the braille display prototype, it was verified that all braille contacts of the braille display had a support force of more than 150 mN, the response speed was 27.9 ms, the temperature was stable at 32°C for an extended continuous operation, and the display accuracy of braille characters reached 100%, thus meeting all of the design requirements.

The above experimental results demonstrate the practicality and stability of the electromagnetic braille display developed in this study. Depending on the electromagnetic type of actuation used, its structure dictated that, to continuously maintain a raised contact, the coil of the solenoid must be continuously energized to maintain the electromagnetic force, thereby resulting in continuous heating, and in turn a high power consumption. In future research, we will aim to resolve this issue by incorporating a self-locking structure, i.e., the disconnection current will be able to maintain a predetermined height when the contact is raised to a predetermined position, and the braille characters can be redisplayed by unlocking them when the visually impaired person is finished reading, thereby further reducing the power consumption and heat generation.

References

1. World health organization, Global data on visual impairments 2010. Accessed 28 Dec 2020. https://www.who.int/blindness/GLOBALDATAFINALforweb.pdf
2. Xie, X., Zaitsev, Y., Velásquez-García, L.F., et al.: Scalable, MEMS-enabled, vibrational tactile actuators for high resolution tactile display. J. Micromechan. Microeng. **24**(12), 125014 (2014)
3. Metec, A.: Braille-cell B11. https://www.metec-ag.de/downloads/b11-rohs.pdf. Accessed 13 Dec 2021
4. Voelkel, T., Weber, G., Baumann, U.: Computers Helping People with Special Needs. In: International Conference on Computers for Handicapped Persons, Linz, Austria, July. 9–11, pp. 835–842(2008)
5. Russomanno, A., O'Modhrain, S., Gillespie, R. B., et al.: Refreshing refreshable braille displays. IEEE Trans. Haptics. **8**(3), 287–297 (2015)
6. Wu, X., Kim, S., Zhu, H., et al.: A refreshable braille cell based on pneumatic microbubble actuators. J. Microelectromech. Syst. **21**(4), 908–916 (2012)

7. Russomanno, A., Gillespie, R. B., O'Modhrain, S., et al.: Modeling pneumatic actuators for a refreshable tactile display. In: International Conference on Human Haptic Sensing and Touch Enabled Computer Applications, Versailles, France, June. 24–26, pp. 385–393 (2014)

8. Besse, N., Rosset, S., Zárate, J.J., Ferrari, E., et al.: Understanding graphics on a scalable latching assistive haptic display using a shape memory polymer membrane. IEEE Trans. Haptics 11(1), 30–38 (2018)

9. Matsunaga, T., Totsu, K., Esashi, M., et al.: Tactile display using shape memory alloy microcoil actuator and magnetic latch mechanism. Displays 34(2), 89–94 (2013)

10. Masuyama, S., Kawamura., A.: A novel electromagnetic linear actuator with inner and outer stators and one moving winding for tactile display. In: IEEE International Conference on Industrial Technology, Taipei Taiwan, China, May. 26, pp. 628–633 (2016)

11. Izhar, U., Albermani, F., Preethichandra, D.M.G., Sul, J., van Rensburg, P.A.J.: An electrothermally actuated MEMS braille dot. In: Wang, C.M., Ho, J.C.M., Kitipornchai, S. (eds.) ACMSM25. LNCE, vol. 37, pp. 985–993. Springer, Singapore (2020). https://doi.org/10.1007/978-981-13-7603-0_93

12. Chakraborti, P., Toprakci, H., Yang, D., et al.: A compact dielectric elastomer tubular actuator for refreshable braille display. Sens. Actuators A-Phys. 179, 151–157 (2012)

13. Qu, X., Ma, X., Shi, B., et al.: Refreshable braille display system based on triboelectric nanogenerator and dielectric elastomer. Adv. Func. Mater. 31, 2006612 (2021)

14. VersaBraille. https://www.aph.org/. Accessed Jan 2022

15. Kim, J., Han, B.K., Pyo, D., Ryu, S., et al.: Braille display for portable device using flip-latch structured electromagnetic actuator. IEEE Trans. Haptics 13(1), 59–65 (2021)

16. Runyan, N.H., Carpi, F.: Seeking the 'holy Braille' display: might electromechanically active polymers be the solution. Expert Rev. Med. Devices 8(5), 529–532 (2011)

17. Zarate, J.J., Shea, H.: Using pot-magnets to enable stable and scalable electromagnetic tactile displays. IEEE Trans. Haptics 10(1), 106–112 (2017)

18. Blazie, D.: Refreshable Braille now and in the years ahead, Braille Monitor 43(1). https://www.nfb.org/Images/nfb/Publications/bm/bm00/bm0001/bm000110.htm. Accessed Jan 2022

19. Chinese Braille, GB/T 15720–2008. https://www.bzko.com/std/180890.html. Accessed Jan 2022

20. King, H. H., Donlin, R., Hannaford, B.: Perceptual thresholds for single vs. multifinger haptic interaction. In: 2010 IEEE Haptics Symposium, 08 April, pp. 95–99 (2010)

21. Dosher, J., Hannaford, B.: Human interaction with small haptic effects. Teleoperators Virtual Environ. 14(3), 329–344 (2005)

22. Louw, S., Kappers, A.M.L., Koenderink, J.J.: Active haptic detection and discrimination of shape. Perception Psychophys. 64(7), 1108–1119 (2002)

23. Dewhirst, M.W., Viglianti, B.L., Lora-Michiels, M., Hanson, M., Hoopes, P.J.: Basic principles of thermal dosimetry and thermal thresholds for tissue damage from hyperthermia. Int. J. Hyperthermia 19(3), 267–294 (2003)

Modality-Specific Effect of Cueing on Inter-Manual Coordination in Bimanual Force Control Tasks with Accentuated- or Attenuated-Force Production

Cong Peng[1]([✉]), Xin Wang[1], Xingwei Guo[2], Jin Liang[1], and Dangxiao Wang[3,4,5]

[1] China Institute of Marine Technology and Economy, Beijing, China
Conpeng2017@sina.com, hapticwang@buaa.edu.cn
[2] School of Sports Engineering, Beijing Sport University, Beijing, China
[3] State Key Laboratory of Virtual Reality Technology and Systems, Beihang University, Beijing, China
[4] Beijing Advanced Innovation Center for Biomedical Engineering, Beihang University, Beijing, China
[5] Peng Cheng Laboratory, Shenzhen, China

Abstract. Little is known about how perceptual modality affects the inter-manual coordination in bimanual force control tasks with accentuated- or attenuated-force production. This study examined the effects of relative phase patterns on the inter-manual coordination in a bimanual force control task with visual/vibrotactile cues. In the proposed force control task, both index fingers were required to simultaneously produce congruent accentuated- or attenuated-force pulses in the in-phase pattern, and produce incongruent ones in the anti-phase pattern. According to visual or vibrotactile cues, participants were prompted to quickly perform the bimanual force control task by pressing with their index fingers on force sensors from the same background force level. The inter-manual coordination performance was indexed by the delayed reaction time and timing difference of the index fingers. Results demonstrated that the advantage of the inter-manual coordination with vibrotactile cues in the in-phase patterns was significant over the anti-phase patterns. The inter-manual coordination of the index fingers could differentiate the in-phase patterns from the anti-phase patterns in the vibrotactile modality while the visual modality showed shorter delayed reaction time and less timing difference of the index fingers in the proposed force control task. Consequently, these findings suggested that the modality-specific effect of cueing on the advantage of the inter-manual coordination existed in the bimanual force control task with accentuated- or attenuated-force production using both index fingers simultaneously. This study would be referential for designing interactive applications leveraging inter-manual spatial coordination for in-phase and anti-phase patterns during bimanual synchronized force production.

Keywords: Sensory Modality · Vibrotactile Cue · Relative Phase Pattern · Timing Difference · Mirror-Symmetrical Kinetics

© The Author(s), under exclusive license to Springer Nature Switzerland AG 2023
D. Wang et al. (Eds.): AsiaHaptics 2022, LNCS 14063, pp. 28–40, 2023.
https://doi.org/10.1007/978-3-031-46839-1_3

1 Introduction

Although bimanual coordination has recently become the subject of intensive investigation, the focus of related studies is now shifting towards overcoming the elementary coordination constraints by means of task symbolization or perceptual transformation rules [1]. Most previous studies have investigated inter-manual coordination in mirror-symmetrical movements with respect to either timing or kinematics [2, 3]. However, little study on the inter-manual coordination has been done with respect to mirror-symmetrical kinetics. Many motor activities used daily, such as those in sports and playing musical instruments, might require both an accentuation and attenuation of force produced by fingers [4]. Contextual effect on force control by single-finger tapping was observed under the accentuated-force conditions but not the attenuated-force conditions. Traditionally, bimanual tapping to an isochronous pacing sequence is a common paradigm for investigating the role of visual and auditory stimulation in music contexts [3]. Whereas, the vibrotactile cue has great potential to be applied in some special military application scenarios at night. Taken together, it is necessary to explore the effect of accentuated- and attenuated-force patterns cued by vibrotactile stimulation on the inter-manual coordination during synchronizing force production of bimanual fingers.

In this study, the first question to study is whether the mirror-symmetrical advantage also resides in the inter-manual coordination when synchronizing force production of bimanual fingers from the same background force level. In classical kinematic tasks requiring symmetrical movements, the in-phase pattern with a relative phase of 0° could be temporally defined by the synchronized actions, or spatially defined by unidirectional actions [1]. In the kinematic tasks requiring asymmetrical movements, the anti-phase pattern with a relative phase of 180° could be temporally defined by the asynchronized actions, or spatially defined by bidirectional actions. For example, symmetrical patterns requiring bidirectional actions were observed to be much more stable than parallel patterns requiring unidirectional actions, and the symmetry tendency in bimanual movements was proposed to be purely perceptual [5]. Similarly, it was also found that in-phase tapping had the highest stability of relative phase but the lowest asynchrony stability in bimanual timing tasks, specifically at the higher frequencies [2, 6]. Actually, two limbs did not perform simultaneously for some anti-phase patterns in the bimanual timing tasks wherein the relative phase was defined by the relative temporal delay [7]. Moreover, the symmetric mass manipulation was faster than the asymmetric mass manipulation in bimanual movement control tasks [8]. Spatially, the two arms under the asymmetric mass manipulation pattern moved synchronously in the same directions rather than in the opposite directions. Interestingly, little research has been done on the kinetic analysis of force production in the bimanual finger coordination paradigm with respect to the in-phase and anti-phase patterns. Inui observed the advantage of an in-phase pattern in the speed of force production finding in the bimanual production of finger tapping with asymmetrical forces [9]. Whereas, Inui also employed a temporal anti-phase pattern as used in the bimanual timing tasks. Therefore, one remaining issue is whether the in-phase pattern still has an advantage of the inter-manual coordination over the spatial anti-phase pattern when the forces of bimanual fingers are demanded to deviate inversely from the same background force level.

The second question of interest is whether the mirror-symmetrical advantage in the inter-manual coordination would be affected by the sensory modality of cue for the coordinated phase pattern. Researchers proposed that information about the relative phase in bimanual coordination was modality-specific [10]. Retention performance for the visual metronome condition was less accurate and more variable than for the auditory and audio-visual modality conditions [11]. Moreover, it was revealed that the asynchrony and stability of the inter-manual coordination were affected by the modality of the stimuli. More precisely, for the in-phase and antiphase patterns, audio-visual stimulation improved asynchrony stability and auditory stimulation improved the relative phase stability, whereas visual stimulation led to the worst inter-manual coordination [2]. Accordingly, considering the different performances of the inter-manual coordination between sensory modalities is valuable to researchers of human-computer interaction and designers of engineering applications. Several studies testified that the perception of tactile stimuli was crucial to the bimanual advantage in temporal regularity during bimanual finger tapping tasks [12, 13]. Our previous paper confirmed the feasibility of accurately perceiving two vibrotactile cues on both arms, which provided the foundation for comparing visual and haptic modalities in present work [14].

To answer the two above questions, we investigate the effects of relative phase patterns on the inter-manual coordination in a bimanual force control task with visual or vibrotactile cues. The inter-manual coordination performance was measured with the delayed reaction time and inter-manual timing difference of the index fingers, as defined and used in a previous study [15]. Similar to relative phase patterns used extensively in kinematics [5], two typical bimanual coordination patterns were adopted in this study: the in-phase pattern and the anti-phase pattern. The former required both index fingers to accentuate or attenuate force simultaneously from the same background force level, and the latter required one index finger to accentuate force whilst the other to attenuate force. We expected to reveal the performance difference of the inter-manual coordination sensory modalities between the visual and vibrotactile cueing for the in-phase and anti-phase patterns in the bimanual force control task. The emphasis on self-produced timing distinguishes the present task from studies of finger tapping in which extrinsic timing sources have been used [16]. This work would be of great benefit to make full use of multi-finger pressing force synergy in keystroke human-machine interaction, finger motor rehabilitation, and related fields [1].

2 Methods

2.1 Participants

Fifteen participants for three experiments were college students from Beihang University (aged 21 ~ 25 years, average 23.33 years, standard deviation 1.4, including 6 females). Thirteen of them are right-handed and others are left-handed according to their preferential use of the hand during daily activities such as writing, drawing, and eating. All participants reported normal or corrected-to-normal vision acuity. None of them had a previous history of overt autonomic and sensorimotor neuropathies with dysfunction in the hand or finger activity. All the participants were informed of their rights to terminate their participation at any time. Each participant gave his or her written informed consent

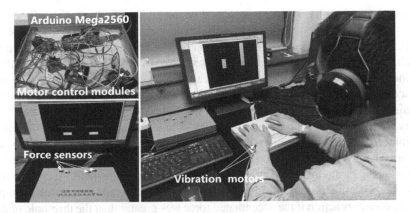

Fig. 1. Platform for exploring the synchronized force control capability of paired fingers.

before taking part in the study. This research complied with the tenets of the Declaration of Helsinki and was approved by the Institutional Review Board at China Institute of Marine Technology and Economy.

2.2 Apparatus

As shown in Fig. 1, a customized platform for multi-finger force acquisition was modified from the single-finger force measurement system used in previous research [17]. For each finger, the amplitude of finger force was measured by a force sensor (FSG15N1A, Honeywell International Inc., Morris Plains, NJ, USA) embedded in a customized rectangular box. The amplified signal from the force sensor was sampled and digitized at a frequency of 200 Hz by a 12-bit A/D converter (PCI FY6210, FYYING V10.0, Beijing, China). A GUI program displayed a set of visual cues to the participants. Each visual cue consisted of two white boundary lines, signifying the allowable variability range W of the finger force relative to the target amplitude A. Two identical visual cues of the target-centered ranges $[A, W]$ were presented for the index fingers. Two white vertical bars with the same initial heights stayed near the bottom of the GUI. The real-time force output of each finger was linearly mapped to the increased height of the bar on a black background. To generate different vibration modes, two vibration actuators were separately driven by a pair of motor control modules using pulse width modulation (PWM) from a microcontroller (Arduino Mega2560, Shenzhen, China). The microcontroller providing the PWM was communicated with the graphic user interface (GUI) programming of the host computer through a serial protocol.

2.3 Task Design

A bimanual force control task was designed to observe the effects of relative phase patterns with visual or vibrotactile cues. Figure 2 showed the definition of temporal parameters for an anti-phase pattern with visual cues in a trial, which was consistent in trials of the in-phase pattern with the vibrotactile cues. Four boundary lines of the target-centered range [*A*, *W*] were presented on the GUI at the beginning of each trial. The target amplitude *A* of 2 N and the allowable variability range *W* of 0.2 N were adopted as our previous finding [17]. Force outputs of both index fingers were required to reach and maintain within the target-centered range [*A*, *W*] for a dwell time of 400 ms once the visual cue popped up. Once the expiration of the dwell time, a pure black interface lasting 400 ms appeared immediately to wait for the upcoming cues whilst still maintaining the finger forces within the [*A*, *W*]. Subsequently, two red squares lasting 800 ms were presented with different brightness to act as the visual cues for spatially coordinated patterns of the index fingers. In each trial, the total action time of each finger was defined as the time from the appearance of the visual cues to the completion of accentuating or attenuating the finger forces to the preset threshold. According to the cues in each trial, the finger requiring accentuating the force would successfully complete the force control reaction if the accentuated force was greater than the threshold of 2.6 N in 2000 ms. Similarly, the finger requiring attenuating the force would also successfully complete the force control reaction if the attenuated force was less than the threshold of 1.4 N in 2000 ms. If a finger did not succeed in a trial, the total action time of this finger was recorded as 2000 ms. The trial was terminated only if both index fingers succeeded.

Similar to a previous cueing paradigm [2], four visually cued patterns of spatial coordination between the index fingers were shown for participants. The red square with a relatively high brightness prompted participants to produce an accentuated-force pulse from the current amplitude of the corresponding finger, while the red square with a relatively low brightness prompted participants to produce an attenuated-force pulse. Accordingly, the four patterns of spatial coordination were defined as the in-phase pattern requiring congruent increments or decrements of bimanual finger forces (same directions), and the anti-phase pattern requiring incongruent ones (different directions). For ease of presentation, these four phase patterns were denoted as $D_L D_R$, $D_L I_R$, $I_L D_R$, and $I_L I_R$; where, D = decreasing force, I = increasing force, and the subscripts denoted the hand to which the fingers belong (L = left hand and R = right hand). Specifically, the in-phase patterns of both index fingers consisted of simultaneous attenuated-force pulses ($D_L D_R$) and accentuated-force pulses ($I_L I_R$). The anti-phase patterns of both index fingers consisted of the attenuated-force pulse of the left index finger whilst accentuated-force pulse of the right index finger ($D_L I_R$), and accentuated-force pulse of the left index finger whilst attenuated-force pulse of the right index finger ($I_L D_R$). The participant had to perform bimanual finger force production using the left and right index fingers simultaneously with the left and right red squares, respectively. Each phase pattern was repeated 20 times and therefore 80 trials were pseudo-randomly provided in a session. Protocols of the testing task with vibrotactile cues were the same as those with the visual cues. To generate vibrotactile cues for the in-phase and anti-phase patterns of the index fingers, the brightness of the red squares was replaced by the strength of vibrations from two vibration motors attached to both wrist joints. The order of the 2 sessions with visual and vibrotactile cues was randomized across the participants.

2.4 Procedures

Before the formal experiment, the participants were provided with a detailed description of the experiment to ensure they had understood the required task. Every participant

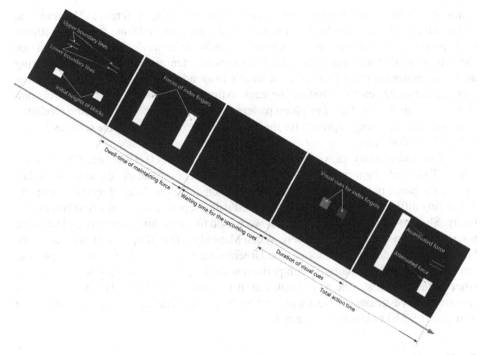

Fig. 2. Definition of temporal parameters in a trial for the anti-phase pattern.

was seated comfortably in a height-adjustable office chair facing the testing computer and both arms retained a consistent posture during the session. The non-tapping fingers were instructed to rest around the force sensors and retain a consistent gesture. The participants were required to perform the force control task according to the cues by pressing two force sensors simultaneously using both index fingers. All participants were allowed to practice a session wherein all phase patterns with visual or vibrotactile cues were involved to ensure they could distinguish the strengths of the two vibrotactile cues on both wrists. Participants were explicitly instructed not to lift tapping fingers off the sensors while pressing with the index fingers. In the formal experiment, a 3-min rest interval was provided between consecutive sessions to avoid fatigue effects. Sessions in which the participant failed to perform as instructed, were repeated after an additional 1-min rest interval.

2.5 Data Analysis

In this study, the inter-manual coordination was taken as a metric for the collective performance in the bimanual force control task. To take the bimanual fingers as a whole, the inter-manual coordination was characterized by the delayed reaction time (DRT) and the timing difference (TD) of the index fingers. Similar to measures of the refractory period [18], the delayed reaction time in each trial was indexed by the larger of the two total action times of the index fingers. Moreover, the difference between the total action times of two fingers of this pair was calculated as the timing difference. The maximal and minimal values of the delayed reaction time were removed from the trials with the same phase patterns in each session. Observations from the previous study indicated that these trials tended to result from unstable states of attention [19]. This preprocessing aimed to minimize the effects of a moment's inattention in the first trial of a session and pre-activated reactions before the cues. After preprocessing, all delayed reaction times of the trials with the same phase patterns were averaged for each cueing modality. The data preprocessing approach for the timing difference remained the same as for the delayed reaction time.

All statistical analyses were completed using SPSS v24.0 (IBM Inc., Chicago, IL, USA). To identify factors influencing the inter-manual coordination, the sensory modality and the phase pattern were varied within participants. The delayed reaction time and the timing difference variables were analyzed using repeated-measures ANOVAs separately. Shapiro-Wilks and Levene's tests were used to check data normality and variance homogeneity ($p < 0.05$), respectively. When Mauchly's Test of Sphericity showed a violation of the sphericity assumption, the Greenhouse-Geisser correction was employed. Furthermore, *Post hoc* pairwise comparison with Bonferroni correction was conducted when a factor was statistically significant at the alpha 0.05 level. The partial η^2 was reported as an estimate of effect size for ANOVAs. The dependent values were reported as means ($\pm$ SE) unless otherwise noted.

3   Results

Figure 3 illustrated the delayed reaction time and the timing difference of the index fingers in the four phase patterns with two sensory modalities. The delayed reaction time and the timing difference variables were statistically analyzed with the phase pattern and the sensory modality, as detailed in Table 1. The statistical analysis revealed that the delayed reaction time was significantly affected by the sensory modality $F(1, 14) = 104.775$, $p < 0.001$, $\eta_p^2 = 0.882$, and the phase pattern $F(1.286, 18.003) = 30.328$, $p < 0.001$, $\eta_p^2 = 0.684$. The fractional degree of freedom was due to the Greenhouse-Geisser correction. Moreover, A two-way ANOVA revealed the significant interaction between the sensory modality and the phase pattern for the delayed reaction time $F(1.164, 16.295) = 27.474$, $p < 0.001$, $\eta_p^2 = 0.662$. As shown in Fig. 3(A), further simple effect analyses showed no significant difference in the delayed reaction time between the two in-phase patterns ($D_L D_R$ and $I_L I_R$) as well as the two anti-phase patterns ($D_L I_R$ and $I_L D_R$) in every sensory modality. In each phase pattern, the delayed reaction time of the index fingers with the visual cues was significantly faster than that with the vibrotactile cues. However, the significant effect of the phase pattern only existed in the vibrotactile modality $F(1.207, 16.893) = 29.256$, $p < 0.001$, $\eta_p^2 = 0.676$, rather than the visual modality $F(3, 42) = 2.567$, $p = 0.067$, $\eta_p^2 = 0.155$. Furthermore, a one-way ANOVA showed that the in-phase patterns had significant advantages in the delayed reaction time over the anti-phase patterns in the vibrotactile modality $F(1, 29) = 64.408$, $p < 0.001$, $\eta_p^2 = 0.69$. Furthermore, the index fingers succeeded in all trials of the inter-finger phase patterns in the visual modality, while the average correct rate of the four inter-finger phase patterns was about 94% in the haptic modality. No interaction between the sensory modality and the inter-finger phase pattern was found, $F(1.755, 24.567) = 2.698$, $p = 0.093$, $\eta_p^2 = 0.162$. Although the inter-finger phase pattern did not have a significant main effect on the correct rate, the main effect of the sensory modality was significant, $F(1.000, 14.000) = 14.751$, $p = 0.002$, $\eta_p^2 = 0.513$.

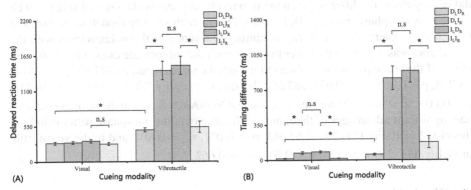

Fig. 3. Delayed reaction times and timing differences in four phase patterns with visual or vibrotactile cues. (A) Means of delayed reaction times of four phase patterns with visual or vibrotactile cues. (B) Means of timing differences of four phase patterns with visual or vibrotactile cues. Error bar denotes standard error of the mean. * denotes significant difference, $p < 0.05$; n.s denotes nonsignificant difference, $p > 0.05$.

Table 1. Statistics for the delayed reaction time and the timing difference.

Pattern	Cueing	Variable	Mean	SEM	Cueing	Pattern	Variable	Mean	SEM
D_LD_R	Visual	DRT	289.36	21.54	Visual	D_LD_R	DRT	296.67	20.03
	Vibrotactile	DRT	494.02	31.32		D_LI_R	DRT		
D_LI_R	Visual	DRT	297.84	20.90		I_LD_R	DRT		
	Vibrotactile	DRT	1418.51	145.86		I_LI_R	DRT		
I_LD_R	Visual	DRT	321.53	25.86		D_LD_R	TD	47.31	5.63
	Vibrotactile	DRT	1498.20	140.88		D_LI_R	TD		
I_LI_R	Visual	DRT	277.95	20.84		I_LD_R	TD		
	Vibrotactile	DRT	539.17	88.17		I_LI_R	TD		
D_LD_R	Visual	TD	16.54	2.85	Vibrotactile	D_LD_R	DRT	987.48	69.68
	Vibrotactile	TD	56.86	9.01		D_LI_R	DRT		
D_LI_R	Visual	TD	73.53	12.19		I_LD_R	DRT		
	Vibrotactile	TD	815.66	116.88		I_LI_R	DRT		
I_LD_R	Visual	TD	81.82	11.04		D_LD_R	TD	485.34	51.26
	Vibrotactile	TD	889.97	117.31		D_LI_R	TD		
I_LI_R	Visual	TD	17.33	1.93		I_LD_R	TD		
	Vibrotactile	TD	178.87	59.89		I_LI_R	TD		

Similarly, the two-way ANOVA on the timing difference revealed significant main effects of the sensory modality $F(1, 14) = 73.571$, $p < 0.001$, $\eta_p^2 = 0.84$, and the phase pattern $F(1.156, 16.183) = 30.301$, $p < 0.001$, $\eta_p^2 = 0.684$. There was interaction between the sensory modality and the phase pattern $F(1.142, 15.989) = 22.957$, $p < 0.001$, $\eta_p^2 = 0.621$. Furthermore, simple effect analyses showed the timing difference did not significantly differ between the two in-phase patterns ($D_L D_R$ and $I_L I_R$) as well as the two anti-phase patterns ($D_L I_R$ and $I_L D_R$) in each sensory modality, as shown in Fig. 3(B). In every phase pattern, the timing difference of the index fingers with the visual cues was significantly lower than that with the vibrotactile cues. The significant effect of the phase pattern was observed in both the visual modality $F(1.995, 27.925) = 23.948$, $p < 0.001$, $\eta_p^2 = 0.631$, and the vibrotactile modality $F(1.143, 16.008) = 26.742$, $p < 0.001$, $\eta_p^2 = 0.656$. Moreover, a one-way ANOVA revealed that the in-phase patterns had significant advantages of the timing difference over the anti-phase patterns in both the visual modality $F(1, 29) = 62.643$, $p < 0.001$, $\eta_p^2 = 0.684$, and in the vibrotactile modality, $F(1, 29) = 56.885$, $p < 0.001$, $\eta_p^2 = 0.662$.

4 Discussion

This study examined the effects of cueing modalities on the inter-manual coordination in bimanual force control tasks with accentual- or attenuated-force production. It was found that the phase pattern had a significant effect on the inter-manual coordination in the visual and vibrotactile modalities. No significant difference in the inter-manual coordination was observed between the two in-phase patterns as well as the two anti-phase patterns. Furthermore, the in-phase patterns of the index fingers had significant advantages in the inter-manual coordination over the anti-phase patterns only in the vibrotactile modality. As we defined above, the in-phase coordinated pattern of the index fingers was also a mirror-symmetrical manipulation with respect to bimanual coordination. As a result, these results provided our answers to the first question raised at the start of this paper. Furthermore, even though the visual modality showed the superiority of both the delayed reaction time and the timing difference over the vibrotactile modality in every phase pattern, the delayed reaction time of the index fingers with visual cues could not differentiate the in-phase patterns from the anti-phase patterns, as shown in Fig. 3. Collectively, the visual and vibrotactile modalities played different roles in the inter-manual coordination in the bimanual force control task with a certain background force level, which answered the second question raised at the start of this paper.

The inter-manual coordination of the index fingers did not significantly differ between the two in-phase patterns as well as the two anti-phase patterns. This finding indicated that the different inter-manual coordination performances may result from the symmetrical and asymmetric phase patterns, rather than the accentual and attenuated forces of both index fingers. Moreover, the in-phase advantage of the inter-manual coordination was more prominent in the vibrotactile modality. Our findings corroborated a proposition that the anti-phase movement might be more independent to utilize homologous muscles mirror-asymmetrically and sequentially, while the in-phase movement was driven by the homologous muscles mirror-symmetrically and simultaneously [20, 21]. Numerous studies found that the anti-phase movement is less successfully performed than the in-phase movement and this becomes evident at fast-cycling frequencies [9]. Previous literature also showed that the performance of the in-phase movement was more accurate and stable when an external timing cue was adopted for Parkinson's disease patients [21]. The instability of anti-phase movements was related to their more complex event representation relative to that associated with in-phase movements [22]. Traditionally this superiority of symmetric movements was attributed to a tendency towards the activation of homologous muscles, which are more strongly involved in symmetric than in asymmetric body movements [23]. However, some researchers suggested that the symmetry tendency in the bimanual finger oscillation task was a tendency towards perceptual, spatial symmetry, rather than towards co-activation of homologous muscles [5]. Therefore, a widely argued hypothesis was that differential neural processes governed the in-phase and anti-phase bimanual coordination [20]. More evidence remains for further study although the present study has revealed the advantage of the inter-manual coordination in mirror-symmetrical kinetics.

There was the modality-specific effect of cueing on the advantage of the inter-manual coordination in the bimanual force control task with accentuated- or attenuated-force production. The inter-manual coordination of the index fingers could differentiate the in-phase patterns from the anti-phase patterns in the vibrotactile modality while the visual modality showed faster reaction speed and less timing difference of the index fingers in the proposed force control task. Similarly, a previous study found different effects of visual and tactile actions on response planning and execution in the bimanual finger-tapping task requiring symmetrically located responses [23]. The advantage of the inter-manual coordination with visual cues might owe to a relatively greater visual modality capacity with respect to the information transmission rate. Previous studies showed that the visual channel capacity was about 10^7 bits/s, while the haptic channel capacity was about 10^2 bits/s [24, 25]. Although the differences between visual and auditory modalities have been revealed in the neural activity underlying rhythm perception [16, 26], the somatosensory underpinnings of the in-phase coordination advantage in the vibrotactile modality also remain to be further in-depth study. It is worthy to note that the visual modality shows the advantage of the in-phase pattern over the anti-phase pattern in the timing difference rather than the reaction speed. This finding, to some extent, supports the hypothesis of asymmetric control of the force and symmetric control of movement timing in the context of a bimanual tapping task [27]. Both neurophysiological and anatomical findings indicated that the timing control in bimanual tasks was more tightly coupled in the motor system than the force control [28]. Therefore when designing an application, the visual cue would be preferable to weaken the difference between phase patterns of the index fingers while the vibrotactile cue would be preferable on the contrary.

However, two potential improvements to this study remain to be explored in future work. Firstly, it would be better to add one more condition for the inter-manual coordination in the auditory modality. A major challenge of using auditory cues is that attentional biases and the right-ear advantage exist in dichotic listening [29, 30]. Two parallel tone cues to instruct the actions of bimanual fingers respectively will introduce an additional inter-manual timing difference. Using a merged tone sequence to cue the actions of bimanual fingers respectively will also produce the starting temporal difference. It may be a candidate method to use four easily distinguishable auditory cues and provide participants with longer perception time. Secondly, it might be better to take the role of working memory in the performance difference between visual and haptic modalities into consideration [31, 32]. In the current study, the visual modality showed the superiority of both the delayed reaction time and the correct rate of trials. It should be noted that the visual cues may have immediacy in prompting the requested reaction, while the perception of tactile vibrations might become vague when performing under time pressure. Tactile working memory capacity was generally more limited and showed more variability than visual memory in participants with normal vision [33]. One of our ongoing studies has preliminarily verified the decay of tactile working memory and sensory attenuation during haptic interaction.

5 Conclusion

This study demonstrated the modality-specific effect of cueing on the advantage of the inter-manual coordination in the bimanual force control task with accentuated- or attenuated-force production. The phase pattern had a significant effect on the inter-manual coordination in the visual and vibrotactile modalities. The in-phase patterns of the index fingers had prominent advantages of the inter-manual coordination over the anti-phase patterns in the vibrotactile modality. Even though the visual modality showed the superiority of both the delayed reaction time and the timing difference over the vibrotactile modality in every phase pattern, the delayed reaction time of the index fingers with visual cues could not differentiate the in-phase patterns from the anti-phase patterns. Consequently, the visual and vibrotactile modalities played different roles in the inter-manual coordination of the index fingers during the bimanual synchronized force production with a certain background force level. The findings of this study provided an important addition to understanding the inter-manual coordination of the index fingers in bimanual synchronized force control tasks and theoretical references for designing interactive applications using both the in-phase and anti-phase bimanual coordination.

References

1. Swinnen, S.P., Wenderoth, N.: Two hands, one brain: cognitive neuroscience of bimanual skill. Trends Cogn. Sci. **8**(1), 18–25 (2004)
2. Blais, M., Albaret, J.-M., Tallet, J.: Is there a link between sensorimotor coordination and inter-manual coordination? Differential effects of auditory and/or visual rhythmic stimulations. Exp. Brain Res. **233**(11), 3261–3269 (2015)
3. Repp, B.H.: Sensorimotor synchronization: a review of the tapping literature. Psychon. Bull. Rev. **12**(6), 969–992 (2005)
4. Inui, N.: Contextual effects on force control and timing in a finger-tapping sequence with an accentuated- or attenuated-force tap. Mot. Control **8**(3), 255–269 (2004)
5. Mechsner, F., Kerzel, D., Knoblich, G., Prinz, W.: Perceptual basis of bimanual coordination. Nature **414**(6859), 69–73 (2001)
6. Whitall, J., Forrester, L., Song, S.: Dual-finger preferred-speed tapping: effects of coordination mode and anatomical finger and limb pairings. J. Mot. Behav. **31**(4), 325–339 (1999)

7. Kelso, J.A.: Phase transitions and critical behavior in human bimanual coordination. Am. J. Physiol.-Regul., Integr. Comp. Physiol. **246**(6), R1000–R1004 (1984)

8. Marteniuk, R.G., MacKenzie, C.L., Baba, D.M.: Bimanual movement control: information processing and interaction effects. Q. J. Exper. Psychol. Sect. A **36**(2), 335–365 (1984)

9. Inui, N.: Coupling of force variability in bimanual tapping with asymmetrical force. Mot. Control **9**(2), 164–179 (2005)

10. Bingham, G.P., Snapp-Childs, W., Zhu, Q.: Information about relative phase in bimanual coordination is modality specific (not amodal), but kinesthesis and vision can teach one another. Hum. Mov. Sci. **60**, 98–106 (2018)

11. Kennedy, D.M., Boyle, J.B., Shea, C.H.: The role of auditory and visual models in the production of bimanual tapping patterns. Exp. Brain Res. **224**(4), 507–518 (2013)

12. Drewing, K., Hennings, M., Aschersleben, G.: The contribution of tactile reafference to temporal regularity during bimanual finger tapping. Psychol. Res. **66**(1), 60–70 (2002)

13. Studenka, B.E., Eliasz, K.L., Shore, D.I., Balasubramaniam, R.: Crossing the arms confuses the clocks: sensory feedback and the bimanual advantage. Psychon. Bull. Rev. **21**(2), 390–397 (2014)

14. Wang, D., Peng, C., Afzal, N., Li, W., Wu, D., Zhang, Y.: Localization performance of multiple vibrotactile cues on both arms. IEEE Trans. Haptics **11**(1), 97–106 (2018)

15. Peng, C., Yao, N., Wang, X., Wang, D.: Interfinger synchronization capability of paired fingers in discrete fine-force control tasks. Mot. Control **26**(4), 608–629 (2022)

16. Repp, B.H., Su, Y.-H.: Sensorimotor synchronization: a review of recent research (2006–2012). Psychon. Bull. Rev. **20**(3), 403–452 (2013)

17. Peng, C., Wang, D., Zhang, Y.: Quantifying differences among ten fingers in force control capabilities by a modified meyer model. Symmetry **11**(9), 1–18 (2019)

18. Buckingham, G., Carey, D.P.: Rightward biases during bimanual reaching. Exp. Brain Res. **194**(2), 197–206 (2009)

19. Peng, C., Peng, W., Feng, W., Zhang, Y., Xiao, J., Wang, D.: EEG correlates of sustained attention variability during discrete multi-finger force control tasks. IEEE Trans. Haptics **14**(3), 526–537 (2021)

20. Shih, P.-C., Steele, C.J., Nikulin, V., Villringer, A., Sehm, B.: Kinematic profiles suggest differential control processes involved in bilateral in-phase and anti-phase movements. Sci. Rep. **9**(3273), 1–12 (2019)

21. Johnson, K.A., Cunnington, R., Bradshaw, J.L., Phillips, J.G., Iansek, R., Rogers, M.A.: Bimanual co-ordination in Parkinson's disease. Brain **121**(4), 743–753 (1998)

22. Spencer, R.M.C., Ivry, R.B.: The temporal representation of in-phase and anti-phase movements. Hum. Mov. Sci. **26**(2), 226–234 (2007)

23. Janczyk, M., Skirde, S., Weigelt, M., Kunde, W.: Visual and tactile action effects determine bimanual coordination performance. Hum. Mov. Sci. **28**(4), 437–449 (2009)

24. Gallace, A., Spence, C.: In Touch with the Future: The Sense of Touch from Cognitive Neuroscience to Virtual Reality. Oxford University Press, Oxford, UK (2014)

25. Rau, P.-L.P., Zheng, J.: Modality capacity and appropriateness in multimodal display of complex non-semantic information stream. Int. J. Hum. Comput. Stud. **130**, 166–178 (2019)

26. Hove, M.J., Fairhurst, M.T., Kotz, S.A., Keller, P.E.: Synchronizing with auditory and visual rhythms: an fMRI assessment of modality differences and modality appropriateness. Neuroimage **67**, 313–321 (2013)

27. Inui, N., Hatta, H.: Asymmetric control of force and symmetric control of timing in bimanual finger tapping. Hum. Mov. Sci. **21**(2), 131–146 (2002)

28. Maki, Y., Wong, K.F.K., Sugiura, M., Ozaki, T., Sadato, N.: Asymmetric control mechanisms of bimanual coordination: an application of directed connectivity analysis to kinematic and functional MRI data. Neuroimage **42**(4), 1295–1304 (2008)

29. Bryden, M.P., Munhall, K., Allard, F.: Attentional biases and the right-ear effect in dichotic listening. Brain Lang. **18**(2), 236–248 (1983)
30. Ianiszewski, A., Fuente, A., Gagné, J.-P.: Association between the right ear advantage in dichotic listening and interaural differences in sensory processing at lower levels of the auditory system in older adults. Ear Hear. **42**(5), 1381–1396 (2021)
31. Gallace, A., Tan, H.Z., Haggard, P., Spence, C.: Short term memory for tactile stimuli. Brain Res. **1190**, 132–142 (2008)
32. van Erp, J.B.F., Paul, K.I., Mioch, T.: Tactile working memory capacity of users who are blind in an electronic travel aid application with a vibration belt. ACM Trans. Accessible Comput. **13**(2), 1–15 (2020)
33. Bliss, I., Hämäläinen, H.: Different working memory capacity in normal young adults for visual and tactile letter recognition task. Scand. J. Psychol. **46**(3), 247–251 (2005)

Creation of Realistic Haptic Experiences for Materialized Graphics

Hiroyuki Shinoda[(⊠)]

The University of Tokyo, 5-1-5 Kashiwano-Ha, Kashiwa 277-8561, Chiba, Japan
hiroyuki_shinoda@k.u-tokyo.ac.jp

Abstract. Aerial images that can interact with the hands and fingers inducing realistic tactile sensations and behave as though they are composed of physical substances are referred to as materialized graphics. Materialized graphics provides a natural interface that humans can handle and manipulate using skills that are inherent in any human. The technology also enables us to confirm and enjoy the tactile feeling and mediates human–human communication. This paper reports the ten-year progress of materialized graphics based on airborne ultrasound tactile displays. Early symbolic demonstrations of materialized graphics are presented, and the recent technological advances in haptic rendering that improve the realism are summarized. It explains the current non-contact display covers the sensations of static pressure and thermal interaction in addition to vibratory sensations.

Keywords: Midair Haptics · Airborne Ultrasound Tactile Display · Haptic Reproduction · Materialized Graphics

1 Introduction

Visual display technologies for creating 3D experiences are progressing, and ordinary people are already familiar with head-mounted displays. Such progress is evoking a need for haptic displays for directly touching and manipulating aerial images. Realistic haptic stimulation enables complex operations, such as deforming and assembling virtual objects, in addition to grasping and moving them. Moreover, reproducing various tactile sensations enables us to confirm the feel of the displayed objects, enjoy touching the aerial image itself, and send emotional information to others by virtual touch. Noncontact tactile presentation technology originating from [1–3] has advanced recently and is beginning to have the ability to reproduce such tactile sensations.

Aerial images, which can interact with the hands and fingers inducing realistic tactile sensations, behave as though they are composed of physical substances [4]. In this paper, we refer to such VR images as "materialized graphics" and introduce their current status [5]. Wearable devices are another promising option for haptic displays combined with such graphical images. However, in this paper, we focus on the airborne ultrasound tactile display (AUTD), which does not require the user to wear any device.

Ultrasound-based noncontact tactile presentation synchronized with aerial video was first demonstrated in 2009 [6]. By around 2015, HaptoMime [7], a midair touch panel that

D. Wang et al. (Eds.): AsiaHaptics 2022, LNCS 14063, pp. 41–52, 2023.
https://doi.org/10.1007/978-3-031-46839-1_4

allows users to operate buttons and icons in the air while feeling tactile feedback, a tactile projector [8, 9] that superimposes noncontact tactile sensations on projector images, and HaptoClone [10] that synchronizes 3D images with airborne tactile presentation were demonstrated, as well. Although these demonstrations provided new experiences of noncontact tactile stimulation, the tactile sensations reproduced were limited to a few types of special sensations. However, recent research is changing this situation, and the range of presentable tactile sensations is expanding considerably. The first half of this paper provides an overview of the above-mentioned demonstrations, whereas the second half summarizes the recent advances to improve the realism of the presented tactile sensations.

This manuscript focused on the earliest demonstrations and recent essential problems in materialized graphics. The general applications of noncontact tactile stimulation are broader as summarized in a comprehensive survey by Rakkolainen et al. [11]. Note that this manuscript does not cover gesture-interface applications [3] and other general use-cases. Instead, it focuses on the latest important results of realistic tactile presentation.

2   Materialized Graphics Before 2016

2.1   Single-Focus Amplitude Modulation

The most primitive method of reproducing tactile sensations with ultrasound is to make a single focus with an ultrasound phased array. The amplitude and position of the radiation pressure at the focus are modulated, creating a tactile sensation. The radiation force proportional to the ultrasound power is perceivable by the skin when it is properly modulated [1, 2]. The force required on the skin surface determines the approximation of the minimally required electric power. For example, if an ultrasonic wave with a power of 10 W is perpendicularly incident on a certain area of the skin, most of the sound is reflected on the skin, resulting in a radiation pressure of 60 mN or 6 g-force.

The used wavelength provides the theoretical limit for the spatial resolution. The wavelength of 40-kHz ultrasound, which is typically used in noncontact tactile displays, is 8.5 mm, and it provides an approximate estimate of the focal-spot size. Higher ultra-sonic frequencies increase the spatial resolution, but also increase the attenuation of the ultrasonic waves in air, which in return reduces the workspace size. It should also be noted that air currents called acoustic streaming [12] are generated in a space where a strong sound field is generated. The presence of wind is perceived and the pressure due to airflow is added to the presented radiation pressure.

The following subsections present examples of studies in which the focus of such simple focused ultrasound is generated with amplitude modulation (AM) and superimposed on an aerial image.

2.2   Midair Touch Panel

Figure 1 shows the first demonstration system of an airborne touch panel called Hap-toMime [7]. An image of the touch panel was generated in air and operated by a user. The locations of the buttons and icons were visually transmitted to the user. When the user's finger touched the surface of the aerial touch panel, the finger position was detected by an infrared sensor. The phased array produced the focus at the finger-pad. Contact with the button was experienced through a vibratory sensation created by AM. The vibratory stimulation was sustained when the finger and virtual touch-panel are in contact. Multiple arrays were used to provide a strong tactile sensation, and the finger sensing using an infrared touch screen sensor was precise and robust.

Such a noncontact touch panel is hygienic. During surgery, a doctor can proceed with the operation while inputting information with his/her unclean hands. By producing the intensity contrast of the tactile sensation, a clicking sensation can also be provided [13].

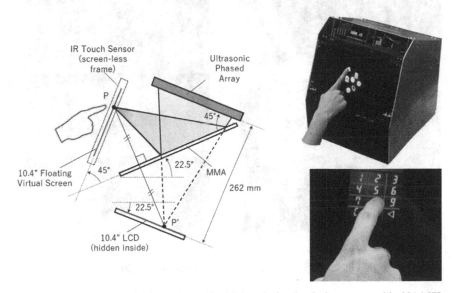

Fig. 1. Haptomime, a midair touch panel with haptic feedback demonstrated in 2014 [7].

2.3 Tactile Projector

The tactile projector proposed in [8] and [9] is another example of audiovisual superimposition. As depicted in Fig. 2, tactile stimuli are provided in conjunction with the visual images projected on the user's skin. In the first demonstration in 2013, an ordinary video projector projected images including those of small creatures, on which ultrasonic tactile stimuli were superimposed. The temporal waveforms were tested through trial-and-error to determine the suitable ones. The spatial pressure distribution was a single focus of approximately 1-cm diameter superimposed on the visual image. The position and motion of the haptic image were predetermined, and feedback from the sensor was not required.

The system was demonstrated in conferences, exhibitions, and open labs on campus. Even though the signals were not designed on a physical basis, the system appeared to provide a certain sense of reality to the tactile stimuli. The participants were often surprised when told that the displayed pattern was only a single focal point 1-cm in diameter because they perceived finer and complex spatial patterns, influenced by the visual information.

The pressure of ultrasonic radiation and the flow of air due to acoustic flow not only create tactile sensations, but also physical interactions with the surrounding lightweight or flexible objects. For example, ultrasound can move the surface of water or sand. This visually reinforces the sense of reality as though the entity is physically present.

 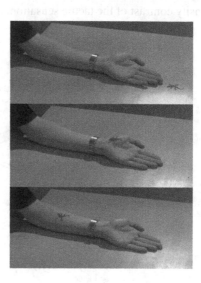

Fig. 2. Tactile projector [8, 9] demonstrated in 2013.

2.4   HaptoClone

HaptoClone (Haptic & Optical Clone) [10] is an interaction system that generates high-definition 3D visual objects with tactile feedback, as shown in Fig. 3. Side-by-side booths were optically connected, and the 3D image of an object in one booth was copied to the other booth. Ultrasonic tactile feedback was combined with the transferred 3D image to enable real-time interaction.

A pair of micro-mirror array plates (MMAPs) was used to reconstruct the 3D images in adjacent booths. As illustrated schematically in Fig. 3, the 3D object image in one booth was optically transferred to the other booth through reflection by the two MMAPs, twice. The booths were perfectly symmetrical. For example, if a balloon was placed in the booth on the right and the user touched the reconstructed image of the balloon in the booth on the left, the real balloon in the right booth appeared to be touched and moved by the image of the hand in the left booth.

The 3D shapes of the objects in each booth were measured by sensors, and tactile sensation was reproduced by forming an ultrasonic focus in the area where it was determined that the hand touched the virtual object in the image. In the first version of the

HaptoClone, the acoustic energy was distributed equally to the detected contact points. No processing was involved to fine-tune the magnitude or temporal variation of the force according to the contact depth. Even with such simple tactile stimulation, two people sitting in adjacent booths could enjoy the mutual touch experience. Such a device can be used as a scientific tool to clarify the role of tactile modality in nonverbal communication. The effect of the sense of touch on the mind and body when a human touches another's hand is an interesting theme for future research.

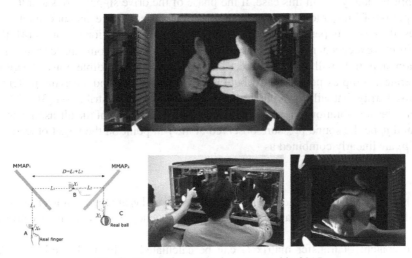

Fig. 3. HaptoClone [10] demonstrated in 2015.

3   Tactile Reproduction Through Ultrasound

3.1   Recent Progress of Haptic Feel Creation

As mentioned above, the potential of materialized graphics had been demonstrated by the mid-2010s. However, it was still in a primitive stage in tactile presentation. To advance the materialized graphics, the 3D shape of a real object needs to be more precisely measured to identify the contact area with the virtual object. Interaction is then created by reproducing the proper pressure distribution corresponding to the deformation and the motion of the virtual image in response to the force. Further, the reproduction of the force distribution needs improvement for effective stimulation.

In this section, the significant advancements of such tactile rendering problems are summarized. First, the method of forming spatial patterns of the pressure distribution is described below. Furthermore, we extend the reproduced haptic perception based on the perceptual characteristics of the human tactile sensation. We also introduce a temperature display using ultrasound in addition to mechanical stimulation.

3.2 Spatial Pressure Pattern Generation

Scanning a single focal point at high-speed is a method for reproducing the contact and pressure distribution at multiple points, as previously described. If the ultrasonic transducer is non-resonant and the phase can be switched instantaneously, the scanning method can be used for a wide range of applications. However, in many transducers, resonant elements are used to match the solid vibrator impedance with air. For example, in the case of a typical 40-kHz transducer, which is being extensively used, the quality factor Q is approximately 30. In this case, if the phase of the drive signal varies significantly over a period of 1 ms or less, the physical oscillation phase of the resonator cannot follow it. Thus, there is an upper limit to the frequency of the focal position updates [14]. If the upper limit is exceeded, not only will the focal point position become inaccurate, but the vibration amplitude will also decrease, generating unwanted audible noise. Therefore, to generate a complex pressure distribution, it is necessary to find a driving pattern for the phased array that will form the desired radiation pressure distribution [3].

Let v_i be the vibration velocity of the i-th transducer surface of the ultrasonic phased array and p_j be the sound pressure observed at the j-th point on the target object; then, v_i and p_j are linearly combined as

$$p = Gv, \tag{1}$$

where $p = [p_1 p_2 \ldots p_M]^\top$ and $v = [v_1 v_2 \ldots v_N]^\top$. p_j and v_i are the complex representations of the amplitude and phase at the ultrasonic frequency. This is the inverse problem we should solve here.

The content of transfer matrix G can be calculated easily if the reflections and diffraction are neglected. However, in recent years, some studies have reported tactile sensation improvement by using G taking these factors into account [15, 16].

Another factor contributing to the difficulty of this inverse problem is the considerable limitation of the maximum power of a single transducer. Solving Eq. (1) alone often yields a useless solution in which only a limited number of elements are strongly driven while the other elements are at rest. In many cases, the power from most transducers must be aggregated to finally produce a significant tactile sensation. Therefore, certain constraints must be imposed on the amplitude of each element $|v_i|$ to find an acceptable solution [17–20]. The most extreme constraint is to maintain $|v_i|$ constant and vary only its phase to determine the most favorable solution [16]. Although this constraint appears too strong, but it has been used in many practical cases in our laboratory.

It should be noted that the human skin feels the radiation pressure at point j:

$$P_j = \frac{A}{\rho c^2} |p_j|^2, \tag{2}$$

where only the amplitude of the ultrasonic sound pressure must have a desired value on the target surface and the phase may be arbitrary. Therefore, instead of setting p as the target value, we solve an optimization problem that selects the phase of v_i and the overall amplitude such that P_j approaches a target value. Utilizing this arbitrariness of the phase, a good solution can be obtained even under the strong constraint that $|v_i|$ must be constant. Although these methods are not perfect, they are useful in many practical cases. This is an important recent achievement.

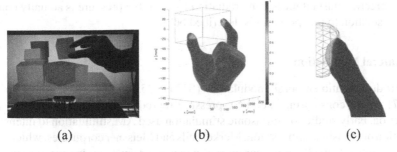

(a)   (b)   (c)

Fig. 4. Creation of a pressure distribution [16, 22, 24].

3.3 Problems in Pressure Pattern Rendering

Figure 4 (a) displays an example of a tactile interaction system using 3D computer graphics (CG). Glassless 3D CG is created by a parallax barrier display developed by the Hideki Kakeya Laboratory of the University of Tsukuba [21]. The workspace is a cube with a side of approximately 30 cm, and a total of 16 units of ultrasonic phased arrays are installed on the top, bottom, left, and right walls to surround the workspace.

In this system, the pressure distribution reflecting the depth of contact between the finger and the virtual object is reproduced at the fingertip. In earlier studies [22, 23] by Matsubayashi et al., as shown in Fig. 4 (a), the contact surface spread was represented by rotating the focal point on a circular path on the finger belly. With this system, it was possible to pick-up a virtual object placed in a 20 cm × 15 cm area and move it to a specified point without vision. Later, they demonstrated a method for reproducing the spatial distribution in a finger-pad as described in the previous section [16]. When phased arrays surround the workspace from all sides, the ultrasonic waves can be focused down to approximately half a wavelength, enabling the generation of various pressure distributions on the fingertips, using 40-kHz ultrasound with a wavelength of 8.5 mm. It has been shown that various local shapes can be reproduced, including the contact distribution on a flat surface as depicted in Fig. 4 (b) [16]. As shown in Fig. 4 (c), a study also verified that the differences in the elasticity can be presented by the differences in the contact area when a finger contacts a virtual (very) flexible body [24].

These studies confirmed that the state-of-contact could be perceived and recognized based on differences in the pressure distribution on the fingertip-skin. Human fingers are sensitive to changes in the pressure distribution, through which the direction and curvature of the surface, hardness of the surface, etc. are perceived. Reproducing these changes would create the feeling of a physical entity. However, this distribution changes sensitively in response to slight differences in the positional relationship between the finger and the object, which requires quick and accurate measurement of the fingertip surface. This is a remaining challenge for reproducing such an experience.

Another crucial issue in haptic rendering is the reproduction of the static pressure sensation. When an object is grasped with the fingertip, the main temporal component of the force is static pressure with a time constant of several hundred milliseconds or longer. As the human perception threshold of such a slowly varying force is high, humans cannot perceive constant ultrasound radiation forces if the pressure is actually constant. A recent solution to this problem is described below.

3.4 Lateral Modulation

We introduce spatiotemporal modulation (STM) [25] and lateral modulation (LM) [26, 27] before considering the static-pressure reproduction mentioned in the previous section. Early studies on ultrasonic stimulation used AM stimulation to intensify the perception of ultrasonic stimulation. Merkel cells and Meissner corpuscles, which are relatively superficial, and Pacinian corpuscles, which are deeper, are known as mechanoreceptors in human glabrous skin. Because the threshold for the vibratory component at 100–200 Hz, to which the Pacinian corpuscle is sensitive, is the lowest, 200-Hz AM is often used in ultrasonic haptic stimulation.

In contrast, recent studies have found that LM and STM, in which the force is maintained constant, and the spatial position is moved vibrationally (LM) or nonvibrationally (STM), can significantly increase the subjective intensity. When the maximum ultrasound power of the device is set to 0 dB, the LM threshold is more than 10 dB less than that of AM, as shown in Fig. 5 (a) on a palm. With this stimulation method, stronger stimulation can be felt even at low frequency. When the frequency of LM stimulation is reduced to 10 Hz or lower, the sensation is clearly different from that of vibration and is closer to static pressure sensation [28]. The similar phenomenon was reported by Konyo et al. in 2005 [29].

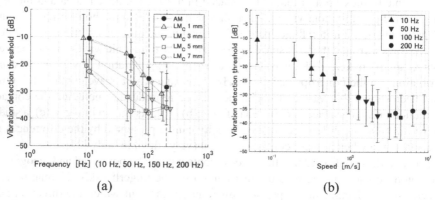

(a)   (b)

Fig. 5. Threshold of lateral modulation (LM) [26] at the palmar region. "LM$_C$ d mm" indicates that the ultrasound focus is rotated along a circle with a radius of d mm on the skin.

3.5 Static-Pressure Presentation

As described in the previous section, static pressure presentation has been considered difficult in conventional airborne ultrasound tactile presentation, and the presentation stimuli has been mainly vibratory. For example, AM modulation of the pressure at

200 Hz has often been applied. However, the perceived sensation is clearly a "vibration" which is different from the tactile sensation felt when gently touching or grasping an object.

A recent study by Morisaki et al. revealed that in LM modulation, pseudo pressure sensation could be realized by setting the motion frequency to 10 Hz or lower and by setting the focal displacement step sufficiently fine such that no unnecessary vibration components were perceived [28].

When a physically static pressure is applied to a certain area on the skin, the sensation weakens with time due to adaptation. In contrast, this pseudo-pressure perception maintains its perceptual intensity for the duration of the stimulus. We compared the perceptual intensity of this pseudo-pressure and the ordinary static pressure produced by pushing-up a force gauge with the hand. We confirmed that the pseudo pressure sensation was more than five-times greater than the physical force in a typical case.

In a series of studies in our laboratory, a phased array that can control multiple units in coordination was developed and used [30]. Although the generated radiation pressure is not very weak, lack of static pressure sensation was a problem. Now that the static pressure sensation can be reproduced, the basic tactile elements originating from mechanical quantities are already covered. Although there are certain restrictions on the spatial resolution, force direction, and maximum force, it is possible to reproduce various tactile sensations with certain versatility.

3.6 Cooling-Sensation Presentation

The main components of the physical stimuli that compose a tactile sensation are mechanical and thermal stimuli. The temperature change when an object is touched enables the differences in the thermal conductivity to be distinguished, which plays an important role in the estimation of the object material. In addition, temperature perception strongly influences tactile impressions and mental effects. Noncontact display of the warming sensation has already been proposed based on infrared irradiation by Saga [31]. However, the noncontact presentation of a cooling feel has been considered challenging. Nakajima et al. recently confirmed that when ultrasonic waves are focused on the skin in the presence of a normal-temperature mist of water, the temperature decreases by 3 K in the first

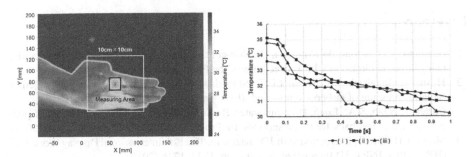

Fig. 6. Display of cooling sensation: temporal change of the skin temperature immediately after ultrasound irradiation [32].

0.5 s on the skin surface of a hand located 500 mm away from the device, as shown in Fig. 6. This temperature drop is due to accelerated vaporization by the ultrasound near the skin-surface [32]. The cooling rate is comparable with that of conventional Peltier cooling devices, and enables remote cooling with high-spatiotemporal resolution. Furthermore, it has been confirmed that the cooling spot can be moved by controlling the focal point position and its movement can be perceived.

4 Summary

The progress of materialized graphics was presented in this paper. Early attempts to superimpose ultrasonic tactile stimuli on interactive aerial video images were summarized, and the recent progress in tactile presentation technology was described as well. Recent studies have shown that it is possible to present the main components of tactile perception, from mechanical to thermal sensations, in a noncontact manner.

The significance of materialized graphics can be understood through the analogy of humanoid robots as a multimodal interface with humans. The human-like behavior and shape of humanoid robots enable communication with humans even if the users do not possess special prior knowledge. Materialized graphics provides a natural interface that humans can handle and manipulate using their inherent skills. It may embody a passive object or a living being, including a human. It mediates human–human communication and sometimes facilitates ergonomic testing to evaluate the usability of a product before it is manufactured.

Though this manuscript focused on the earliest demonstrations and recent essential problems in materialized graphics, airborne ultrasound tactile displays have many other applications, including gesture interfaces [11]. The same device can also control smell [33] with acoustic streaming [12]. The sound-image icon [34] is an example of a haptic entity with no visual images, which is a combination of a touchable virtual object and audible sound created by ultrasound [35]. Motion guidance using ultrasound [36] is another example where synchronization with video is not always necessary. The emotional effects [37-39] have not yet reached specific applications but are potentially significant, even without vision. Thus, materialized graphics is a part of the midair haptics, but that part contains the current main problems of cutaneous tactile reproduction.

References

1. Iwamoto, T., Tatezono, M., Shinoda, H.: Non-contact method for producing tactile sensation using airborne ultrasound. In: Proceedings of the Eurohaptics, pp. 504–513 (2008)
2. Hoshi, T., Takahashi, M., Iwamoto, T., Shinoda, H.: Noncontact tactile display based on radiation pressure of airborne ultrasound. IEEE Trans. Haptics 3(3), 155–165 (2010)
3. Carter, T., Seah, S.A., Long, B., Drinkwater, B., Subramanian, S.: UltraHaptics: multi-point mid-air haptic feedback for touch surfaces. In: Proceeding UIST 2013, pp. 505–514 (2013)
4. Shinoda, H.: Tactile interaction with 3D images. In: The 17th International Display Workshops (IDW 2010), INP4: 3D Interactive Systems, pp. 1743–1746 (2010)
5. https://materialized-graphics.hapislab.org/. JST CREST, Materialized Graphics Project (since 2018)

6. Hoshi, T., Takahashi, M., Nakatsuma, K., Shinoda, H.: Touchable holography. In: Proceeding of the ACM SIGGRAPH 2009 Emerging Technologies, New York, NY, USA, Article No. 23. ACM (2009)
7. Monnai, Y., Hasegawa, K., Fujiwara, M., Yoshino, K., Inoue, S., Shinoda, H.: HaptoMime: mid-air haptic interaction with a floating virtual screen. In: Proceeding of the 27th Annual ACM Symposium on User Interface Software and Technology (UIST 2014), pp. 663–667 (2014)
8. https://www.youtube.com/watch?v=Bb0hNMxxewg. "Visuo-Tactile Projector" video produced by Keisuke Hasegawa in Shinoda laboratory
9. Hasegawa, K., Shinoda, H.: Aerial display of vibrotactile sensation with high spatial-temporal resolution using large-aperture airborne ultrasound phased array. In: Proceeding of the IEEE World Haptics Conference 2013, pp. 31–36 (2013)
10. Makino, Y., Furuyama, Y., Inoue, S., Shinoda, H.: HaptoClone (Haptic-Optical Clone) for mutual tele-environment by real-time 3D image transfer with midair force feedback. In: Proceeding of the 2016 CHI Conference on Human Factors in Computing Systems, pp. 1980–1990 (2016)
11. Rakkolainen, I., Freeman, E., Sand, A., Raisamo, R., Brewster, S.: A survey of mid-air ultrasound haptics and its applications 14(1), 2–19 (2021)
12. Hasegawa, K., Qiu, L., Noda, A., Inoue, S., Shinoda, H.: Electronically steerable ultrasound-driven long narrow air stream. Appl. Phys. Lett. 111(064104) (2017)
13. Ito, M., Kokumai, Y., Shinoda, H.: Midair click of dual-layer haptic button. In: Proceedings of the 2019 IEEE World Haptics Conference, Tokyo, Japan, 9–12 July 2019, pp. 349–352 (2019)
14. Suzuki, S., Fujiwara, M., Makino, Y., Shinoda, H.: Reducing amplitude fluctuation by gradual phase shift in midair ultrasound haptics. IEEE Trans. Haptics 13(1), 87–93 (2020)
15. Inoue, S., Makino, Y., Shinoda, H.: Mid-air ultrasonic pressure control on skin by adaptive focusing. In: Proceedings of the Eurohaptics, pp. 68–77, 4–8 July 2016, London, UK (2016)
16. Matsubayashi, A., Makino, Y., Shinoda, H.: Rendering ultrasound pressure distribution on hand surface in real-time. In: International Conference on Human Haptic Sensing and Touch Enabled Computer Applications (Euro Haptics), 6–9 September 2020, pp. 407–415 (2020)
17. Wyrowski, F.: Iterative quantization of digital amplitude holograms. Appl. Opt. 28(18), 3864–3870 (1989)
18. Long, B., Seah, S.A., Carter, T., Subramanian, S.: Rendering volumetric haptic shapes in mid-air using ultrasound. ACM Trans. Graph. 33(6), 1–10 (2014)
19. Marzo, A., Drinkwater, B.W.: Holographic acoustic tweezers. Proc. Nat. Acad. Sci. 116(1), 84–89 (2019)
20. Plasencia, D.M., Hirayama, R., Montano-Murillo, R., Subramanian, S.: Gs-pat: high-speed multi-point sound-fields for phased arrays of transducers. ACM Trans. Graph 39(4) (2020)
21. Kakeya, H., Okada, K., Takahashi, H.: Time-division quadruplexing parallax barrier with subpixel-based slit control. ITE Trans. Media Technol. Appl. 6(3), 237–246 (2018)
22. Matsubayashi, A., Makino, Y., Shinoda, H.: Direct finger manipulation of 3D object image with ultrasound haptic feedback. In: Proceedings of the 2019 CHI Conference on Human Factors in Computing Systems, Paper No. 87, pp. 1–11 (2019)
23. Matsubayashi, A., Oikawa, H., Mizutani, S., Makino, Y., Shinoda, H.: Display of haptic shape using ultrasound pressure distribution forming cross-sectional shape. In: Proceeding of the 2019 IEEE World Haptics Conference, Tokyo, Japan, 9–12 July 2019, pp. 419–424 (2019)
24. Matsubayashi, A., Yamaguchi, T., Makino, Y., Shinoda, H.: Rendering softness using airborne ultrasound. In: Proceedings of the 2021 IEEE World Haptics Conference, pp. 355–360 (2021)
25. Frier, W., et al.: Using spatiotemporal modulation to draw tactile patterns in mid-air. In: Proceedings of the EuroHaptics 2018, Part I, pp. 270–281 (2018)

26. Takahashi, R., Hasegawa, K., Shinoda, H.: Lateral modulation of midair ultrasound focus for intensified vibrotactile stimuli. In: Proceedings of the EuroHaptics 2018, Part II, pp. 276–288 (2018)
27. Takahashi, R., Hasegawa, K., Shinoda, H.: Tactile stimulation by repetitive lateral movement of midair ultrasound focus. IEEE Trans. Haptics 13(2), 334–342 (2020)
28. Morisaki, T., Fujiwara, M., Makino, Y., Shinoda, H.: Non-vibratory pressure sensation produced by ultrasound focus moving laterally and repetitively with fine spatial step width. IEEE Trans. Haptics 15(2), 441–450 (2022)
29. Konyo, M., Tadokoro, S., Yoshida, A., Saiwaki, N.: A tactile synthesis method using multiple frequency vibrations for representing virtual touch. In: 2005 IEEE/RSJ International Conference on Intelligent Robots and Systems. IEEE, pp. 3965–3971 (2005)
30. Suzuki, S., Inoue, S., Fujiwara, M., Makino, Y., Shinoda, H.: AUTD3: scalable airborne ultrasound tactile display. IEEE Trans. Haptics 14(4), 740–749 (2021)
31. Saga, S.: Thermal-radiation-based haptic display using laser-emission-based radiation control. In: Proceedings of the IEEE World Haptics 2019, WP2P.10 (Work-in-Progress Papers) (2019)
32. Nakajima, M., Hasegawa, K., Makino, Y., Shinoda, H.: Spatiotemporal pinpoint cooling sensation produced by ultrasound-driven mist vaporization on skin. IEEE Trans. Haptics 14(4), 874–884 (2021)
33. Hasegawa, K., Qiu, L., Shinoda, H.: Midair ultrasound fragrance rendering. IEEE Trans. Vis. Comput. Graph. 24(4), 1477–1485 (2018)
34. Rim, S., Suzuki, S., Toide, Y., Fujiwara, M., Makino, Y., Shinoda, H.: Sound-image icon with aerial haptic feedback. In: Proceedings of Euro Haptics 2020, pp. 497–505 (2020)
35. Ochiai, Y., Hoshi, T., Suzuki, I.: Holographic whisper: rendering audible sound spots in three-dimensional space by focusing ultrasonic waves. In: Proceedings of the 2017 CHI Conference on Human Factors in Computing Systems, pp. 4314–4325 (2017)
36. Suzuki, S., Fujiwara, M., Makino, Y., Shinoda, H.: Midair hand guidance by an ultrasound virtual handrail. In: Proceedings of the 2019 IEEE World Haptics Conference, pp. 271–276 (2019)
37. Obrist, M., Subramanian, S., Gatti, E., Long, B., Carter, T.: Emotions mediated through mid-air haptics. In: Proceedings 33rd Annual ACM Conference on Human Factors in Computing Systems (CHI 2015), pp. 2053–2062 (2015)
38. Eid, M.A., Osman, H.A.: Affective haptics: current research and future directions. IEEE Access 26–40 (2016). https://doi.org/10.1109/ACCESS.2015.2497316
39. Vi, C.T., Ablart, D., Gatti, E., Velasco, C., Obrist, M.: Not just seeing, but also feeling art: mid-air haptic experiences integrated in a multisensory art exhibition. Int. J. Hum.-Comput. Stud. 108, 1–14 (2017)

Vibrotactile Encoding of Object Features and Alert Levels for the Visually Impaired

Liwen He[1](✉), Yun Wang[1], Hu Luo[1,2], and Dangxiao Wang[1,2]

[1] School of Mechanical Engineering and Automation, Beihang University,
Beijing 100191, China
buaaheliwen@163.com, wang_yun@buaa.edu.cn
[2] State Key Lab of Virtual Reality Technology and Systems, Beihang University,
Beijing 100191, China

Abstract. Representation of object features can help visually impaired people better comprehend their surrounding environment. Tacton (Tactile Icon) is an effective method to extract and express information non-visually, utilizing users' tactile perception capacities. However existing vibrotactile displays mainly place emphasis on directional guidance, and the number of representable object features is very limited. To leverage the egocentric spatial cognition habit and high tactile perception sensitivity of visually impaired users, this research proposes a user-centered vibrotactile cueing strategy to convey 30 kinds of spatial information through 30 tactons played by 4 vibrators on the back and front side of a pair of gloves. Three parameters including vibration sequence, stimulus location, and intensity are used to encode 10 typical objects located in 3 directions with 2 alert levels. User tests in both laboratory and natural settings are conducted to evaluate the validity of the strategy. The recognition accuracy of the designed tacton has reached 98.99% within a recognition time of less than 0.6s, indicating that this strategy can provide practical assistance for visually impaired users to perceive and respond to the pre-defined spatial information. The multi-parameter tactons provide possibility to encode a wide variety of spatial information by exploiting the communication capacities of the tactile channel of visually impaired users.

Keywords: Tacton · Vibrotactile Display · Visually Impaired

1 Introduction

Independent activity in public spaces can encourage social participation and develop social identity of the visually impaired group [1]. Relevant research has found that 36% of visually impaired people go out every day [2], and 94% of them move within 500 m of their home, and are highly dependent on close and familiar community spaces over safety concerns [3,4]. The public spaces familiar to the visually impaired refer to the sites they visit frequently or regularly in their daily lives, such as supermarkets and parks. To reduce safety risks in complex places, it is necessary to provide them with more real-time, high-precision, and comprehensive spatial information [2].

© The Author(s), under exclusive license to Springer Nature Switzerland AG 2023
D. Wang et al. (Eds.): AsiaHaptics 2022, LNCS 14063, pp. 53–67, 2023.
https://doi.org/10.1007/978-3-031-46839-1_5

Many researchers have attempted to use tactile signal to help visually impaired users to move more safely, and most of them mainly focused on directional guidance [5,6]. Being aware of what type of object they are about to encounter is as important as knowing in which direction the object is located, because the specific features of objects help visually impaired people build a better spatial understanding of their surrounding environment [4]. Representation of various features of objects in the environment is not a trivial task, as it may require a multi-parameter vibrotactile encoding with a wider expression range, and without increasing users' memory load. It is necessary to design a solution that is consistent with the mental model of the visually impaired. Moreover, knowing only the type and direction of the objects may not be sufficient enough to ensure the safety of visually impaired users. Tactile warning or alert has been proven to improve people's responding ability and speed [7,8,9], and it may also help visually impaired users react faster as they move.

In this study, the author adopted an agile development method to design a novel vibrotactile cueing strategy which encodes 30 types of spatial information to visually impaired users, with the aim of expanding the expression range and richness of vibrotactile display.

1.1 Contributions

This paper proposes a user-centered vibrotactile encoding with high recognition accuracy and fast response speed. The main contributions include:

- Inspired by the egocentric spatial cognition habit of visually impaired users in familiar environments, a set of 30 tactons encoding direction (in which way), semantic features (what), and alert level (how risky) of 30 kinds of spatial information in a public park. The above three types of information are conveyed to users in a temporal order that is consistent with visually impaired users' egocentric reference strategy to construct sequential route representation.
- Leveraging the high tactile perception sensitivity of visually impaired users, three haptic parameters including vibration sequence, stimulus location, and intensity were used to construct tactons played by 4 vibrators on a pair of gloves. The demo is tested in both lab and natural settings after a 90-min quick training. A 98.99% recognition accuracy of designed tactons has been achieved, and the recognition time of each tacton is less than 0.6s.

2 Related Work

2.1 Tactile Travel Aids for the Visually Impaired

Existing travel aids for visually impaired users include seeing-eye dogs, white canes, and electronic travel aids (ETAs) [10], with various limits and pain points. A seeing-eye dog costs approximately $42,000 to raise and train, which results in low accessibility. White canes are widely available but label people as visually impaired. ETAs [10] use auditory cues to communicate spatial information, but they occupy the auditory channel and cause high cognitive load[11,12].

Unobstructed hearing is required for safe walking on the street, even for sighted people [5]. For visually impaired people, the addition of tactile feedback has a supplementary effect on auditory feedback in information transmission [13], while not interfering with users' normal hearing. The sensitivity of tactile perception of the visually impaired can have a substitution effect on vision [14,15,16], so that tactile feedback can be used for non-visual expression of spatial information with low cognitive load. Furthermore, tactile feedback can fulfill visually impaired users' need for privacy. The key difficulty in related researches is to determine what type of information can be presented tactually, and which parameters of stimulation can be used to convey these messages effectively [17].

2.2   Mental Model of the Visually Impaired

In terms of spatial cognition, the congenital blind uses an egocentric reference strategy to construct a sequential route representation, and the acquired blind tends to use an external reference strategy to construct an accurate spatial representation [4]. Visually impaired participants who better grasp the relationship between objects and adopt a relevant pathfinding strategy that can find direction faster in unfamiliar spaces.

Specific features of objects help visually impaired users build a better spatial representation or cognitive map of their surrounding environment [4], which encourages them to move with more security and autonomy. In that case, telling them in a higher voice that there is a pond in front of them on the left might work better than just telling them to turn right.

2.3   Vibrotactile Cues for Semantic Features Representation

Using tactile signals to represent objects in the environment can be achieved in two ways: (1) abstract mapping between tactile signals and semantic features of objects; and (2) rendering of physical features of objects. The latter is widely used in VR scenarios; however, it takes up lots of computing resources. Furthermore, the perception of physical features may require a longer time in object identification, and it is also unable to communicate non-haptic information, such as object direction. In contrast, abstract mapping can provide the possibility to expand information-carrying capacity and optimize the communication performance of the users' tactile channel.

Tacton (Tactile Icon) is an effective tool to extract and express information non-visually, utilizing users' tactile perception capacities. Brewster first put forward the concept of Tacton in 2004 (Tactile Icon) [18]. Tacton is an encoded vibration sequence that represents particular semantic information for enhancements of desktop interfaces, provides guidance for visually impaired users, and mobile and wearable device displays. For example, iOS users can distinguish different types of notifications based on received tactons without looking. Lin et al. [19] developed a tacton-based navigation method in a pedestrian environment. Barralon and others use wearable tactons to convey 36 vital situations of patients for anesthesiologists during medical operations [20]. Tacton can be very useful to represent complex information, however, it normally requires a long time to learn. Optimizing the encoding structure of tacton might lower the learning cost and improve its usability.

2.4   Direction Identification and Alert Delivery

Many researchers have also attempted to use tactile signals to inform users of risks in their environment, which are very intuitive to perceive an external direction when receiving tactile stimulation from a single point on the body [21]. In an automatic driving scenario, the users' tactile channel is not occupied as much as visual and auditory channels, hence relatively clear for incoming alerts [22]. Tactile feedback can significantly reduce users' reaction time in error identification [23], braking response, and create larger safety margins [8].

The location of vibrotactile stimuli can be used to map directional spatial information, especially in the driving scenario. The existence of robust cross-modal links in spatial attention between vision and touch [24], and makes it possible to use spatially-distributed vibrotactile warning signals to direct car drivers' attention [7,25]. Vibrotactile alerts have already been suggested as effective modalities for Take-Over Requests (TOR) in terms of reducing reaction times in Highly-Automated Driving (HAD), such as communicating directions and temporal distances to safety hazards [26].

3   Design and Implementation

3.1   Design Objectives

This paper proposes a cueing strategy which aims to inform visually impaired people of the objects they are about to encounter in their familiar public spaces. It functions by transmitting vibrotactile signals to help users quickly grasp the direction (in which way), semantic features (what), and the alert level (how risky) of objects they are about to encounter, as shown in Fig. 1. To achieve the above objectives, tactons should be easily perceived, identified and memorized.

The interaction model of this cueing strategy is shown in Fig. 2. It should be noted that this paper mainly focuses on the design and evaluation of the tacton display, while the input method for detecting environment has not been elaborated. During the tests, the information about the objects in the park was inputted manually into the development board by the experimenter.

3.2   Target Space and Objects

Six indicators such as the visit frequency and risk level were used to evaluate common public spaces for visually impaired people, and a typical public park (Lvyuan Park of Beihang University) was selected as the typical environment in this study. By scoring 67 questionnaires, the 10 most safety-relevant objects in the park were identified for vibrotactile encoding, including pond boundary, pedestrian, ascending steps, etc.

3.3   User-Centered Agile Design Development

This work adopted the user-centered agile software development (UCASD) [27], which integrates the iteration process of agile software development and the user-centered design approach to ensure the usability of the design. The iteration of the design is

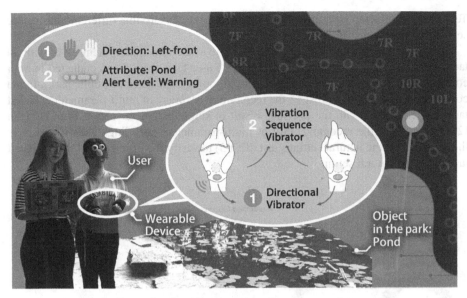

Fig. 1. Example of user's experience when encountering a pond

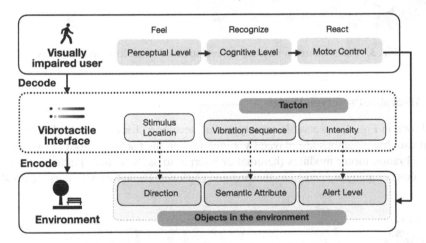

Fig. 2. Interaction model of the vibrotactile interface

driven by small-scale user tests (as shown in Fig. 3), including exploratory tests in the conceptual design stage and confirmatory tests [28] for design evaluation. Firstly, two user tests were conducted to construct design principles. Test 1 was to explore the user's intuitive correlation tendency between objects in the environment and vibrotactile cues by using existing vibration sequences in smartphones. In Test 2, participants' coping strategies when encountering target objects (such as instant stop or slowing down) were collected from questionnaires and further used as important reference for alert level design. Based on these two pre-tests, the first version of tactons were constructed. Then,

Test 3 was conducted by a different group of users to ensure that different vibrotactile sequences can be clearly distinguished.

In the evaluation stage, the participants were asked to acquaint themselves with 30 tactons for 30 min per day for three days. Two user tests were then conducted in both controlled laboratory and uncontrolled natural settings (the selected public park). In the controlled laboratory test (Test 4), the recognition accuracy of multi-parameter encoded tacton is compared with the previous result of single-parameter tacton from Hoggan [29], to evaluate the recognizability of multi-parameters encoding. Then it serves as the baseline for the natural settings test (Test 5) to verify the efficiency of the designed tactons in the natural setting.

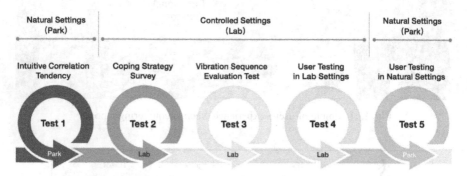

Fig. 3. User-centered agile design iteration based on multi-round user tests

3.4 Wearable Prototype Design

As shown in Fig. 4, a wearable prototype was developed for tactons display in subsequent user tests. Tactons are played by 4 vibrators on the back and front of two gloves. Four vibration motor modules (hereinafter referred to as "vibrators") manufactured by YwRobot company are driven by the Arduino platform. These four vibrators are divided

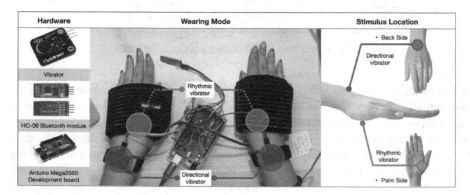

Fig. 4. Hardware composition of the prototype

into two groups, Directional vibrator*2, and Sequence vibrator*2, respectively fixed on two groups of elastic Velcro telescopic belts:

- **Directional vibrator:** Fixed on a thin telescopic belt and worn on the backs of both hands. Convey the direction of the object to be encountered based on the egocentric reference strategy of visually impaired users.
- **Sequence vibrator:** Fixed on a wide telescopic belt and worn on the palms of both hands. Convey the semantic feature and its alert level of the object to be encountered, which is acquired by users during the learning stage.

3.5   Construction of Tacton

Tactons communicate two levels of information: (1) key features of objects in the environment, including the direction and the semantic attribute; (2) two alert levels which are Warning and Caution. Three vibrotactile parameters including stimulus location, vibration sequence, and its overall intensity, which are used to encode the direction, semantic attribute, and alert level of the object to be encountered.

The multi-parameter encoding is designed to transmit vibrotactile signals in a temporal order consistent with the users' coping process to the object they are about to encounter. Firstly, visually impaired users need to ensure, based on the egocentric reference strategy, in what direction they are going to encounter the change and devote their attention to that direction. Then they identify what the object is and trigger necessary reactions. The transmission order of vibrotactile signals is consonant with this process: direction information comes first, and then the semantic attribute of the object appears together with the alert level. This consistency is expected to improve the task performance of tacton.

The mappings between the information of objects in the environment, vibrotactile parameters, and designated vibrators are shown in Table 1. The allocation principles of the three types of signals are:

- The direction information of objects is mapped with the stimulus location (left, right, or both hands) which could be firstly perceived and recognized, as shown in Table 1. The direction vibrator is at the back of the hand.
- Different vibration sequences refer to the semantic attributes of objects which can be learned by users beforehand. The detailed sequence design is shown in Table 2.
- Two alert levels are mapped with the overall intensity of the vibration signal. The vibration from both hands refers to the Warning level, indicating that users are suggested to stop instantly or to slow down significantly. One hand vibration refers to the Caution level, indicating that users should consider appropriate deceleration or keep moving forward with caution.

Composition of Vibration Sequence. The vibration sequence is composed of three types of vibration units: short signal, long signal, and interval unit. As shown in Fig. 5, the adjustable features of the three vibration units are (1) Short signal (dot): intensity; (2) Long signal (line): maximum intensity and duration; (3) Interval (blank): duration.

Table 1. Multi-parameter encoding of tacton

Information category		Parameter category	Designated vibrator	Location of vibrator
Object feature	Direction	Stimulus location	Directional vibrator	Back of hand
	Attribute	Vibration sequence	Sequence vibrator	Palm
Alert level		Intensity	Sequence vibrator	Palm

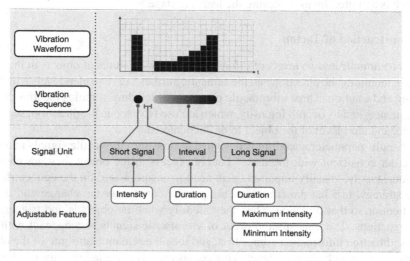

Fig. 5. Composition of vibration sequence

Table 2. Parameter design of attribute and alert

	Attribute Category	Vibration Sequence	Alert Level	Intensity
1	Pond boundary	....	Warning	High (double hands)
2	Descending steps	.•• ▬	Warning	High (double hands)
3	Bridge	•▬▬•	Caution	Gentle (single hand)
4	Ascending steps	▬ ▬	Warning	High (double hands)
5	Entrance and exit	▬▬ ▬▬	Caution	Gentle (single hand)
6	Wall	▬▬• ▬▬•	Warning	High (double hands)
7	Fork	• ▬	Caution	Gentle (single hand)
8	Paving switching	▬▬	Caution	Gentle (single hand)
9	Pedestrian	•• ▬	Warning	High (double hands)
10	Bench	••• ••	Caution	Gentle (single hand)

In this design, the vibration sequence expressing the semantic attribute of the object (what is) is the most difficult feature for users to identify. A critical aspect of designing tactons is to creat patterns that are easy to identify and learn [17]. Different vibration sequences need to vastly differ from each other to lower the cognitive burden of users and improve the recognizability of tactons. Therefore, in Test 3, 5 blindfolded participants were asked to wear the prototype gloves, and use dots and lines to draw the 10 designed vibration sequences after experiencing them. The result showed that the vibration sequence of "descending steps" and "crowd" are highly similar, hence are iterated to be more distinguishable.

Two user tests (Test 4 and Test 5) were then conducted to evaluate the tacton design, which is discussed in the next chapter.

4 Evaluation

4.1 Test 4: User Testing in Lab Settings

In previous studies, the recognition accuracy of tacton encoded only with rhythm has reached 96% [29], which can be considered as a reference for evaluating the performance of single-parameter-tacton. Multi-parameter tacton should reach a similar level of efficiency to ensure eligible usability for users. In Test 4, the recognition accuracy of semantic attributes and of object direction are tested in lab settings.

Participants. 4 participants (ages 20–25, 3 females) were recruited for tactons learning and laboratory test all undergraduate, without visual impairment, and right-handed. All participants were familiar with the selected public space (Lvyuan Park, Beihang) and the target objects within. Test 4 was carried out in a quiet indoor laboratory without a complex acoustic environment, and pedestrians, etc.

Procedure. A three-day learning process was conducted before the test. Experimenters introduced the correlations between tactons and features of objects to the participants, and the participants need to learn and practice by themselves for 30 min per day for three consecutive days. During the learning process, participants can independently send the serial number to play tactons, or be assisted by experimenters.

At the end of the learning process, the participants were invited to complete 120 (30 kinds, 4 times for each kind) tacton recognition tests in the laboratory in random order. Each tacton is played twice at two-second intervals. The participants were asked to recognize and speak out the direction and semantic attribute encoded in the tacton.

Result and Discussion. The data collected in this test include: (1) The overall recognition accuracy of tactons; (2) The respective recognition accuracy of direction and attribute information; (3) The recognition time of tactons (if the participant had given the answer before the completion of tacton playing, the recognition time was recorded as 0.5 s).

After three days of learning, all three types of data have reached a high level. As shown in Fig. 6, in the controlled settings user test, the average recognition accuracy is 97.5% for tacton overall, 98.33% for direction, and 99.17% for semantic attribute. The recognition completion time of all 30 tactons is within 2 s, and 70% of the recognition time is within 0.5 s.

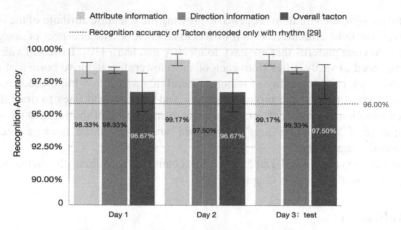

Fig. 6. Recognition accuracy during 3-day learning

The results show that the tactons designed in this study have good performance in recognition accuracy and time. After three days of learning, the recognition accuracy of 83.3% of 30 tactons in the controlled settings user test has reached 100%, which can preliminarily verify that our design requires a relatively low memory load.

4.2 Test 5: User Testing in Natural Settings

On the basis of the controlled settings user test, the tactons were tested in natural settings (Test 5), which was the Lvyuan Park in Beihang University. This test was designed to explore the following two questions:

- Whether the complex acoustic environment in the natural settings can affect the participants' perception and recognition of tactons.
- Whether the prior experience of the geometric distribution of objects can improve recognition accuracy and shorten recognition time of the participants, in such a familiar space.

Procedure. Four participants of the precious test were invited back to carry out the natural settings user test in the Lvyuan Park on a sunny day. During Test 5, participants were asked to wear the prototype gloves blindfolded, and move along a path with a total distance of 250m that covered all 10 target objects. Figure 7 shows the walking path of one of the participants. The participants were all with normal sight and couldn't walk alone blindfolded, and therefore were supported and protected by experimenters. The experimenters manually put in the serial number of the object to be encountered by the prototype to play the encoded tacton, and then the participants identified and spoke out the received tactons directly.

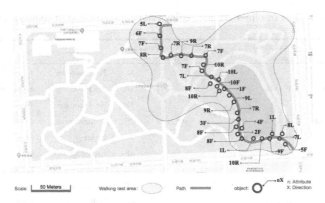

Fig. 7. Encoded objects along the participant's walking path

Result and Discussion. The data collected from the natural settings test were the same as the lab test. The results are shown in Table 3. The recognition accuracy of the 10 objects in the park has reached 100%, and the recognition accuracy of direction was 98.99%, both of which were higher than the controlled settings results, as shown in Fig. 8. The recognition time of all 21 tactons appeared in the natural settings test was less than 1 s, and 33.33% tactons' recognition time was within 0.5 s. The recognition time of 95% of tactons in natural settings was shorter than that in controlled settings, indicating that the participants' prior understanding of space may have a positive effect on their recognition speed of tactons. During the tests, all the participants have not failed to perceive tactons, and the recognition of tactons did not affect participants' normal walking.

The alert level could also be identified by users based on the experimenter's close observation and recording. The participants decelerated or paused significantly when receiving the Warning alert, and made fewer behavior adjustments when receiving the Caution alert during the test.

Table 3. Test results in natural settings and comparison with controlled test

	Attribute	Recognition accuracy		Direction		Recognition accuracy			Tacton		Recognition time*
								1L	Pond boundary	Left front	0.5s =
1	Pond boundary	100.00%	=					1R	Pond boundary	Right front	0.5s =
								1F	Pond boundary	Front	0.5s =
2	Descending steps	100.00%	=	L	Left front	100.00%	+	2F	Descending steps	Front	0.5s =
3	Bridge	100.00%	=					3F	Bridge	Front	0.5s =
4	Ascending steps	100.00%	=					4F	Ascending steps	Front	0.5s +
5	Entrance and exit	100.00%	=					5L	Entrance and exit	Left front	0.5s +
								5F	Entrance and exit	Front	0.6s =
6	Wall	100.00%	=					6F	Wall	Front	0.6s -
								7L	Fork	Left front	0.5s =
7	Fork	100.00%	=	R	Right front	100.00%	+	7R	Fork	Right front	0.5s =
								7F	Fork	Front	0.5s +
8	Paving switching	100.00%	=					8L	Paving switching	Left front	0.5s =
								8R	Paving switching	Right front	0.5s =
								8F	Paving switching	Front	0.5s =
								9L	Pedestrian	Left front	0.5s +
9	Pedestrian	100.00%	=					9R	Pedestrian	Right front	0.5s =
				F	Front	97.95%	-	9F	Pedestrian	Front	0.5s =
								10L	Pedestrian	Left front	0.5s =
10	Bench	100.00%	+					10R	Pedestrian	Right front	0.5s +
								10F	Pedestrian	Front	0.5s =
Recognition accuracy		**100.00%**	**+**	**Recognition accuracy**		**98.99%**	**+**	**Recognition accuracy**		**98.99%**	**+**

* " = " indicates that two results are the same; " + " indicates that the result of natural settings is better; "-" indicates the result of natural settings is worse.

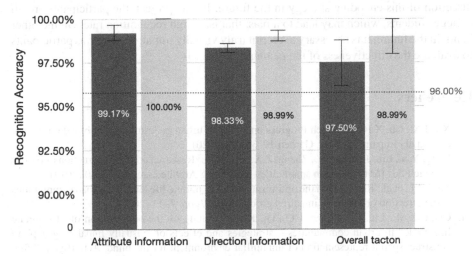

Fig. 8. Recognition accuracy comparison between lab settings and natural settings

5 Conclusion and Future Works

This paper proposes a vibrotactile cueing strategy, utilizing abstract and structured tactons to encode the direction, semantic attribute, and alert level of objects to be encountered when visually impaired users travel in a familiar public space. It aims to enhance their perception and response ability to their traveling environment, and to improve their safety and autonomy.

A series of user tests were carried out to show that tactons functioned well in both controlled settings and natural settings. In the latter, the recognition accuracy of tactons reached over 98.9%, and the recognition time for each tacton was shorter than 0.6s, indicating that this vibrotactile encoding strategy achieved high task performance without affecting the user's normal walking. The result showed that the multi-parameter tactons provide a possibility to optimize the usability of blind guidance system and explore the communication capacities of the tactile channel for visually impaired users.

In natural settings, the psychological mechanism of how previous experience improved users' response to the objects they are about to encounter in a familiar public space remained unclear. Providing prior knowledge for visually impaired people may help them travel more independently in unfamiliar spaces.

The distance of the object to the users also affects their reaction, and different vibration intensities may convey the distance information. This means that a more complex intensity pattern combing the distance information and alert levels needs to be developed and tested in further studies. In the meantime, how to effectively combine different tactile cues to create usable tactons has been a challenge for lots of researchers [17].

Furthermore, the torso part close to the center of the body may be more compatible with the direction of objects and further lower the reaction time, because of its large surface and its possible ego-centric 'view' [21]. This could also be an interesting iteration direction of this encoding strategy in the future. In this project, the participants are all college students, which may lead to a bias, that is, a high recognition rate. On the other hand, in the future, it is necessary to recruit truly visually impaired people as participants to evaluate the effectiveness of the tactons.

References

1. Xu, J.X., Gu, X.R.: Research Progress on safety of urban pedestrian space based on the use of visually impaired people. Garden **10**, 36–40 (2020)
2. Yang, Y.N., Liu, J., Wang, Y., Zhang, Z.X., Dai, Y.R.: Research on the construction of barrier free facilities for the blind in smart cities. Huazhong Architecture. **37**, 36–40 (2019)
3. Yu, Y.M., et al.: Research on the optimization of "15 minute life circle" in urban communities -- the direction of "visually impaired groups, vol. 17, pp. 7–11 (2020)
4. Chen, X.M., Liu, C.L., Qiao, F.Q., Qi, K.M.: A study on the optimization of "15 minute life circle" in urban communities – strategies and effects of "visually impaired group" to construct spatial representation of unfamiliar environment for the blind. Acta Psychol. Sin. **48**, 637 (2016)
5. Kaul, O.B., Rohs, M., Mogalle, M., Simon, B.: Around-the-head tactile system for supporting micro navigation of people with visual impairments. ACM Trans. Comput.-Hum. Interact. **28**, 27 (2021). https://doi.org/10.1145/3458021
6. Flores, G., Kurniawan, S., Manduchi, R., Martinson, E., Morales, L.M., Sisbot, E.A.: Vibrotactile guidance for wayfinding of blind walkers. IEEE Trans. Haptics **8**, 306–317 (2015). https://doi.org/10.1109/TOH.2015.2409980
7. Ho, C., Tan, H.Z., Spence, C.: Using spatial vibrotactile cues to direct visual attention in driving scenes. Transport. Res. F: Traffic Psychol. Behav. **8**, 397–412 (2005)
8. Ho, C., Reed, N., Spence, C.: Assessing the effectiveness of "intuitive" vibrotactile warning signals in preventing front-to-rear-end collisions in a driving simulator. Accid. Anal. Prev. **38**, 988–996 (2006). https://doi.org/10.1016/j.aap.2006.04.002
9. Scott, J.J., Gray, R.: A comparison of tactile, visual, and auditory warnings for rear-end collision prevention in simulated driving. Hum. Factors **50**, 264–275 (2008). https://doi.org/10.1518/001872008X250674
10. Lévesque, V.: Blindness, technology and haptics. Center for Intelligent Machines, pp. 19–21 (2005)
11. Faria, J., Lopes, S., Fernandes, H., Martins, P., Barroso, J.: Electronic white cane for blind people navigation assistance. In: 2010 World Automation Congress, pp. 1–7. IEEE (2010)
12. Yuan, D., Manduchi, R.: Dynamic environment exploration using a virtual white cane. In: 2005 IEEE Computer Society Conference on Computer Vision and Pattern Recognition (CVPR2005), vol. 1, pp. 243–249 (2005). https://doi.org/10.1109/CVPR.2005.136
13. Zhao, Y., et al.: Enabling people with visual impairments to navigate virtual reality with a haptic and auditory cane simulation. In: Proceedings of the 2018 CHI Conference on Human Factors in Computing Systems, pp. 1–14 (2018)
14. Bach-y-Rita, P., Kercel, S.W.: Sensory substitution and the human–machine interface. Trends Cogn. Sci. **7**, 541–546 (2003)
15. Bach-y-Rita, P.: Tactile sensory substitution studies. Ann. N. Y. Acad. Sci. **1013**, 83–91 (2004)

16. Lenay, C., Canu, S., Villon, P.: Technology and perception: the contribution of sensory sub-stitution systems. In: Proceedings Second International Conference on Cognitive Technology Humanizing the Information Age, pp. 44–53. IEEE (1997)

17. Jones, L.A.: Chapter 8 - Tactile communication systems: optimizing the display of informa-tion. In: Green, A., Chapman, C.E., Kalaska, J.F., Lepore, F. (eds.) Progress in Brain Research, pp. 113–128. Elsevier (2011). https://doi.org/10.1016/B978-0-444-53355-5.00008-7

18. Brewster, S.A., Brown, L.M.: Non-visual information display using tactons. In: CHI2004 Extended Abstracts on Human Factors in Computing Systems, pp. 787–788 (2004)

19. Lin, M.-W., Cheng, Y.-M., Yu, W.: Using tactons to provide navigation cues in pedestrian situations. In: Proceedings of the 5th Nordic Conference on Human-Computer Interaction: Building Bridges, pp. 507–510 (2008)

20. Barralon, P., Ng, G., Dumont, G., Schwarz, S.K.W., Ansermino, M.: Development and eval-uation of multidimensional tactons for a wearable tactile display. In: Proceedings of the 9th International Conference on Human Computer Interaction with Mobile Devices and Services, pp. 186–189. Association for Computing Machinery, New York, NY, USA (2007). https://doi.org/10.1145/1377999.1378005

21. van Erp, J.B.F.: Tactile navigation display. In: Brewster, S. and Murray-Smith, R. (eds.) Haptic Human-Computer Interaction. Haptic HCI 2000. LNCS, vol. 2058, pp. 165–173. Springer, Heidelberg (2001). https://doi.org/10.1007/3-540-44589-7_18

22. Petermeijer, S.M., De Winter, J.C., Bengler, K.J.: Vibrotactile displays: a survey with a view on highly automated driving. IEEE Trans. Intell. Transp. Syst. **17**, 897–907 (2015)

23. Enriquez, M., Afonin, O., Yager, B., Maclean, K.: A pneumatic tactile alerting system for the driving environment (2002). https://doi.org/10.1145/971478.971506

24. Spence, C., Driver, J.: Crossmodal space and crossmodal attention (2004). https://doi.org/10.1093/acprof:oso/9780198524861.001.0001

25. Meng, F., Spence, C.: Tactile warning signals for in-vehicle systems. Accid. Anal. Prev. **75**, 333–346 (2015). https://doi.org/10.1016/j.aap.2014.12.013

26. Krüger, M., Wiebel-Herboth, C.B., Wersing, H.: Tactile encoding of directions and temporal distances to safety hazards supports drivers in overtaking and intersection scenarios. Transport. Res. F: Traffic Psychol. Behav. **81**, 201–222 (2021). https://doi.org/10.1016/j.trf.2021.05.014

27. Brhel, M., Meth, H., Maedche, A., Werder, K.: Exploring principles of user-centered agile software development: a literature review. Inf. Softw. Technol. **61**, 163–181 (2015). https://doi.org/10.1016/j.infsof.2015.01.004

28. Sharp, H.: Interaction design. Wiley (2003)

29. Hoggan, E., Brewster, S.: New parameters for tacton design. In: CHI2007 Extended Abstracts on Human Factors in Computing Systems, pp. 2417–2422 (2007)

Haptic Rendering Algorithm for Manipulating Tiny Objects Attached on Adhesive Surface of Rigid Objects

Xiaohan Zhao[1]([✉]), Quanmin Guo[4], and Dangxiao Wang[1,2,3]

[1] State Key Lab of Virtual Reality Technology and Systems, Beihang University,
Beijing 100191, China
zhaoxiaohan_buaa@163.com, hapticwang@buaa.edu.cn
[2] Beijing Advanced Innovation Center for Biomedical Engineering, Beihang University,
Beijing 100191, China
[3] Peng Cheng Laboratory, Shenzhen 518055, China
[4] Xinjiang Medical University Stomatological College, Urumchi 830011, China

Abstract. Manipulating tiny objects adsorbed onto irregular objects is a typical simulation application, such as adjusting brackets in orthodontic training. The operator firstly places the bracket on tooth surface covered with adhesive, and then adjusts its posture with probe. There are two challenges in realizing the above simulation scenes with force feedback. Firstly, the tiny object can be affected by multiple forces when manipulating it, making it difficult to build the dynamic model. Secondly, interaction among the tool, the tiny object and the supporting object is complicated. In addition to embedding between the tool and the objects, embedding between the objects should also be avoided. In our previous work we constructed an orthodontic simulation system with force feedback. However, the haptic operation of adjusting brackets was not ideal, as serious penetration and motion chaos often occurred. In this paper, we analyzed various forces in the process of adjusting the bracket with probe to refine the dynamic model, and introduced viscous force to erase motion chaos to accurately control the bracket's motion. In addition, we optimized the bracket's posture through the shape matching constraint to ensure that the bracket can closely contact the tooth surface without embedding into it. The subjective assessment and objective assessment were implemented to validate the system. The experimental results indicated that the system allowed to precisely move the tiny object while maintaining its close contact with the supporting object.

Keywords: Haptic Simulation · Position Manipulation · Shape Matching

1 Introduction

Manipulating tiny objects adsorbed onto irregular objects is a typical simulation application, such as adjusting brackets in orthodontic training. As shown in Fig. 1, the operator pushes the bracket with probe to adjust its posture (position and orientation) after placing it on tooth surface covered with adhesive. The position difference with the standard position is required to control within 2 mm [1]. Traditionally the students practices bonding brackets on plaster models, which not only consumes materials, but also shows poor training effect [2]. We constructed a bracket bonding training system with force feedback to simulate the whole process of bracket bonding [3]. The bottleneck of the training system was that the simulation effect of adjusting bracket with haptic device was not ideal. Serious penetration and motion chaos often occurred when adjusting the posture of the bracket.

Apply adhesive on tooth   Place brackets   Adjust brackets with probe

Fig. 1. Adjust the bracket with probe on tooth

There are two challenges in simulating manipulating tiny objects adsorbed onto irregular objects. Taking adjusting bracket as an example, the first challenge is that the bracket is subjected to a variety of external forces during motion, including push force of the probe, adhesion of the adhesive, support force from the tooth and gravity. Consequently it is difficult to build the dynamic model. The second challenge arises from the complicated interaction situations among the probe, the tiny object (bracket) and the supporting object (tooth). When adjusting the bracket on tooth with probe, it is necessary to avoid not only the embedding between the tool and the object, but also the embedding among the tiny objects and the supporting objects.

In addition to the orthodontic training system mentioned above, Iskandar et al. also developed a simulation system for bracket positioning training [4]. The system could help users experience the force feedback of clamping and placing brackets. However, it didn't support accurately adjusting the bracket in real time. Yue Huang et al. built a virtual orthodontic teaching system, which was operated and controlled through the HTC handle. And thus it didn't support real-time force feedback operation [5].

As for research of rigid body interaction, the research topics focused on interaction stability instead of posture adjustment [6]. In the open source engine Chai 3D, we found some demos of dynamically adjusting the posture of objects, all of which were relatively simple and didn't help much [7].

Compared with previous works, we achieved precise posture manipulation of tiny objects absorbed onto irregular objects with force feedback. The contribution of our work can be summarized as the following two aspects.

1. We built the dynamic model of adjusting the bracket taking account of push force, viscous force and gravity. Viscous force was important in preventing the location of the bracket from changing too much, and gravity could force the bracket to closely contact the tooth. In addition, we solved the dynamic model through implicit method to improve stability.

2. We optimized the bracket' posture based on the shape matching constraint. The bracket was abstracted as a series of particles. When pushing it, we firstly computed the coordinates of these particles according to the above dynamic model. Then we found the non-penetration locations of these particles through greedy strategy. At last we managed to restore the shape matching constraints among these particles.

The rest of this paper is organized as follows. In Sect. 2, we introduced the dynamic model for moving the bracket. In Sect. 3, we introduced how to construct the virtual environment and how to optimize the posture of the bracket. In Sect. 4, experiments results were provided to validate the effectiveness of the simulation system. Finally in Sect. 5, we conclude the paper and pointed out several future research topics.

2 Dynamics Model

The operator needs to adjust the posture of the bracket with probe after placing it on tooth surface covered with adhesive. When adjusting the bracket, the user puts the probe on different parts of the bracket to make it translate or rotate in the expected direction. Figure 2 shows the adjustment results of the same bracket with the same force when the applying positions are different.

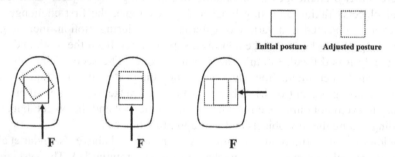

Fig. 2. Illustration of the bracket postures when pushed from different points

2.1 Force Analysis

The physics based method was utilized to describe the motion of the bracket. As shown in Fig. 3, when constructing the dynamic model of pushing the bracket, the bracket was abstracted as a regular rectangle without thickness. In each frame of the haptic thread, the system would calculate the resultant force and resultant moment acting on the bracket. The brackets were mainly affected by the probe thrust, viscous resistance and gravity. In this chapter we explained how to calculate these forces.

Thrust. The thrust acting on the bracket mainly comes from the probe. When the user pushes the bracket, the thrust of the probe is the reaction force of the virtual force felt by the user through the force feedback device. In the constraint based 6-DoF haptic rendering algorithm, we calculated the virtual feedback force based on the posture differences

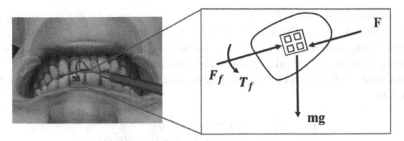

Fig. 3. Force analysis of the bracket

between the virtual tool and physical tool. As shown in Eq. 1, k is the stiffness factor, $q_g(x_g, y_g, z_g, \alpha_g, \beta_g, \gamma_g)$ and $q_h(x_h, y_h, z_h, \alpha_h, \beta_h, \gamma_h)$ represent the 6-DoF posture of the physical tool and the graphic tool respectively.

$$F = k(\mathbf{q_g} - \mathbf{q_h}) \tag{1}$$

When the push force does not pass through the geometric center of the bracket, moment that can rotate the bracket will be generated. The calculation formula of the moment is as the following, where r is the distance vector from the rotation center to the action point of the push force. We assume that the bracket always rotates around its geometric center, and the rotation axis is perpendicular to the contact surface between the bracket and the tooth.

$$T = r \times F \tag{2}$$

Viscous Resistance. As the contact surfaces of the tooth and the bracket are smooth, the resistance when the bracket moves mainly comes from the viscous resistance of the adhesive. When constructing the dynamic model for adjusting the position and orientation of the bracket, viscous resistance should be considered to increase motion stability and prevent the bracket from moving too much. Because the movement speed of the bracket is slow, we use the idealized formula for calculating the viscous resistance. As shown in Eq. 3, F_f is the viscous resistance, C_D is the drag coefficient, and μ is the motion speed of the bracket.

$$F_f = -C_D\mu \tag{3}$$

When the bracket rotates, it will also be subjected to the viscous resistance torque from the adhesive. The viscous resistance is calculated through integration. As shown in Eq. 4, D is the contact area between bracket and adhesive, ω is the angular velocity of the rotated bracket, and $r(s)$ is the distance from the current position to the rotation center.

$$T_f = -C_D \iint_D \omega d r^2(s) \tag{4}$$

Gravity. Tooth surface is arching. In order to ensure that the bracket closely contacts the tooth surface during movement, gravity should also be applied to the bracket to prevent it from leaving the tooth.

$$G = mg \tag{5}$$

In addition to the above forces, the bracket is acted upon by the supporting force from the tooth in reality. The main effect of supporting force is to prevent the bracket from penetrating into the tooth. As we could achieve the same effect through posture optimization, we neglected this item when constructing the physical model.

Combined with Eqs. (1)–(3), the stress model of moving the bracket can be established:

$$\begin{cases} \boldsymbol{F}_s = k\big(\mathbf{q}_g - \mathbf{q}_h\big) - C_D \mu + mg \\ \boldsymbol{T}_s = kr \times \big(\mathbf{q}_g - \mathbf{q}_h\big) - C_D \iint_D \omega dr^2(s) \end{cases} \tag{6}$$

2.2 Dynamic Model

When the bracket moves, we use Eq. (7) to update its position and orientation. In Eq. (7), $\mathbf{x}^t$ and $\mathbf{x}^{t+1}$ represent the posture of the bracket at the current cycle and the next cycle respectively, θ^t and θ^{t+1} represent its rotation angle around the contact surface normal at the current cycle and the next cycle, and J is the moment of inertia of the bracket.

$$\begin{cases} \mu^{t+1} = \mu^t + (F_s/m)dt \\ \mathbf{x}^{t+1} = \mathbf{x}^t + \mu^{t+1}dt \\ w^{t+1} = w^t + (T_s/J)dt \\ \theta^{t+1} = \theta^t + w^{t+1}dt \end{cases} \tag{7}$$

In order to improve motion stability, we proposed an implicit integration method to solve the bracket's velocity. Implicit method could reduce the integration error by considering the velocity at the next time. Assuming that the motion state of the bracket can be expressed as $y = (\mathbf{u}, w)^T$, the implicit integral expression of the motion state of the bracket is:

$$y^{t+1} = y^t + \Delta t \cdot \dot{y}^{t+1} \tag{8}$$

where the superscript t represents the state of the current cycle, t + 1 represents that of the next cycle, and Δt is the selected time step. It can be seen from Eq. (6) that $\dot{y}^{t+1}$ can be approximated by Taylor expansion:

$$\dot{y}^{t+1} = \dot{y}^t + \Delta y \cdot \frac{\delta f^t}{\delta y^t} \tag{9}$$

where f represents the resultant force effects acting on the bracket currently, i.e. $f = (F_s, T_s)^T$. Combined with the above formula, the motion state change Δy of the bracket can be solved.

$$(I - \frac{\delta f^t}{\delta y^t})\Delta y = \Delta t \cdot \dot{y}^{t+1} \tag{10}$$

Finally we could solve the position and orientation of the bracket by substituting Δy into Eq. (7).

3 System Design

3.1 Construction of the Virtual Scene

The first step to construct the virtual scene is to build the visual models and the physical models offline. The format of the visual models is triangular mesh that is widely used in graphic rendering. The physical model adopts hierarchy octree due to its high efficiency in collision detection. The hierarchical sphere-tree models and mesh models of typical objects are shown in Fig. 4. It can be seen from the figure that three-layer sphere-tree models approach the mesh models quite well.

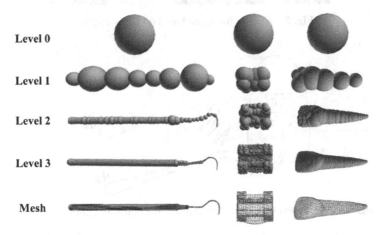

Fig. 4. Hierarchy sphere-tree and mesh models of probe, bracket and tooth

After building the models, the system runs in real time to update the virtual scenarios. The online-running part consists of two modules, the graphic thread and the physical thread. The main task of the graphics thread is to update the visual effects of the virtual scene. The system utilizes Unity 3D as the rendering engine to realize various graphical rendering effects. As shown in Fig. 5, the unity engine can help render a real surgical operating environment by setting the lighting and viewing angles.

The main work of the physical thread is to perform collision detection and collision response to solve the optimized posture of the virtual tool and the virtual objects, and to calculate feedback force. The core part of this module is the 6-DoF haptic rendering algorithm based on configuration optimization [8]. The algorithm is able to simulate the multi-point and multi-region interactions between the virtual tool and the virtual objects without penetration (Fig. 6).

Once the optimized posture of the graphic tool is solved, we can calculate the virtual force transmitted to the user based on the spring force model. The virtual force is the reaction force of the thrust force applied to the tooth and the bracket by the user.

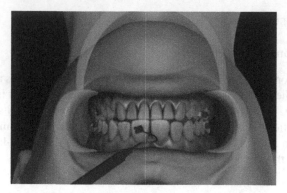

Fig. 5. The graphic scene based on Unity engine

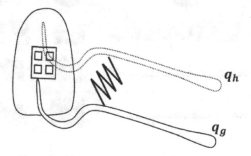

Fig. 6. Illustration of the haptic posture and the optimized graphic posture

3.2 Optimization of the Bracket's Posture

While the constraint based 6-DOF haptic rendering algorithm prevents the virtual tool from penetrating into the virtual objects, it cannot deal with the self-intersections between the objects. Actually every time after pushing the bracket, it may be separated from or embedded into the tooth. In order to correctly display the bracket, it is necessary to optimize its posture after pushing it. We introduced the idea of shape matching to optimize the bracket's posture. Shape matching constraint is a common constrain in position based dynamics for simulating soft bodies [9]. This method assumes that the soft bodies are composed of particles, and the particles are connected by invisible implicit constraints. In this paper, we applied it to force feedback.

The physical model of the bracket is octree, which could be directly regarded as the input particles set. The coordinates of the input particles set can be expressed as $x = [x_1^T, x_1^T, \cdots, x_n^T]^T$. When the bracket moves, we update the input particle coordinates according to Eq. (7) to obtain its intermediate state $x\prime$. Because we add gravity to the dynamic model, these particles will embed into the tooth or pass through the tooth, as shown in the Fig. 7. It should be noted that only four particles are drawn in Fig. 7 to clearly demonstrate the process. Actually the number of input particles may be up to hundreds. Because these intermediate particles don't contact closely with the tooth, it is necessary to optimize the position and orientation of the bracket based on shape matching constraint.

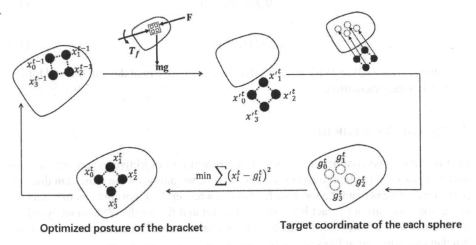

Optimized posture of the bracket   Target coordinate of the each sphere

Fig. 7. Flow chart of optimizing the bracket's posture

The first step to optimize the bracket's posture based on shape matching constraint is to calculate the non-penetration particles set $g = [g_1^T, g_1^T, \cdots, g_n^T]^T$ for each particle respectively. In this paper, we calculated the non-penetration location of each particle through greedy strategy. For each input particle, we firstly found its closest tooth octree sphere, and then we push the target particle to the tooth surface along the connection line of the closest sphere center and its location.

After calculating the non-penetration coordinates of the input particles set, the shape matching constraint between particles is broken. The second step of optimizing the bracket's posture is to restore the shape matching constraints between particles. As the brackets are rigid, the shape matching constraints between these particles are rigid. Rigid constraints can be expressed through the homogeneous coordinate matrix $T = \{ \begin{matrix} R & 0 \\ D & 1 \end{matrix} \}$.

For any particle, it can naturally follow the shape matching constraint by representing its current coordinate x_i^t through Eq. (11), where x_i^o the initial coordinate of the particle, R is the rotation matrix, and D is the translation vector.

$$x_i^t = Rx_i^o + D \tag{11}$$

After calculating the target coordinates set g^t of the input particles, the optimization goal of shape matching is to solve the minimum coordinate change between the two point sets x^{t-1} and g^t by optimizing the homogeneous matrix of the bracket. The optimization goal can be expressed as:

$$\min f(t, R) = \sum (Rx_i^o + D - x_i^{t-1})^2 \tag{12}$$

Formula (12) is an extreme value problem of multivariate function, and it can be solved by making the partial derivative zero.

$$\nabla_t f(t, R) = 0 \tag{13}$$

$$\nabla_R f(t, R) = 0 \tag{14}$$

Through Eqs. (13) and (14) we can solve the motion matrix of the bracket, and further its position and orientation.

4 System Assessment

In this section, we conducted subjective experiment and objective experiment to validate the proposed haptic rendering method. Firstly, we analyzed the minimum distance between the bracket and the tooth surface to test whether the algorithm can maintain the close non-penetration contact between the bracket and the tooth. We also analyzed the response time to see whether the algorithm can ensure stable force output when multiple brackets are adjusted at the same time.

We further conducted the user experiment. We invited 7 subjects to participate in the experiment. Each subject needed to complete the bracket adjustment experiment based on the ordinary adjustment algorithm and the improved adjustment algorithm respectively. The sequence of the two experiments was random for each participant. In each experiment, the user needs to adjust 20 brackets to standard positions. The system recorded the operation time of each subject and scored their operation results. We also inquired users about their operation feelings of the two systems.

4.1 Subjective Data Analysis

In order to analyze whether the algorithm could ensure that the bracket kept in contact with the tooth surface under different conditions, we selected incisor and molar for experiments. In the movement process of the bracket, the penetration distance of the bracket into the tooth was calculated. We regulated that the positive direction of the penetration distance was the direction of the outward tooth normal. The penetration distance was negative if the bracket penetrated into the tooth, and it was positive if the bracket floated above the tooth.

The experimental results are shown in Fig. 8. Although the bracket and tooth surface do not always fit closely due to calculation errors, the results are acceptable as the penetration depth can be kept within a small range. In fact, such errors are hard to perceptible. In addition, it can be seen from Fig. 8 that penetration depth is related to the arching degree of the tooth. Compared with the incisor, the arching degree of the molar is larger, making the bracket easier to penetrate into or detach from it.

During the above experiments, the computation time of the physical thread was kept within 1ms, satisfying the requirements for stable haptic simulation.

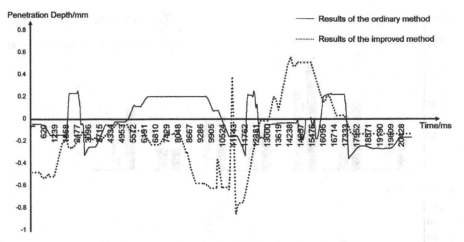

Fig. 8. Penetration depth of the bracket into the tooth

4.2 Objective Data Analysis

In clinical practice the bracket's distance to standards position is restricted to less than 2 mm. We implemented objective experiment to explore whether the improved method could promote the bracket adjustment effect in practice. We recruited seven testers to participate in the experiment. Each tester was required to complete the operation of adjusting 20 brackets to standards position twice. One time under the ordinary algorithm and the other under the improved algorithm. The test sequences of the two algorithms were random to reduce side effects.

Before the experiment, the user was asked to complete the pre procedure of bounding brackets on teeth to get familiar with the virtual system. They were required to bond 20 brackets for each test. After bonding the bracket, they used the probe to adjust these brackets. The system automatically measured the location difference between the current position and the standard position. If the distance to the standard position was less than 2 mm, the user got 5 points, otherwise they got zero. As there were 20 brackets, the final results ranged from 0 to 100.

Figure 9 shows the operation time and final scores of each tester with two different methods. As can be seen from the figure, the improved algorithm helped users to achieve higher adjustment accuracy in less time, which effectively validated the efficiency of the improved algorithm.

After the experiment, we also asked users to compare their operation feelings of the two algorithms. According to the comments from users, the improved algorithm could effectively ensure the stability of bracket adjustment, as well as reduce vibration. In addition, the viscous feelings were more evident.

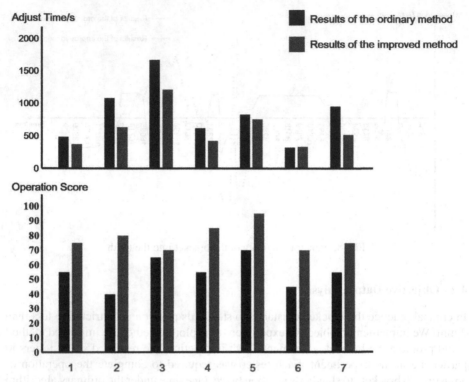

Fig. 9. Adjust time and final scores of testers during the two experiments

5 Conclusion and Future Work

In this paper we achieved posture manipulation of tiny objects attached on adhesive surface of rigid objects. We managed to overcome two challenges. Firstly, we built the dynamic model for describing the motion of tiny objects under various forces including push force, viscous force and gravity. Secondly, we optimized the posture of the adjusted object through the shape matching constraint to prevent it from penetrating or detaching from the attached object. Results of the experiments proved that the improved method could maintain penetration depth within an ideal range, and help users to promote their operations.

A limitation of this work is that we ignored the self-interactions between the tiny objects. It has little impact on brackets adjustment as only one bracket is allowed to put on a tooth. However, it may affect the simulation effects in other applications where more than one object is required to manipulate at the same time. We would focus on this problem later. We will also try to develop more applications with the haptic rendering method, such as manipulating small irons attached by magnetic.

References

1. Alrbata, R.H.: Accurate bracket positioning as a prerequisite for ideal orthodontic finishing. Int. J. Orthod. Rehabil. **8**, 3–4 (2017). https://doi.org/10.4103/2349-5243.200223
2. Brown, M.W., Koroluk, L., Ko, C.C., et al.: Effectiveness and efficiency of a CAD/CAM orthodontic bracket system. Am. J. Orthod. Dentofac. Orthop. **148**(6), 1067–1074 (2015). https://doi.org/10.1016/j.ajodo.2015.07.029
3. Ye, F., Liu, L., Yan, B., Zhao, X., Hao, A.: Orthodontic simulation system with force feedback for training complete bracket placement procedures. Virtual Reality Intell. Hardware **3**(4), 261 (2021). https://doi.org/10.1016/j.vrih.2021.08.001
4. Rao, G.K.L., Mokhtar, N.B., Iskandar, Y.H.P.: An integration of augmented reality technology for orthodontic education: case of bracket positioning. In: 2017 IEEE Conference on e-Learning, e-Management and e-Services (IC3e), pp. 7–11. IEEE (2017). https://doi.org/10.1109/IC3e.2017.8409230
5. Huang, Y., et al.: Virtual reality approach for orthodontic education at school of stomatology, Jinan University. J. Dent. Educ. **86**(8), 1025–1035 (2022). https://doi.org/10.1002/jdd.12915
6. Wang, Y., Feng, L., Andersson, K.: Haptic force rendering of rigid-body interactions: a systematic review. Adv. Mech. Eng. **13**(9), 168781402110415 (2021). https://doi.org/10.1177/16878140211041538
7. CHAI3D Homepage (2023), https://www.chai3d.org/
8. Wang, D., Zhang, X., Zhang, Y., Xiao, J.: Configuration-based optimization for six degree-of-freedom haptic rendering for fine manipulation. IEEE Trans. Haptics **6**(2), 167–180 (2013). https://doi.org/10.1109/TOH.2012.63
9. Müller, M., Heidelberger, B., Teschner, M., Gross, M.: Meshless deformations based on shape matching. ACM Trans. Graph. **24**(3), 471–478 (2005). https://doi.org/10.1145/1073204.1073216

Ocular Tactile Vibration Intervention in VR and Its Modeling Coupled with Visual Fusion

Pei Kang[1], Yan Liu[1], Hang Wang[1], Enshan Ouyang[2], and Tao Zeng[1(✉)]

[1] Department of Instrumental and Electrical Engineering, Xiamen University, Xiamen 361000, Fujian, China
tao.zeng@xmu.edu.cn
[2] Fujian Branch of China United Network Communication Co., Ltd., Fuzhou 350001, Fujian, China

Abstract. The main application of virtual reality (VR) is to immerse users in the three-dimensional simulation environment and experience the virtual reality world. At present, VR products and content on the market have some problems to be solved, such as location information error, dizziness and discomfort, stereo vision error, sound mismatch and so on. Moreover, most VR applications use stereo vision perception, but that alone is not enough to fully immerse users in the VR environment. For a long time, the single way of information transmission makes people over rely on the visual channel, which leads to visual information overload. Compared with the receptive visual information obtained by a single channel, haptic interaction system is more bidirectional. The employment of tactile feedback technology in VR can provide better immersion and interaction, and expand the scope of user experience. Among the four main tactile stimuli-vibrant stimulus, pressure stimulus, electric stimulus and temperature stimulus, vibrant stimulus has higher comfort, consistency and better response speed and adjustable range. Therefore in this paper, combined with specific VR scene, external vibration was applied around the eyes to provide periocular stimulation, so as to explore the role of vibration in enhancing the immersion of VR equipments. A mathematical model of human visual-haptic interaction process is established, and it is verified that the artificial neural network model has good fitting effect in simulating human visual-haptic nervous system.

Keywords: Ocular tactile intervention · artificial neural network · virtual reality. visual-haptic

1 Introduction

Science Facebook's $2 billion acquisition of Oculus VR in 2014, the entire global VR industry has been booming. However, apart from the novelty brought by 360-degree immersion, the biggest experience for users is the dizziness and discomfort after taking off the eyemask device [1–3]. Most VR systems only provide visual feedback through head-mounted display (HMD) tracking of head posture and position, to achieve 3D perception and interaction with the simulated environment [4]. If the VR environment is

D. Wang et al. (Eds.): AsiaHaptics 2022, LNCS 14063, pp. 80–96, 2023.
https://doi.org/10.1007/978-3-031-46839-1_7

not properly used, it may cause headaches, dizziness, nausea and other symptoms. This is called the VR disease [5]. At present, the improvement of VR equipment mainly focuses on hardware and optical imaging [6]. However, the problem of insufficient resolution and refresh rate cannot be solved in a short time, which requires the improvement of industry hardware level as the cornerstone. In general, user experience improvement has a long way to go.

In the way people interact with virtual environments, the use of vision and hearing has been saturated. Sherman and Craig [7] mentioned that in order to bring users an immersive interactive experience, a multi-sensory feedback system, such as visual, sound and tactile feedback, is needed. Although tactile feedback is hardly required during the naked eye's interaction with the environment, the visual field imaging is confined to a closed space after wearing the VR device, and the limited frequency of computer rendering greatly reduced the immersion of visual interaction, which needs tactile feedback to eliminate these deficiencies. With the introduction of tactile feedback, the gap between VR devices in space and time and the actual situation can be made up, so as to better improve the system performance, greatly expand the communication with the external environment, and give users a richer and more realistic feeling.

Several research projects showed that haptic-enhanced virtual reality leads to an increased level of immersion [8–12]. In particular, some studies have incorporated haptic feedback into HMD. Gugenheimer et al. used the gyroscopic effect to simulate kinesthetic force by connecting the flywheel to user's head (front of the HMD) [13]. The designed device can render inertia in VR. Pamungkas and Ward proposed a feedback system based on hand electric tactile feedback combined with Oculus Rift device [14]. It consists of gesture interface, stereo vision head-wearing device and electric tactile feedback system. It can provide various feedback sensations to users and enhance the immersion and interaction of VR users. Peiris et al. have designed ThermoVR which is the first attempt to integrate thermal feedback with HMD [15]. The system integrates five thermal modules that provide thermal stimulation directly on the user's face. The results showed that the significance between no stimulus and cold/hot stimulus conditions indicated that thermal stimulation significantly improved participants' immersion experience. Most participants mentioned that the stimulus suddenly reminded them of different situations: "feels like wind", "feels like I'm underwater" were some of the comments about the cold stimulus, and "feels like I'm turning on the oven" was one of the comments about the hot stimulus. Kaul and Rohs proposed a system that utilizes 20 vibrating motors distributed in three concentric ellipses around the head to provide intuitive tactile guidance and increase immersion for VR and AR applications [16]. In [17], the study proposes a portable tactile system, which can be used by anyone to transmit various tactile feedback easily and cheaply. The system first identifies the left and right hands, and then sends tactile sensations (vibrations and heat) to each fingertip (thumb and index finger), providing a variety of tactile responses to enhance interactive immersion.

Above researches, in order to improve the immersion experience of VR, have developed related devices to provide sensations other than visual and auditory sensations, such as inertia sensation, thermal sensation, navigation hints, and electrical stimulation sensation. However, there is no systematic study of vibration tactile sensation and its integration with vision in VR.

In this study, we explore the relationship between ocular vibration and immersion during VR viewing by applying physical vibration stimulation with different frequencies and amplitudes around human eyes, so as to find the means to enhance the immersion and improve the subjective feelings of VR users. The experimental results showed that the vibration tactile intervention on the upper eyelid of the human eye can greatly improve the VR experience. Therefore, the integration of semi-periocular tactile stimulation devices in HDM can reduce the device complexity and make it more portable. In addition, in order to further explore the mechanism of tactile intervention on human visual nervous system, this study uses the artificial neural network model, which is widely used in decision-making, to carry out mathematical modeling of the intervention process. According to the inverse biomimetic structure of human visual cells, the transmission network of human visual-haptic system is established. Detailed verification shows that the artificial neural network model is feasible to analyze the human visual-haptic nervous system.

This paper is organized as follows: in Sect. 2, psychophysical experiments were conducted to verify the effect of tactile vibration on human vision; in Sect. 3, an inverse bionic artificial neural network was established to simulate human visual-tactile nervous system by using the experimental data; Sect. 4 gives the conclusions and future work.

2 Psychophysical Experiments

In this paper, the relationship between stimulation and response of human eye visual-haptic system is explored through psychophysical experiments. For the purpose of improving the immersion of VR equipment and reducing the vertigo of users, the experiments employed vibrations with different frequencies and amplitudes to stimulate the eye area in specific VR scenes so as to explored the effects of physical intervention on human vision in VR environment. In order to quantify the subjective feelings of the users and facilitate the subsequent modeling process, the classical psychological threshold scale Borg CR10 and Likert subjective scale were used in data processing.

2.1 Experiment 1

The effects of different amplitudes of stimulation on the subjective feelings of the participants, including vertigo, ambiguity and immersion, were tested under VR environment.

Subjects
The experiment was conducted by 30 healthy participants (30 college students aged 19–22, male to female ratio 1:1). All the participants have good eyesight and are naïve to the purpose of the experiment. Each participant watched a VR video four times at four vibration amplitudes of the vibrator. At the end of the video experience, all the participants were asked to complete the required sensory output scale.

Stimuli
Haptuator Planar (@Tactile Labs Inc. Canada) is chosen as the vibrator in the experiment,

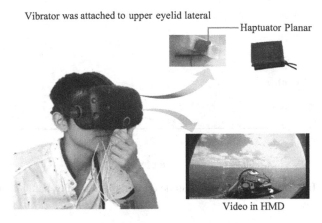

Fig. 1. Experimental setup in Exp.1.

as shown in Fig. 1. It has the advantages of high accuracy, fast response and wide frequency bandwidth. It can output various stimulations with different types, intensity and frequency. In addition, its surface is flexible and it can directly act on human skin. The vibrator provides four amplitudes of vibration: 0 μm, 2.31 μm, 4.71 μm, and 10.60 μm at 0V, 0.5V, 1V, and 1.5V input voltage respectively (at the frequency of 30 Hz). It was attached to the upper eyelid lateral of the participants. The used HDM was HTC VIVE. The used software is "Eisenhower VR" 360 degree panoramic video released by HTC virtual reality software platform Viveport. The content of the VR video is a record of the entire visit of journalists of USA Today on the USS Eisenhower. It consists of five parts: the island, the flight deck, the hangar and the stern. Each part includes several panoramic videos, in which the experiencer can rotate his/her head 360 degrees to watch. For consistency, all the subjects are required to watch the same video—the take-off and landing process of the F18 fighter jet, as shown in Fig. 1.

Procedure

In order to quantify the subjective feelings of the participants, including vertigo, ambiguity and immersion, a classical psychological threshold scale named Borg CR10 was employed. In this experiment, five orders of magnitude were used for each subjective output. In the initial stage of the experiment, the participants were asked to wear the HDM and randomly select videos for warm-up experience. The purpose was to eliminate the negative emotions such as tension and discomfort when the participants first used the equipment, so as to prevent interference with the subsequent subjective feedback. After the warm-up, all the participants would take off the HDM, rest for ten minutes freely, and wear vibrators. Then the participants will take the HDM again and watch four videos (under four vibration amplitudes of the vibrators). To avoid any bias due to unwanted cues, the order of four vibrational stimuli was randomized and counterbalanced. At the end of the video experience, all the participants were asked to complete the required sensory output scale.

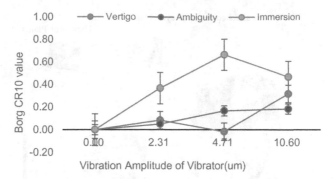

Fig. 2. Influence of vibration amplitude on vertigo, ambiguity, and immersion.

Results and Discussion

The Borg CR10 values were calculated. The values under the input voltage of the vibrator is 0V (that is, the sensory value of the participants without external stimulus) were as the reference. Then the reference value was subtracted from the sensory value under different stimulation amplitude (0 um, 2.31 um, 4.71 um, and 10.60 um) and 30 sets of data were processed. The average values were presented in Fig. 2 which showed that when the vibration amplitude is 4.71 um, the vertigo degree is relatively small and at the same time, the user immersive ascension achieved the maximum level. However, the immersive ascension is accompanied by the sacrifice of picture quality. When the vibration amplitude rises, the participants feel that the ambiguity of the picture increases under more violent vibration.

In addition to the above three indicators, this paper also received two feedbacks with high value for follow-up research. The first one is about the ambiguity of the picture. Although the ambiguity of all the samples involved in the experiment shows an upward trend in data, about 1/3 of the 30 participants involved in the experiment reported that the ambiguity decreased significantly with the increase of vibration amplitude. Almost all the participants with this kind of experience have moderate or high myopia (wearing glasses with a degree more than 300°). The second is about vertigo. The pictures presented to the participants can be roughly divided into two types: static and dynamic pictures. The static steady-state picture refers to the flat flight period after the F18 fighter takes off from the deck, in which the turbulence of the aircraft is less and the scene changes little, while the dynamic picture refers to the acceleration in the take-off stage and the interception deceleration in the landing stage of the F18 fighter. In the dynamic picture, along with the increase of vibration amplitude of the vibrating plate, all the participants presented the feeling of "absolute immersion", that is, the human eye and brain could not distinguish the reality from the virtual.

2.2 Experiment 2

This experiment explores the influence of different vibration frequencies on improving human eye recognition ability and recognition accuracy in VR environment.

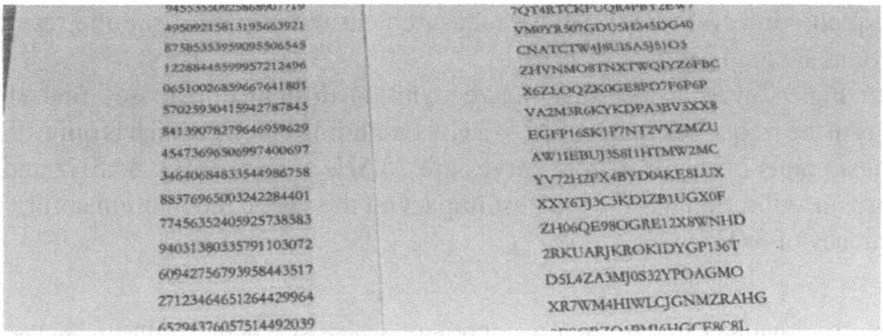

Fig. 3. Random number table and random alphabet.

The participants identified a random alphabet under natural light and VR equipment respectively.

Subjects
In this experiment, 6 participants (3 males and 3 females, aged 18–24) were asked to complete the prescribed sensory output scale after recognized a random alphabet under natural light and VR environment. The participants were naive to haptic and they did not know the content and purpose of the experiment. And they did not receive relevant training, so as to ensure the objectivity of the experimental results.

This experiment aims to verify the feasibility of vibration affecting human eye recognition ability and accuracy in virtual reality environment, so only a small number of participants were conducted. In the future work, we will increase the number of participants to obtain more accurate and reliable data.

Stimuli
Haptuator Planar was selected as the vibrator. The random alphabet used in the experiment is shown in right panel of Fig. 3. It is designed with a large number of rows to avoid memory behavior. Richter Subjective Scale [18] was used to measure the comfort rating scale: 1 is extremely uncomfortable and 5 is very comfortable. Borg CR10 Psychological Scale [19] was used to measure the degree of recognition difficulty.

Procedure
Firstly, participants were asked to read the random number table (left panel of Fig. 3) naked (without VR HDM) and each person recognized 20 numbers. The distance between the table and the human eye was appropriate for a person to recognize all the numbers clearly and effortlessly, so as to exclude the different diopters of each person. Secondly, the vibrator was fixed on the outer side of the upper eyelid and actuated by sinusoidal signal. The interference of the vibrator to human vision was tested at different input frequencies. The Richter Subjective Scale and Borg CR10 Psychological Scale were filled in. This step was pilot measurement; therefore, the frequency interval of input signals was relatively large. The data record is as shown in Table 1.

As can be seen from Table 1, within 20–60 Hz, the recognition difficulty shows a trend of rising first and then declining. Therefore, the frequency of this section was set at a smaller interval (3Hz). Above measurement was repeated and the results were collected, as shown in Fig. 4.

From Fig. 4, we can see that the recognition difficulty increases first and then decreases in the frequency range of 22–43 Hz. Excluding curve 2 which is quite different, the highest points of the other five curves are 28.5Hz, 34Hz, 34Hz, 34.5Hz and 37Hz. Therefore, the vibration has the greatest impact on the vision recognition ability around the frequency of 34Hz.

Table 1. The relation between input signal frequency and recognition difficulty and comfort.

Signal frequency	Recognition difficulty	Comfort evaluation	Subjective feeling description
5Hz	0	4	Vibrator beating can be clearly experienced
10 Hz	0	4	Beating speed is slightly faster and amplitude is smaller, which does not affect the recognition
20 Hz	0.5	3	From beating to vibration
40 Hz	3	3	Visual jitter, no strong discomfort
60 Hz	1	2	Vibration is stronger, but not affect recognition
80 Hz	1	1	Vibration is so strong that the scalp became tense, and vibrator is easy to heat in this case
100 Hz	1	1	

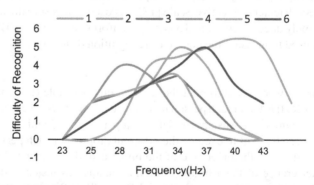

Fig. 4. The relationship between frequency and difficulty of recognition at the range of 20-60Hz.

Above steps were repeated in the VR scene to explore the impact of vibration on the degree of recognition difficulty. Firstly, VR scene was set up: a scene as shown in Fig. 5 was designed in Unity3D, in which the location of camera was the location of eyes in VR.

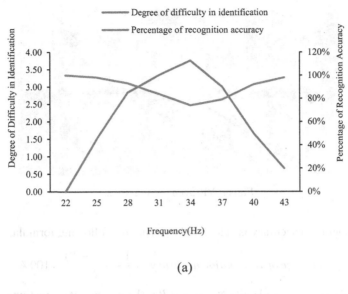

(a)

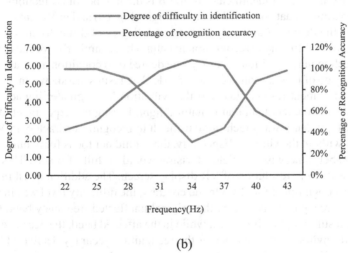

(b)

Fig. 5. Influence of vibration frequency on the accuracy percentage and difficulty degree of recognition. (a) in natural light; (b) in VR environment.

The main purpose of the ruler on the ground was to record the human standing position in order to avoid being unable to return to that position. After installing the vibrator, the participants wore a VR HDM and watched the random alphabet. The experimental data was recorded. Six groups of data were averaged and the recognition accuracy was calculated.

Results and Discussion

The recognition difficulty measured by Borg CR10 Psychological Scale is shown in

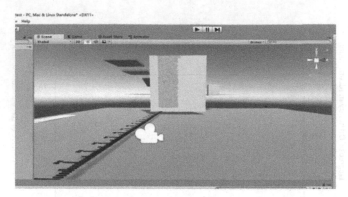

Fig. 6. VR Scenario in Exp. 2.

Fig. 6b. Recognition accuracy is calculated by using the following formula:

$$percentage\ of\ recognition\ accuracy = \frac{1 - (A - B)}{B} * 100\% \tag{1}$$

where, A is the number of identifications and B is the number of corrections.

By comparing the data obtained in natural light (Fig. 6a) and in VR environment, we can calculate the degree of difficulty increase: the degree of difficulty in recognition in VR - the degree of difficulty in recognition in natural light; similarly, we can calculate the degree of decline in recognition accuracy: the degree of recognition accuracy in natural light - the degree of recognition accuracy in VR. The results are shown in Table 2.

Above experiment results indicated that vibration has a greater impact on human vision in VR environment than that in natural light. During the experiment, the participants pointed out that it was much more difficult to recognize characters in VR than in reality, even without the vibrator. Especially, they could not focus for a long time on the random alphabet; otherwise the field of vision would be full of pixels. This is mainly due to the insufficient resolution of VR display screen. The addition of vibration could not alleviate recognition difficulty. On the contrary, the difficulty level was increased by about 2.5. For recognition accuracy, the original unaffected frequency band (23-28Hz, 40-43Hz) still suffered little influence, while in the affected band, the decrease was more severe in VR environment, such as that the recognition accuracy decreased by 43% at 34Hz. The significance of this experiment is to explore the extent and trend of vibration influence on human recognition of text, so as to lay a research foundation for improving VR immersion in the future.

Table 2. Recognition difficulty and accuracy comparision in VR and natural light.

Frequency (Hz)	23	25	28	31	34	37	40	43	23
Increase in Difficulty	2.50	1.50	1.67	2.33	2.58	3.00	1.83	1.83	2.50
Decrease in accuracy	0%	−2%	2%	22%	43%	35%	3%	0%	0%

2.3 General Discussion

Psychological experiments were carried out to quantitatively measure human vision changes in VR and reality under vibration tactile stimulation. Experiment 1 proves that in VR environment, the addition of tactile vibration stimulation (with amplitude as variable) has a significant effect on improving immersion and reducing vertigo of VR equipment. Experiment 2 shows that vibration stimulation (with frequency as variable) has a greater impact on human vision in VR environment than in natural light, and increases the recognition difficulty and reduces the accuracy significantly at around 34Hz.

In order to explain mathematically the process of tactile vibration stimulation affecting human subjective feelings in VR environment and to guide the application of tactile vibration in improving the immersion of VR, we used the collected feedback data of participants' subjective feelings to construct a mathematical model and evaluate its performance in the following section.

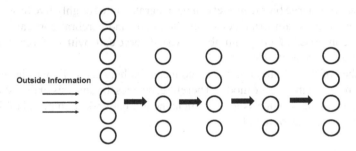

Retinal hierarchy Bipolar cells Amacrine cells Ganglion cells Cortical cells

Fig. 7. Bionic network of optic nerve.

3 Modeling

3.1 Theoretical Basis of Modeling

Artificial neural network model was adopted in this study. As a tool originally used to analyze and explain the mechanism of human brain operation, the basic source model of artificial neural network is to simulate the flow and thinking mode of human nerve information by combining multiple operators into a huge network with a certain logical connection, and then make corresponding decision tree and prediction analysis. Among the three main components of artificial neural network (input layer, hidden layer and output layer), the structure of hidden layer is the most important part of the whole network. The quality of its structure directly determines the quality of the network performance indicators. Therefore, we decide to use artificial neural network reversely and apply its bionic structure to the research and modeling of visual nerve structure. The main basis of the modeling is the existing visual nerve physiological structure.

When the human eye processes the external optical signal, the specific signal transmission path is as follows: the optical signal from the outside enters the eye through the pupil, then the optical signal is received by the retina through the refraction of lens and vitreous body; the retina will carry out the necessary signal conversion and information preliminary processing. The task is performed by M and P cells in the retina. M cells have a wide range of receptive domains, which mainly deal with the outline and shape information of the outside world, while P cells mainly accept the details of color and objects. After that, ganglion cells in the retina transmit signals from these two types of cells to the visual center through the optic nerve crossing and the optic tract, which is called the lateral geniculate body. The lateral geniculate body transmits information directly to the cerebral cortex with its necklace, and finally the cerebral cortex performs a more complex process of information decomposition and processing. According to this physiological and anatomical structure, this paper constructs a fully connected neural network model, and uses the neural network model to analyze the user's experience on virtual reality devices.

Based on a large amount of evidence from the anatomy of the medicine, this paper argues that the optic nerve bionic model can be integrated into roughly five levels: retinal hierarchy, bipolar cells, amacrine cells, ganglion cells and cerebral cortical cells. The five levels are composed of a large number of visual nerve cells with different functions. Its schematic structure is shown in Fig. 7.

The number of neural hierarchies and connections between cells will have a great impact on the performance of the model. Therefore, besides the analysis of the established model, the performance comparison of artificial neural networks composed of different numbers of neurons is also included.

3.2 Modeling Process and Data Fitting

The BP network is used. The layers of the artificial neural network are set to five, which correspond to the layers of the human visual neural network mentioned above. The number of neurons in each layer is 7, 4, 4, 4 and 4 from the retinal level to the cortical level.

The activation function of the network is Sigmoid, and its expression is as follows:

$$S(x) = \frac{1}{1 + e^{-x}} \tag{2}$$

In the training process of artificial neural network, the back propagation algorithm is used for errors. The core idea of back propagation algorithm is to propagate training errors layer by layer. The weights between each layer of neurons and its lower layer of neurons are adjusted by the method of the fastest gradient of errors. In the training process of multi-layer artificial neural network, the input of data will first propagate forward, and its mathematical expression is as follows:

$$a^{m+1} = f^{m+1}\left(W^{m+1}a^m + b^{m+1}\right), m = 0, 1, \ldots, M - 1 \tag{3}$$

where, M is the number of layers in the network, W is the weight matrix, a is the m-level data, and b is the unit correction matrix, and f is the transfer function.

s^M is the sensitivity of layer m, and next, it is transmitted back to the network. The directional propagation formula of the sensitivity is as follows:

$$s^M = -2\dot{F}^M(n^M)(t - a) \tag{4}$$

$$s^m = \dot{F}^m(n^m)(W^{m+1})^\top s^{m+1}, m = M - 1, \ldots, 2, 1 \tag{5}$$

where t is the objective function value, a is the network output, t-a is the error, n is the variable.

Finally, the weights and biases of the network are updated by using the approximate steepest descent rule, where, α is the learning rate and k is the number of iterations.

$$W^m(k + 1) = W^m(k) - \alpha s^m (a^{m-1})^\top \tag{6}$$

$$b^m(k + 1) = b^m(k) - \alpha s^m \tag{7}$$

The data fitting of the influence of vibration amplitude on vertigo, ambiguity and immersion was carried out. The used data was that obtained in Experiment 1. The fitting results of the data and the errors in the training process are shown in Figs. 8 and 9.

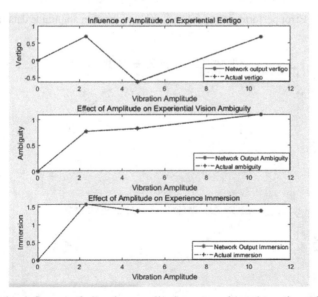

Fig. 8. Data fitting-influence of vibration amplitude on experiencer's vertigo, vision ambiguity and immersion Error performance of network during vibration amplitude data fitting

Similarly, the data fitting of the influence of vibration frequency on recognition difficulty and recognition accuracy was also conducted. The number of layers of artificial neural network and the number of neurons in each layer remained unchanged. The fitting results of the data and the errors in the training process are shown in Figs. 10 and 11.

The fitting results show that in the network training process, mean square error (MSE) decreases gradually with the increase of training times. The data fitting curve of neural network is in line with the distribution of original data.

According to the above two fitting results, the artificial neural network has certain advantages in simulating human visual nervous system. This advantage should be attributed to the characteristics of the artificial neural network itself, which is more adaptable to the fitting of non-linear functions than the traditional mathematical functions. It also proves that the inversed application of artificial neural network of bionics to the analysis of human visual nervous system is feasible.

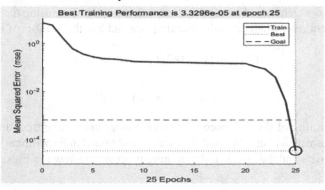

Fig. 9. Error performance of network during vibration amplitude data fitting

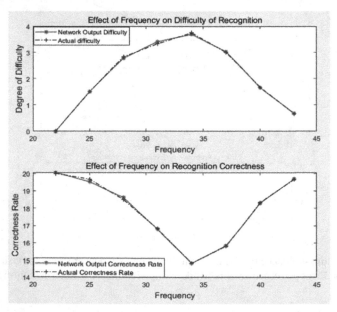

Fig. 10. Data fitting--influence of vibration frequency on recognition difficulty and accuracy.

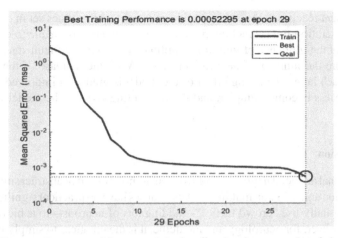

Fig. 11. Error performance of the network in the vibration frequency data fitting process.

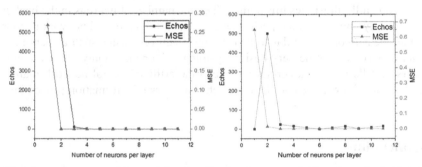

Fig. 12. The performance of the model under vibration frequency (left) and amplitude (right) data

3.3 Model Performance Evaluation

The optic nerve of human eye is composed of tens of millions of cells. The communication, coordination and influence between cells are extremely complex. Therefore, in order to preliminarily discuss the effectiveness and practicability of the artificial neural network constructed in this paper, the number of cells at all levels was adjusted and then the performance of the model was observed by taking the mean square error (MSE) and training time.

The data of the influence of vibration amplitude on user's three subjective experiences and the data of the influence of vibration frequency on the recognition accuracy and difficulty were tested. The numbers of neurons in the second and fourth layers were set to the same value, ranging from 1 to 11. Under different number of neurons, the performances of the model are shown in Fig. 12.

In the above process of using two sets of data to verify the inverse bionic artificial neural network established in this paper, the model error is very large and the required number of iterations is relatively high when the number of neurons is small. For the data of the influence of vibration frequency, the required training process is very long before the cell element reaches 3. Since the maximum weight update times set in the algorithm is 5000, the iteration times reaching 5000 can be considered as unable to converge. As for the data of the influence of vibration amplitude is also in a difficult state of iterative process before the number of neurons reaches 3. With the increase of the number of neurons in each layer, the fitting effect of the model is gradually improved, the weight updating process becomes simpler, and the final fitting error of the model is relatively small.

3.4 Discussion

Since traditional artificial neural network system is mostly used in abstract situations such as classification and decision making, and its neurons have no practical significance, most researchers usually use "crowd tactics"—adding lots of neurons—to achieve the target function. However, for neurology and medicine, it is meaningless to simply increase the number of neurons without considering the cooperation between neurons. For example, the effect of the increase in the number of neurons on the performance of the model in above section fully illustrates this point. When the number of neurons in the back layer network is only one or two, the performance of the artificial neural network is poor. At this time, the network is similar to that of single-cell organisms such as paramecium, and can only achieve some very basic physiological function. Only when the number of layers of cells reaches a certain level, can the artificial neural network realize the diversification of functions and the comprehensiveness of information processing in a real sense.

4 Conclusion

This paper proposes to improve the defects of existing virtual reality devices by using tactile intervention, i.e. physical vibration stimulation, to bring users a third channel of information flow besides vision and hearing. This paper carried out a series of experimental investigations and found that the immersion was significantly improved by employing tactile vibration intervention. In addition, artificial neural network model was used to simulate human visual nervous system. The fitting result has proved the effectiveness of applying inverse bionic artificial neural network to analyze human visual nerve. In terms of network structure, in the case of the number of network layers is tentatively set at 5, only when the neurons in each layer of the last 4 layers reach 4 or more can the experimental data be well fitted.

For the future work, firstly, non-psychological experiments shall be conducted to more accurately quantify the physical performance of users, so as to avoid the interference of subjective factors on the experimental results. Secondly, it is better to constrain the parameters from the physiological perspective. The discussion of models in this paper can only be carried out on the macro-structure for the time being. It needs to constrain some neurons to make them have physiological significance to further study the human eye vision system. The original model full of microscopic uncertainty would have more substantial significance.

Author Contributions. Tao Zeng, Pei Kang and Enshan Ouyang designed the experiments; Yan Liu and Hang Wang performed the experiments and conducted the modeling; Tao Zeng and Pei Kang wrote the paper.

Funding. This research was supported by the Fundamental Research Funds for the Central Universities under Grant 20720220084 and 20720220071.

Conflicts of Interest. The authors declare no conflict of interest. The founding sponsors had no role in the design of the study; in the collection, analyses, or interpretation of data; in the writing of the manuscript; or in the decision to publish the results.

References

1. Zhao, Q.: 10 scientific problems in virtual reality. J. Commun. ACM **54**(2), 116–118 (2011)
2. Dennison, M.: Motion sickness in virtual environments. UC Irvine Electronic Theses and Dissertations (2017)
3. Gregor, G., Lu, H., Jože, G.: Effect of VR technology matureness on VR sickness. Multimedia Tools Appl. 1–17 (2018)
4. Champel, M.L., Renaud, D., Mollet, N.: Key factors for a high-quality VR experience. In: Society of Photo-Optical Instrumentation Engineers (SPIE) Conference Series (2017)
5. Tanaka, N., Takagi, H.: Virtual reality environment design of managing both presence and virtual reality sickness. J. Physiol. Anthropol. Appl. Hum. Sci. **23**(6), 313–317 (2004)
6. Parong, J., Mayer, R.E.: Learning science in immersive virtual reality. J. Educ. Psychol. **110**(6), 785–797 (2018)
7. Sherman, W.R., Craig, A.B.: Understanding Virtual Reality—Interface, Application, and Design. Morgan Kaufmann Publishers Inc, United States, Publisher (2002)
8. Ramsamy, P., Haffegee, A., Jamieson, R., Alexandrov, V.: Using haptics to improve immersion in virtual environments. In: Alexandrov, V.N., van Albada, G.D., Sloot, P.M.A., Dongarra, J. (eds.) ICCS 2006. LNCS, vol. 3992, pp. 603–609. Springer, Heidelberg (2006). https://doi.org/10.1007/11758525_81
9. Yuki, K., Nakamura, T., Kajimoto, H.: HangerOVER: HMD-embedded haptics display with hanger reflex. In: ACM SIGGRAPH 2017 Emerging Technologies ACM (2017)
10. Natalia, C., Milella, F., Pinto, C., Cant, I., White, M., Meyer, G.: The effects of substitute multisensory feedback on task performance and the sense of presence in a virtual reality environment. PLoS ONE **13**(2), e0191846 (2018)
11. Oliveira, V., Brayda, L., Nedel, L., Maciel, A.: Experiencing guidance in 3D spaces with a vibrotactile head-mounted display. In: Proceeding of Virtual Reality, pp. 453–454. IEEE (2017)
12. Amores, J., Benavides, X., Shapira, L.: TactileVR: integrating physical toys into learn and play virtual reality experiences.In: Proceeding of 2016 IEEE International Symposium on Mixed & Augmented Reality, pp. 100–106 (2016)
13. Gugenheimer, J., Wolf, D., Eiríksson, E.R., Maes, P., Rukzio, E.: GyroVR: simulating inertia in virtual reality using head worn flywheels. In: Proceeding of Symposium on User Interface Software & Technology. ACM, Japan (2016)
14. Pamungkas, D.S., Ward, K.: Electro-tactile feedback system to enhance virtual reality experience. Int. J. Comput. Theor. Eng. **8**(6), 465–470 (2016)
15. Peiris, R.L., Peng, W., Chen, Z., Chan, L., Minamizawa, K.: ThermoVR: exploring integrated thermal haptic feedback with head mounted displays. In: Proceeding of 2017 CHI Conference on Human Factors in Computing Systems. ACM, United States, pp. 5452–5456 (2017)

16. Kaul, O.B., Rohs, M.: HapticHead: 3D guidance and target acquisition through a vibrotactile grid. In: Proceeding of 34th Annual CHI Conference on Human Factors in Computing Systems. ACM, pp. 2533–2539 (2016)
17. Kim, M., Jeon, C., Kim, J.: A study on immersion and presence of a portable hand haptic system for immersive virtual reality. J. Sensors **17**, 5 (2017)
18. Likert, R.: A technique for the measurement of attitudes. J. Arch. Psychol. **22**(40), 1–55 (1932)
19. Borg, G.: A general scale to rate symptoms and feeling related to problems of ergonomic and organizational importance. J. Supplemento A, Psicologia **30**(1), 8–10 (2008)

A Texture Display Device Based on Multi-coil Superposition Driving Method

Xuesong Bian[1,2], Yuan Guo[1,2], Yuru Zhang[1,2], and Dangxiao Wang[1,2,3](✉)

[1] State Key Lab of Virtual Reality Technology and Systems, Beihang University,
Beijing 100191, China
hapticwang@buaa.edu.cn
[2] Beijing Advanced Innovation Center for Biomedical Engineering, Beihang University,
Beijing 100191, China
[3] Peng Cheng Laboratory, Shenzhen 518055, China

Abstract. It is a challenge to develop high spatial resolution texture display devices using electromagnetic-driven methods, as the magnetic driving force sharply decreases due to the small size of the actuators. To address this challenge, we report a high spatial resolution texture display device using a novel multi-coil superposition driving method, which consists of 25 tactile units arranged in a 5*5 matrix with a spatial resolution of 2.75mm. Using the vector superposition of magnetic fields, the driving force of the target tactile unit can be effectively enhanced through the joint driving of multiple electromagnetic coils. The experimental result indicates that the upward holding force of the target tactile unit using the proposed multi-coil superposition driving method increases by 36.2% compared to the traditional single-coil driving method.

Keywords: Texture display · High spatial resolution · Magnetic field · Superposition

1 Introduction

Haptics plays a crucial role in human interaction with the external environment. Various properties of interactive objects, such as hardness, texture, and temperature, are primarily transmitted through haptics [1]. As one of the physical properties of object surface, texture is critical for human to recognize and manipulate objects. How to present the texture information of interactive objects to humans and simultaneously guarantee the fidelity of the rendered texture by tactile feedback device has been a hot issue in the field of human-computer interaction and virtual reality [2–6].

There are numerous driving methods in the design of texture display device, among which the electromagnetic driving method has been widely adopted due to its rapid, safe and stable characteristics [7–10]. The texture display devices developed by Khoudja et al. [11] and Streque et al. [12] used an electromagnetic coil to drive the permanent magnet above it, of which the driving magnetic field generated by single electromagnetic coil is relatively weak and cannot provide sufficient driving force. Cho et al. [13] proposed a

D. Wang et al. (Eds.): AsiaHaptics 2022, LNCS 14063, pp. 97–104, 2023.
https://doi.org/10.1007/978-3-031-46839-1_8

texture display device using electromagnetic-pneumatic hybrid driving method, which solved the problem of insufficient driving force provided by single electromagnetic coil. However, the pneumatic actuation demands sophisticated chamber design and component assembly, hindering the tactile device from high spatial resolution. Pece et al. [14] proposed an electromagnetic-locked driving method, which maintained large holding force of the tactile units. But the electromagnetic-locked structure increases the volume of the tactile unit, limiting further improvement of the spatial resolution. Therefore, it remains an open challenge to increase the driving force of small-sized tactile units in the electromagnetic-driven texture display device and thus to achieve high spatial resolution.

In this study, we propose a high spatial resolution texture display device based on a multi-coil superposition driving method. Through the superposition of magnetic field generated by multiple electromagnetic coils, the driving force of the target tactile unit can be significantly enhanced. We validate the multi-coil superposition driving method through COMSOL simulation and quantitative experiment. Finally, we summarize exploration of the proposed texture display device and look into the distance.

2 System Design

2.1 Device Design

The texture display device integrates 25 tactile units, which are arranged in a 5*5 matrix with a spatial resolution of 2.75 mm (Fig. 1). Its overall structure is mainly composed of nine parts: among which the coil fixing structure, the coil base structure and the permanent magnet fixing structure are fabricated by 3D printing. The cylindrical holes of the coil fixing structure are used to limit the radial movement of the coil (Fig. 1.g). Meanwhile, the axial movement of the coil is limited by the coil base structure (Fig. 1.h). The cylindrical ladder holes of the permanent magnet fixing structure are designed to limited the vertical displacement of the permanent magnet, on which a pin is fixed (Fig. 1.c). In addition to the above parts, the skeleton structure of the texture display device also includes base structure (Fig. 1.i) and finger guide structure (Fig. 1.a). The base structure ensures the stability of the device, and the finger guide structure guides the user to touch within an appropriate range through the continuous surface which has the shape of middle depression.

The contact part between texture display device and user's finger is an integrated flexible structure of film and bracket (Fig. 1.b), of which the flexible film and the flexible bracket respectively ensure the flatness and the softness of the device surface. The thickness of the film is 0.15 mm, and the cavities of the bracket are designed to provide free space for the moving part of the tactile unit. The integrated flexible structure simplifies the assembling process of the film and the bracket, whose fabrication process is depicted in Fig. 2. First, Part A and Part B of Ecoflex 00–30 are mixed in a 1:1 mass ration. Then, the well-mixed silica gel is placed in a vacuum chamber to remove the air bubbles. Next, the silica gel is poured into a 3D printed mold and placed in a drying chamber for curing. After 5 h, the integrated flexible structure is peeled off from the 3D printed mold.

The working principle of the proposed texture display device is depicted in Fig. 3. When the electromagnetic coils are powered on, the permanent magnet drives the pin to move upward with the action of electromagnetic force, forming a protrusion on the surface of the texture display device. When the electromagnetic coils are powered off, the permanent magnet and the pin return to its initial position with the action of film elastic force.

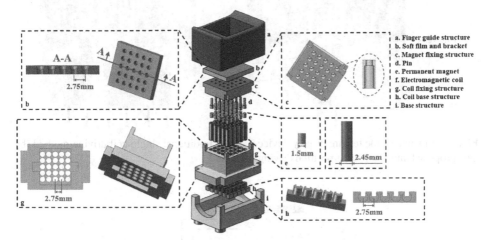

Fig. 1. Architecture of the texture display device.

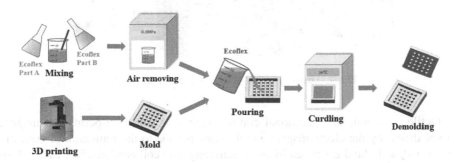

Fig. 2. Fabrication process of the integrated flexible structure.

The driving system is depicted in Fig. 4. There are 25 branches in the driving system, which can independently control any tactile unit in the 5*5 matrix. In the process of texture display, the position of target tactile units in the array is first determined according to the shape of the desired texture. According to the position, PC sends control commands to the microcontroller to activate the corresponding branches, which drive the tactile units connected to them. Then, target tactile units form protrusions on the surface of the texture display device to present the desired texture.

2.2 Driving Method

As a key parameter in the design of texture display device, the holding force can resist the press exerted by users in the interactive process, effectively providing users with

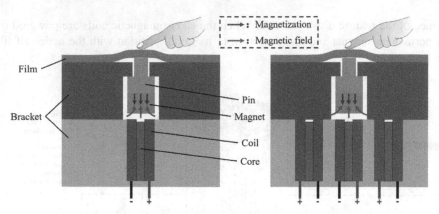

Fig. 3. Principle of the texture display device. (a) The traditional single-coil driving method (b) Our proposed multi-coil superposition driving method.

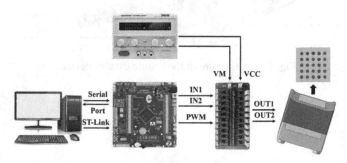

Fig. 4. Driving system of the texture display device.

the tactile sensation. The traditional control method is that each permanent magnet is only driven by the electromagnetic coil below it. Due to the limitation of size, the driving magnetic field generated by the electromagnetic coil is relatively weak, failing to provide a sufficient holding force [15, 16]. To address this challenge, we propose a multi-coil superposition driving method, based on the vector superposition of magnetic field, to control the target tactile unit. As depicted in Fig. 5(a), two electromagnetic coils with iron cores are arranged side by side. Since the magnetic permeability of the iron core is much larger than that of the air, the external magnetic flux generated by the left coil mostly concentrate to the iron core inside the right coil. Consequently, the left electromagnetic coil can generate vertical magnetic flux intensity B_1 at the point P above the right electromagnetic coil.

In addition, we carry out a simulation using COMSOL on the above mentioned condition. With the left electromagnetic coil energized, we obtain the distribution of magnetic field lines in the cylinder space, of which different colors represent different levels of magnetic flux intensity (Fig. 5(b)). The distribution of magnetic field lines indicates that there is a certain amount of magnetic flux in the right iron core, which can generate vertical magnetic flux intensity B_1 at the point P.

When the right electromagnetic coil is energized with opposite current to the left electromagnetic coil, it generates vertical magnetic flux intensity B_2 with the same direction as B_1 at the point P (Fig. 5(c)). According to the vector superposition of magnetic field, the actual magnetic flux intensity at the point P can be expressed as

$$B_P = B_1 + B_2 \qquad (1)$$

Compared with the single coil, the magnetic flux intensity generated by two coils at the point P is significantly enhanced. To quantify the superimposed magnetic field, three conduction modes of the two electromagnetic coils are simulated respectively (Table 1). Figure 6 depicts the magnitude distribution of the magnetic flux intensity along the horizontal line l (Fig. 5(c)) at a height of 0.5 mm above the coils. When only the right coil is powered on, the magnetic flux density at the point P is 97.16 mT (mode 1, Fig. 6(a)). When an opposite current of 0.4 A is applied to the left coil for the meanwhile, the magnetic flux density at the point P reaches 104.27 mT (mode 2, Fig. 6(b)), which is 7.32% higher than that in mode 1. When the current of the left coil increases to 0.8 A, the magnetic flux density (111.37 mT) at the point P (mode 3, Fig. 6(c)) is increased by 14.63% compared with mode 1. The simulation results indicate that multi-coil superposition driving method can generate larger driving magnetic field while maintaining high spatial resolution of the texture display device.

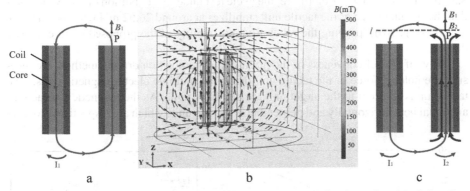

Fig. 5. Principle of the magnetic field superposition. (a) Magnetic flux intensity of the left coil at the point P. (b) Distribution of the magnetic field lines in the cylinder space. (c) Superposition of the magnetic flux intensity at the point P.

Table 1. Current modes of the electromagnetic coils.

Current modes	The left coil (I_1)	The right coil (I_2)
Mode 1	0 A	0.8 A
Mode 2	0.4 A	0.8 A
Mode 3	0.8 A	0.8 A

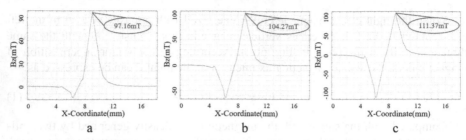

Fig. 6. Magnitude distribution of the magnetic flux intensity along the line *l* above the coils. (a) Mode 1. (b) Mode 2. (c) Mode 3.

3 Experiment

To evaluate the reliability of the proposed texture display device, we measure the holding force of the tactile unit under different conditions. In one working cycle, the electromagnetic coil was powered on for 1 s, then powered off for 4 s. For each condition, eight working cycles were repeated and the holding force was recorded by the force sensor (Nano 17, ATI Industrial Automation Inc., America). As depicted in Fig. 7(a), the holding force of the tactile unit is positively correlated with the current. When the current increases from 0.5 A to 0.8 A, the holding force correspondingly increases from 8.33 mN to 26.52 mN. Furthermore, the cycle test under the condition of 0.8 A indicates that the holding force of the tactile unit stabilizes at around 26.52 mN with the variance of 1.04 (Fig. 7(b)), proving the reliability and stability of the proposed texture display device.

To verify the effectiveness of the multi-coil superposition driving method, we measure the holding force of the tactile unit driven by multiple electromagnetic coils. Two tactile units adjacent to the target unit are auxiliary units. As the magnetic interactions are equal both horizontally and perpendicularly, two units which are respectively located

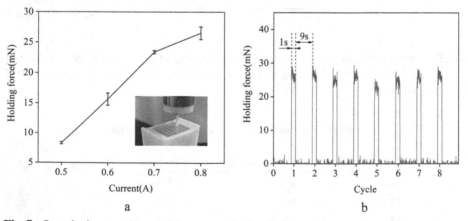

Fig. 7. Quantitative experiment of the texture display device. (a) Holding forces under different current conditions. (b) The cycle test under the condition of 0.8 A.

above and to the left of the target unit are randomly set as auxiliary units. It is assumed that the current direction of the target unit is positive. The current of the target unit was set to 0.8 A, while the current of the auxiliary units were set to -0.5 A. As depicted in Fig. 8, the holding force of the target tactile unit adopting multi-coil superposition driving method is 36.12 mN, which increases by 36.2% compared to the single-coil driving method. In addition, the protrusion height of the target tactile unit driven by multiple electromagnetic coils averages 0.2 mm, which can be perceived by human [17].

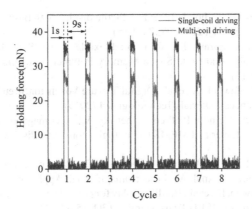

Fig. 8. Comparison of the single-coil driving and multi-coil superposition driving.

4 Conclusion and Future Work

This paper proposes a texture display device based on multi-coil superposition driving method. Each tactile unit can be independently controlled to form protrusions with the interaction between permanent magnet and electromagnetic coils, thereby simulating diverse texture patterns. The target tactile unit can be driven by multiple electromagnetic coils to improve the holding force through the superposition of magnetic field. The quantitative experiments indicate that the proposed texture display device can provide sufficient holding force on the premise of high spatial resolution and thus render finer texture.

To expand the application scenarios of the proposed device and improve the stability and diversity of texture display, we will further explore the optimal currents of the multi-coil superposition driving method. Moreover, we will explore the influence of the iron core shape on the superposition of magnetic field. The driving efficiency of the tactile unit will be improved through a more efficient design of the iron core.

References

1. MacLean, K.E.: Putting haptics into the ambience. IEEE Trans. Haptics **2**(3), 123–135 (2009)
2. Withana, A., Groeger, D., Steimle, J.: Tacttoo: a thin and feel-through tattoo for on-skin tactile output. In: Proceedings - 31st Annual ACM Symposium on User Interface Software and Technology, pp. 365–378 (2018)
3. Dai, X., Colgate, J.E., Peshkin, M. A.: LateralPaD: a surface-haptic device that produces lateral forces on a bare finger. In: 2012 IEEE Haptics Symposium (HAPTICS), pp. 7–14 (2012)
4. Phung, H., Nguyen, C.T., Choi, H.R., et al.: Tactile display with rigid coupling based on soft actuator. Meccanica **50**(11), 2825–2837 (2015)
5. Besse, N., Rosset, S., Zarate, J.J. Shea, H.: Flexible Active Skin: Large Reconfigurable Arrays of Individually Addressed Shape Memory Polymer Actuators. Advanced Materials Technologies 2 (2017)
6. Lamuta, C., He, H., Tawfick, S., et al.: Digital Texture Voxels for Stretchable Morphing Skin Applications. Advanced Materials Technologies 4 (2019)
7. Streque, J., Talbi, A., Pernod, P., Preobrazhensky, V.: New magnetic microactuator design based on PDMS elastomer and MEMS technologies for tactile display. IEEE Trans. Haptics **3**(2), 88–97 (2010)
8. Szabo, Z., Enikov, E.T.: Development of wearable micro-actuator array for 3-D virtual tactile displays. J. Electromagn. Anal. Appl.Electromagn. Anal. Appl. **4**(6), 219–229 (2012)
9. Kim, J., Han, B., Kwon, D., et al.: Braille display for portable device using flip-latch structured electromagnetic actuator. IEEE Trans. Haptics **13**(1), 59–65 (2020)
10. Yu, X., Huang, Y., Rogers, J.A., et al.: Skin-integrated wireless haptic interfaces for virtual and augmented reality. Nature **575**(7783), 473–479 (2019)
11. Benali-Khoudja, M., Hafez, M., Kheddar, A.: VITAL: an electromagnetic integrated tactile display. Displays **28**(3), 133–144 (2007)
12. Streque, J., Talbi, A., Pernod, P., Preobrazhensky, V.: Pulse-driven magnetostatic micro-actuator array based on ultrasoft elastomeric membranes for active surface applications. J. Micromech. Microeng.Micromech. Microeng. **22**(9), 725–734 (2012)
13. Gallo, S., Son, C., Cho, I., et al.: A flexible multimodal tactile display for delivering shape and material information. Sens. Actuators, A **236**, 180–189 (2015)
14. Pece, F., Zarate, J.J., Hilliges, O., et al.: MagTics: flexible and thin form factor magnetic actuators for dynamic and wearable haptic feedback. In: Proceedings - 30th Annual ACM Symposium on User Interface Software and Technology, pp. 143–154 (2017)
15. Zárate, J.J., Shea, H.: Using pot-magnets to enable stable and scalable electromagnetic tactile displays. IEEE Trans. Haptics **10**(1), 106–112 (2017)
16. Zárate, J.J., Tosolini, G., Shea, H., et al.: Optimization of the force and power consumption of a microfabricated magnetic actuator. Sens. Actuators, A **234**, 57–64 (2015)
17. Han, A.K., Ji, S., Wang, D., Cutkosky, M.R.: Haptic surface display based on miniature dielectric fluid transducers. IEEE Robot. Autom. Lett. **5**(3), 4021–4027 (2020)

The Central Mechanism Underlying Extrapolation of Thermal Sensation

Junjie Hua(✉) ⓘ, Masahiro Furukawa, and Taro Maeda

Human Information Engineering Lab, Department of Bioinformatic Engineering,
Graduate School of Information Science and Technology, Osaka University,
Osaka 5650871, Japan
junjie-hua@hiel.ist.osaka-u.ac.jp

Abstract. Extrapolation of thermal sensation (ETS) is a temperature-tuning phenomenon. Heat is felt outside the cold stimulator if given a single warm stimulus for 5 s and then both warm and cold stimulus for 0.5 s, while no such tuning is in reversed condition. The mechanism underlying ETS has not been clarified. We claim a common mechanism based on the transition of the spatiotemporal conditions among ETS, paradoxical heat sensation (PHS), and thermal grill illusion (TGI). We tested whether the addition and unmasking theory in TGI also works in ETS. Percentage hot judgment was found to increase as the temperature difference of stimuli increases, suggesting that hot sensation at extrapolation site can be the result of an addition of non-noxious warm and cold signals. On the other hand, the cold threshold was found to decrease as the distance between warm and cold stimulus increases, suggesting that the unmasking process occurs at the cold site. Our findings suggested that unmasking and addition process involve in the temperature-tuning phenomenon (ETS, TGI, and PHS) at the site with and without physical stimulation, respectively. The co-work of two processes forms a gate control model of temperature.

Keywords: Thermal Illusion · Perception · Human Information Processing

1 Introduction

The sensation of temperature from ascending sensory paths, which are from peripheral to central, are regarded as separate. However, the discovery of thermal illusions, e.g., thermal grill illusion (TGI), paradoxical heat sensation (PHS), and extrapolation of thermal sensation (ETS) challenge this perspective [5,11,19,25,27]. In TGI, a sensation of painful heat is felt by touching interlaced warm and cool bars simultaneously to the skin. In PHS, a sensation of heat occurs if the skin were heated immediately prior to cooling. In ETS, heat is felt outside the cold stimulator if given a single warm stimulus for 5 s and then both warm and cold

This research was supported by JSPS KAKENHI Grant-in-Aid for Scientific Research (A) Grant Number 19H01121.

stimulus for 0.5 s. Of the three illusions, TGI and PHS are temperature-tuning phenomenons in which warm and cold stimulus are convergent temporally and spatially, respectively. While ETS is an in-between phenomenon in the aspect of both time and space. This reveals a spatiotemporal transition among TGI, ETS, and PHS, suggesting that there could be a breakthrough in the mechanism of temperature tuning by investigating ETS. In this study, we investigated the cause of ETS with psychophysical methods.

2 Background

2.1 Temperature-Tuning Phenomenons

Ascending sensory path of thermal sensation, which include warm and cold path, are regarded as separate. This specific theory is now called "labeled lines" [4]. However, the discovery of thermal grill illusion (TGI), paradoxical heat sensation (PHS), and extrapolation of thermal sensation (ETS) challenged this perspective [5,11,19,25,27]. With touching multiple pairs (usually over 3 pairs) of warm and cold bars simultaneously, a painful heat can be felt, and this painful illusion is called thermal grill illusion [5,11]. The discovery of TGI suggests that non-nociceptive temperature channels centrally integrate and moderate nociceptive perception. It also reveals that the spatial pattern of physical stimuli tunes the thermal sensation. On the other hand, a paradoxical heat sensation was observed if the skin was heated immediately before cooling [11,27]. Because of the low possibility of inducement of PHS in healthy participants (about 10%) but high possibility in patients with probable or definite multiple sclerosis [15,27,28], PHS was seldom treated as a temperature-tuning phenomenon on healthy participants. Nevertheless, we could not ignore the tuning of thermal sensation by the temporal pattern of physical stimuli in this illusion. Extrapolation of thermal sensation (ETS) is also a temperature-tuning phenomenon. We encountered this illusion while conducting experiments with two small Peltier thermodes (15 mm × 15 mm for each element). An intense hot sensation was reported outside the cold stimulus if given a single warm stimulus for 5 s and then both warm and cold stimulus for 0.5 s [19]. However, no such illusion was reported if given a single cold stimulus for 5 s and then both warm and cold stimulus for 0.5 s. There was also no report of pain in the simultaneous condition. We consider that both spatial and temporal patterns dominate ETS compared to the illusionary condition with TGI and PHS.

2.2 A Common Mechanism

There has been a perspective that PHS can be interpreted as an instance of TGI [11,25]. The finding partly supports this perspective that PHS is conducted peripherally through C afferents while not $A\delta$ afferents [27]. Green described it as a "paradoxical discharge of warm afferents in a field of cooling would produce a mixture of cold and warm afferent stimulation no different than that produced by TGI". From this perspective, the extrapolation of thermal sensation (ETS)

Table 1. Summary of Spatiotemporal Characteristics of Thermal Illusion

Temperature-tuning Phenomenon	Time	Space
Paradoxical Heat Sensation [14, 15, 27]	Separate	Convergent
Extrapolation of Thermal Sensation [19]	In between	Separate (single pair)
Thermal Grill Illusion [5, 16]	Convergent	Separate (multiple pairs)

may also be interpreted as an instance of TGI and PHS because, in ETS, heat is evoked by cooling the skin, the adjacent of which is pre-heated. If so, ETS would be a spatial form of PHS and a temporal form of TGI.

From this opinion, we summarized the condition when inducing PHS, TGI, and ETS from the point of both space and time. We summarized the temporal pattern of three thermal illusions by separation of thermal stimuli, and the spatial pattern by area of thermal stimuli. As shown in Table 1, in the aspect of time, the cold and warm stimuli are separate in PHS (because of the pre-heating) while converging in TGI (because of simultaneous touch). In ETS, the cold and warm stimuli are partly separate from each other. On the other hand, in the aspect of space, the cold and warm stimuli are convergent in PHS (because of the same stimulation site) and separate in TGI (usually over 3 pairs, area over $100\,cm^2$). ETS is between PHS and TGI (one pair, $4.5\,cm^2$). Thus we can see the spatiotemporal transition when inducing thermal illusion, and the extrapolation of thermal sensation looks like a transitional form between PHS and TGI, suggesting a common mechanism among the three illusions.

2.3 Theories of Thermal Illusion

If we hold the perspective that there is a common mechanism in TGI, PHS, and ETS, the two central theories that explain TGI – "addition theory" proposed by Green and "unmasking theory" proposed by Craig should also explain ETS, although the two theories conflict with each other. We will introduce these two central theories below.

Addition Theory. Green investigated thermal sensation with the mild temperature pairs [10, 11]. Data were collected on the quality of sensation as well as the intensity. Participants rated temperature and pain perception separately, selecting from a list (nothing, cool, cold, warm, hot, burn, sting, pain) the sensation representing the specific quality experienced on each trial. Using 33 °C as a baseline, cooling to 31 °C and warming from 35 °C to 40 °C resulted in a rating of "hot" on 40.6% of trials At temperatures as low as 26 °C, the frequency and intensity of painless heat increased as the CPN threshold was exceeded. Furthermore, another group of participants evaluated the intensity of the sensations produced by these sensations. Gentle temperature differences were set up to measure the intensity of the sensory changes caused by the stimulus pairs. For the range of temperature pairs tested, simultaneous warm and cold stimuli were generally perceived with approximately twice the intensity of either stimulus alone. When the warm (e.g., 36 °C) and cold (e.g., 30 °C) stimuli were presented alone and rated as the same intensity, the perceived intensity was twice as high when the two were presented simultaneously. According to these observations, Green proposed the addition theory [10].

Addition theory claims that "thermal grill illusion is a mixture of simultaneous sensations of warmth and coldness" (see Fig. 1.(a)). According to this theory, the cold bar of the thermal grill activates cold fibers while the warm bar activates warm fibers. Since cold fibers have a paradoxical response to noxious heat, the simultaneous sensation of cold and warmth is interpreted as painful heat. Thus, the addition theory has two premises: 1. the presence of a warm and cold stimulus; 2. the simultaneous sensation of a warm and cold stimulus. Some physiological and psychophysical findings support the addition theory: WDR neurons are found to be involved in the integration of information from multiple modalities in the dorsal horn of the spinal cord, and they respond in a graded manner during the transition from non-noxious warm or cool to noxious heat or cold. Thus, it appears that input signals get added in WDR neurons [22]. On the other hand, Bouhassira found that increasing the intensity of warm and cold stimulus significantly increased TGI, which suggest that TGI can be the result of an addition of non-noxious warm and cold signals [2].

The additive theory predicts two psychological assumptions: 1. the greater the difference between the warm and cold stimuli, the more intense the illusion feels; 2. the small difference between the cold and warm stimuli can produce painless heat.

Unmasking Theory. Craig found STT lamina 1 dorsal horn "cool" neurons in the spinothalamic tract of cats that respond to cold stimulation at 20 °C and get inhibited by the warm stimulation at 40 °C. Craig and Bushnell further showed that the heat-pinch-cold (HPC) lamina 1 neuron activity was not affected by

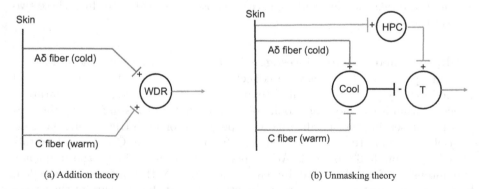

(a) Addition theory   (b) Unmasking theory

Fig. 1. Two central theories for thermal grill illusion. (a) Addition theory. (b) Unmasking theory. Marks (-) indicate inhibitory synapses while marks (+) indicate excitatory synapses.

heating. In human psychophysical experiments, they reported that a grill of 20 °C and 40 °C stimulus caused a "painful thermal sensation similar to a cold sore burn," similar to the sensation produced by cooling to 10 °C. Based on the above results, Craig proposed the unmasking (or disinhibition) theory (see Fig. 1(b)): heat is conducted from the C fiber through the spinothalamic tract to the HPC cells in the thalamus via the lamina 1 of the dorsal horn of the spinal cord. Cold, along with its associated noxious component, is conducted via both pathways, but the $A\delta$ fiber inhibits the C fiber and the cool cells inhibit the HPC cells. Thus, only the cold component is recognized [5,7].

Differ from the addition theory, the unmasking theory predicts two psychological assumptions below: 1. the greater intensity of warm stimuli and the weaker cold stimuli, the more intense the illusion feels; 2. the small difference between the cold and warm stimuli cannot produce painless heat.

3   Materials and Methods

To clarify whether addition theory or unmasking theory works in ETS, we conducted two experiments in this study. Experiment 1 aimed to clarify which theory works for the "extrapolation" phenomenon by observing hot judgment outside the cold stimulus using various temperature pairs. The addition theory predicts that both warm and cold stimulus have a positive effect on the hot judgment, while the unmasking theory predicts that warm and cold stimulus have a positive and a negative effect on the hot judgment.

Experiment 2 aimed to clarify if the perception of the cold stimulus varies, and if so, which theory works for the perception of cold stimulus by observing the cold threshold of the cold stimulus when the location of the warm and cold stimulus varies. The addition theory predicts that no change in the perception of cold stimulus, while the unmasking theory predicts that the cold threshold increases if warm and cold stimulus gets close.

3.1   Participants

14 participants (11 males and 3 females) aged between 23 and 30 participated in experiment 1 and 7 participants (5 males and 2 females)participated in experiment 2. Participants suffering from pain, diseases causing potential neural damage (e.g., diabetes), systemic illnesses, and mental disorders were excluded. All reported being right-hand dominant.

3.2   Apparatus

A thermal display was designed to investigate the mechanism in ETS (see Fig. 2). Two 15×15 mm Peltier thermodes (TEC1-01705T125, Kaito Denshi Co., Ltd.) provide thermal stimuli in this study. Thus, the area of thermal stimulation in this study is 225 mm^2 for each stimulation.

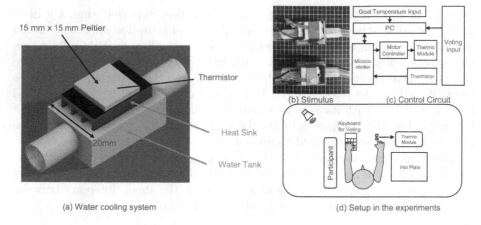

Fig. 2. (a) Water cooling system. (b) Stimulus. (c) Control circuit. (d) Setup in the environment.

A microcontroller (mbed NXP LPC1768, NXP Semiconductors Taiwan Ltd.) sends control signals to the DC motor controller (DBH-12V, MiZOELEC) to drive Peltier elements and receives temperature signals from the thermistors (103JT-025, ATC Semitic, Ltd.). A water cooling system was applied to transfer heat from Peltier elements to the 20-mm wide water tank. To adjust and maintain the skin temperature of participants at a thermally neutral temperature, a hot plate was used in this study (NHP-M30N, New Japan Chemical Co, Ltd.).

3.3   Experiment 1

In this experiment, we aimed to clarify which theory works for the "extrapolation" phenomenon by observing hot judgment outside the cold stimulus using various temperature pairs. The addition theory predicts that both warm and cold stimuli have a positive effect on the hot judgment, while the unmasking theory predicts that warm and cold stimuli have a positive and a negative effect on the hot judgment, respectively.

Prior to the experiment, participants were instructed to put their right hand on the hot plate to adjust skin temperature to $32\,°C$ (baseline temperature). The experiment was conducted in a room with a constant temperature at $25\,°C$. The physical intensities, ΔT, applied were -5, -9, -13, or $-17\,°C$ for cooling and 2, 5, 8, or $11\,°C$ for warming (relative to the baseline temperature).

Perception of the fingertip was observed. The warm stimulus was always given at the distal interphalangeal (DIP) joint, while the cold stimulus was always given at the proximal interphalangeal (PIP) joint[1]. Between every two trials, participants were instructed to place their right hand on the hot plate for at least

---

[1] In the pilot experiment, ETS occurred most frequently when the two stimuli were applied at the DIP and PIP joint.

30 s. Before each trial, they were instructed to place the D3 (middle) finger of the right hand several millimeters above the device. They touched the hot stimulator with the PIP joint first for 5 s and then also touched the cold stimulator with the DIP joint for 0.5 s according to the sound cue. Then they answered the sensation at the fingertip. A two-alternative forced choice (2AFC) standard psychophysical protocol was employed. They answered hot or cold at the observation spot. Five trials were performed under each condition. The stimuli were applied randomly. In total, each participant was given 80 trials.

3.4   Experiment 2

In this experiment, we aimed to clarify if the perception of a cold stimulus varies, and if so, which theory works for the perception of cold stimulus by observing the cold threshold of the cold stimulus when the location of the warm and cold stimulus varies. We defined the cold threshold as the temperature of cold stimulus with 50% hot judgment. When the temperature is below the threshold (physical stimuli are more intense), warm is felt; when the temperature is over the threshold (physical stimuli are weaker), cold is felt. The addition theory predicts no change in the perception of the cold stimulus, while the unmasking theory predicts that the cold threshold increases if the warm and cold stimulus gets close.

Same as the former experiment, the baseline temperature, and the room temperature was controlled. However, in this experiment, we observed the perception at the location where a cold stimulus is given.

Prior to the experiment, we made six marks (0 to 5) on the side face of participants' D3 (middle) finger from the root of finger. 10 mm between every two adjacent marks. During the experiment, the warm stimulus was applied to all the six locations; the cold stimulus was applied to the locations that are at least 20 mm to the warm stimulus (because the water tank of Peltier element is 20 mm wide, see Fig. 2). Using the method of limits, we tested the cold threshold under every location pair. The physical intensity of the warm stimulus was held as 43 °C, while that of the cold stimulus varied from 15 °C to 29 °C. The descending and ascending staircase were conducted in two days.

Participants were instructed to place their right hand on the hot plate for at least 30 s. Before each trial, they were instructed to place the D3 finger of the right hand several millimeters above the device. They were also told to match the location marked with a number and the edge of the warm Peltier element in each trial. They touched the hot stimulator first for 5 s and then also touched the cold stimulator for 0.5 s according to the sound cue. Then they answered the sensation of the cold stimulus is given. A two-alternative forced choice (2AFC) standard psychophysical protocol was employed. They answered hot or cold at the observation spot. In a descending staircase, the temperature of the cold stimulus increased 2 °C till they reported coldness. If they kept reporting heat until 29 °C, the maximum value 29 °C was recorded as the threshold. On the other hand, in an ascending staircase, the temperature of the cold stimulus decreased 2 °C till they reported heat. If they kept reporting coldness until 15 °C, the minimum value 15 °C was recorded as the threshold. The distance between the two stimuli was changed randomly.

4   Experimental Results

4.1   Experiment 1

Geometric means of percentage hot judgment at the fingertip of the D3 finger in Fig. 3 as a function of cold stimulator temperature. Each point is based on 75 observations. The empty circles stand for the percentage hot judgment at the fingertip when the temperature of the cold stimulator at the DIP joint and that of the warm stimulator at the PIP joint varied. The green, blue, red and black dashed line stand for the temperature of warm stimulus as 34 °C, 37 °C, 40 °C and 43 °C, respectively.

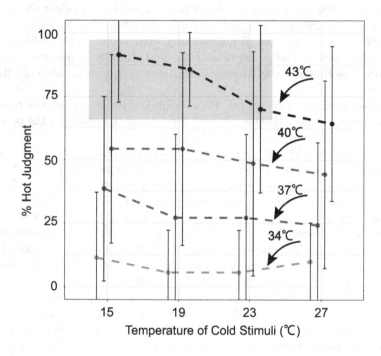

Fig. 3. Percentage hot judgment at the D3 (middle) finger as a function of cold stimulator temperature. The parameter is the temperature of the warm stimulator. Error bars represent standard error of each condition. The pink box stands for the situation the perception of cold stimulus turns to warm (result in experiment 2). (Color figure online)

In general, if the intensity of the warm stimulus is held, the percentage hot judgment increased when the intensity of the cold stimulus increases, indicating

Table 2. Comments from Participants

Comment	Age	Gender
I felt a burn at my fingertip	29	Male
A cold sensation at first, followed immediately by an intense hot sensation	25	Male
I felt a burn at one point on my fingertip, but not at the entire tip	22	Female
Not only is the finger pulp but also the back of the finger is hot	28	Male
Difficult to judgment. I can feel both heat and coldness	27	Male
Sting, but cannot feel heat or coldness	29	Male
I do not know how to answer, but definitely not cold	23	Male

a positive effect of the cold stimulus on the illusion. On the other hand, if the intensity of the cold stimulus is held, the percentage hot judgment also increased when the intensity of the warm stimulus increases, indicating that there is a positive effect of the warm stimulus on the illusion. Percentage hot judgment reached the maximum when the temperature difference reached the maximum.

A two-way ANOVA was performed to analyze the effect of intensity of warm stimulus and cold stimulus on percentage hot judgment. We found a statistically-significant difference in percentage hot judgment yield by both intensity of warm stimulus ($f(3) = 52.963$, $p < 0.001$) and by intensity of cold stimulus ($f(3) = 2.129$, $p < 0.1$) It also revealed that there was not a statistically significant interaction between the effects of the intensity of warm stimulus and cold stimulus ($f = 0.490$, $p = 0.88$). This result suggests that the addition of the warm and cold stimulus occurs. The addition of warm and cold stimulus causes a hot sensation outside the cold stimulus by the direct stimulation at DIP and PIP joints when the physical stimuli are intense enough. Indeed, participants sometimes volunteered comments that "I felt burn at the fingertip" (see Table 2). Also, notice that participants did not touch anything with the D3 fingertip while an illusion is evoked there. The phenomenon of "extrapolation without touching" is different from thermal referral and was never reported [9, 18].

4.2   Experiment 2

Geometric means of the cold threshold at the place where a cold stimulus was given in Fig. 4 as a function of the location of the cold stimulus. The empty circles stand for the cold threshold at the place a cold stimulus was given when the location of the warm and cold stimulus varied. The warm and cold stimuli were applied to the fixed six locations as Fig. 4 shows. The locations were from the root of the finger to the fingertip. Two adjacent locations were 1 cm apart. The dashed lines stand for the location of the warm stimulus as 0 cm, 1 cm, 2 cm, 3 cm, 4 cm and 5 cm, respectively. Considering that each Peltier element is 2 cm wide (see Fig. 2), the number of placeable locations varied when the location of the warm stimulus was held. When the warm stimulus was placed at 0 cm or 5 cm, there were four locations for the cold stimulus. However, there were only three locations for the cold stimulus when the warm stimulus was placed at 1 cm to 4 cm. In this experiment, we defined the cold threshold as the temperature of cold stimulus with 50% hot judgment. When the temperature is below the threshold (physical stimuli are more intense), warm is felt; when the temperature is over the threshold (physical stimuli are weaker), cold is felt.

In general, the data in experiment 2 reveals monotonicity on the same side of the warm stimulus. Once the relative location of the warm and cold stimulus was held (the cold stimulus was always at some side of the warm stimulus), the cold threshold became higher if the cold stimulus got closer to the warm stimulus. This result suggests that unmasking (or disinhibition) occurs and the cold sensation is inhibited because of the warm stimulus.

On the other hand, the data in experiment 2 reveals that the cold threshold is between 16 °C and 23 °C (temperature of warm stimulus is 43 °C). This is also the condition suitable to evoke the hot sensation at the fingertip in experiment 1 (see the black dashed line in Fig. 3). If the temperature of the cold stimulus is over the threshold (feel cold at cold stimulus), there is only a very weak warm image outside the cold stimulus (60% of hot judgment). Once the temperature of the cold stimulus is lower than the threshold, perception at the cold stimulus changes and the warm perception outside the cold stimulus becomes more intense, suggesting that the occurrence of the unmasking process at the cold stimulus promotes the occurrence of the addition process outside the cold stimulus. Considering that this is also close to the onset threshold of HPC cells (25 °C), we speculate that nociceptive component (HPC) also takes part in the evoke of the hot sensation at extrapolation site [6].

5   Discussion

5.1   Principal Findings

The data in this study suggests that perception outside the cold stimulus is dominated by the addition theory (experiment 1), and the cold threshold at the cold stimulus is dominated by the unmasking theory (experiment 2). Our findings indicate that both addition theory and unmasking theory work in the generation of ETS, and in fact, there are two separate processes in the generation of ETS (Fig. 5). One process determines the quality of the resulting thermal sensation by determining the involvement of noxious component. This process is known as unmasking. It requires two premises. One is enough physical stimulus to excite the HPC cells. Another one is the inhibition of the cool cell activity by the warm stimulus. If there is no involvement of HPC, there will be no sting outside the cold stimulus. On the other hand, if there is no inhibition of cool cells, the perception of the cold stimulus could be hot and cold. According to Craig, burning pain can be represented by a result of comparator neurons that receive excitatory inputs from HPC cells and inhibitory inputs from cool cells [5,7,17]. Thus, HPC-cool could be used to calculate the noxious component. The involvement of noxious component HPC-cool indeed forms a gate of nociception. If HPC-cool is over 0, the gate opens and nociception can be clearly perceived; if HPC-cool does not

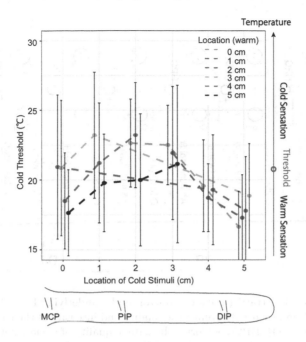

Fig. 4. Geometric means of the cold threshold at the place where a cold stimulus was given in Fig. 4 as a function of the location of the cold stimulus. The warm and cold stimulus were applied to the fixed six locations. The locations were from root of the finger to the fingertip. Cold threshold is defined as the temperature of cold stimulus with 50% cold judgment. When the temperature is below the threshold, warm is felt; when the temperature is over the threshold (physical stimuli is weaker), cold is felt. Error bars represent standard error of each condition.

exceed 0, the gate closes and nociception cannot be clearly perceived. Thus, we call it the gate control model.

The second process is the addition, which determines the intensity of the resulting thermal sensation from the physical stimuli. Here, the component involved in the addition process is not only the innocuous component but also the noxious component HPC-cool. To test our theory that the intensity of the resulting sensation is summated, we investigated the hot judgment at the fingertip when applying various pairs of temperatures in experiment 1. Our data indicated that both warm and cold stimuli have a positive effect on the sensation. In addition, based on the observation that only when it feels hot where a cold stimulus is given, an intense hot sensation is felt outside the cold stimulus, we speculate that the activity of the unmasked HPC cells promotes the addition process. Green conducted the experiment with mild temperature pairs, such as cold stimulus at 26 °C or higher and warm stimulus at 40 °C or lower, and argues that the thermal sensation results from the addition of innocuous warm and cold stimulus [11]. Since the mean onset threshold of HPC cells is not over 25 °C [6], this could explain why there is no noxious component in the addition theory.

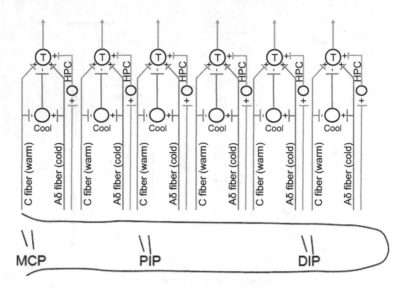

Fig. 5. Diagrams illustrating the gate control model underlying ETS. The unmasking theory and addition theory determine the quality and intensity of the resulting thermal sensation, respectively. HPC-cool forms the gate of quality of nociception. On the other hand, all the inputs projected toward T cells determine the intensity of nociception. Marks (−) indicate inhibitory synapses while marks (+) indicate excitatory synapses.

Besides, the co-work of addition theory and unmasking theory can be also found in the comment of the participants (Table 2). Participants sometimes reported that it is difficult to report because both heat and coldness can be felt at the fingertip. They also reported that nothing is felt except sting.

In this study, the area of thermal stimulation in this study is $225\,mm^2$ ($15 \times 15\,mm$) for each stimulation at finger. Considering the average width of finger of participants is $18\,mm$, the area of thermal stimulation in this study does not have an influence on the experimental result. On the other hand, pressing force in this study was not considered. This is because with the discovery of the TGI and thermal referral without touch [3,8], pressing force is considered no to have an influence on thermal sensation.

A possible application of this study is a new thermal display based on extrapolation of thermal sensation. Usually, thermal sensation is obtained where heat conduction occurs. Past Peltier-based thermal displays offer thermal sensation where Peltier contacts with skin. This means displaying thermal sensation with a large area consumes a lot of heat. However, with the application of extrapolation of thermal sensation, thermal sensation can be felt at the location that no heat conduct occurs. This decreases the consumption of heat. Another application of this study is that, considering the unmasking process at the site of cold stimulation, when displaying thermal gradient at skin with warm and cold stimulation, unmasking process requires to be avoided.

5.2   Adequacy of Gate Control Model

According to the gate control model we proposed, the opening and closing of the gate rely on the balance between the warm and cold signals. The factor that influences this balance may be the spatiotemporal summation of stimulus. A weak temperature signal with poor spatiotemporal summation is insufficient to generate an intense noxious component. A study of paradoxical warmth, the predecessor of paradoxical heat, reported that the greater the area of stimulus, the more heat was felt than warmth, so the name of this illusion was subsequently changed from paradoxical warmth to paradoxical heat sensation (PHS). This is evidence of the change in balance caused by spatial summation.

Cold stimulus plays a very interesting role in this mechanism. According to the above diagram, only a cold stimulus has an inhibitory effect on the perception of the last nociceptive pathway. The function of such peripheral cold stimulation to exert an analgesic effect can be explained by the cold compression that suppresses inflammation by using a cold compress when there is pain due to a sprain. On the other hand, although cold stimulus is subordinate to the formation of temperature sensations, the cold stimulus is indispensable to forming TGI and PHS. Patients with congenital insensitivity to pain (CIP) selectively lack the fibers that transmit temperature and pain sensations, resulting in loss or blunting of both sensations. The presence of CIP proves that cold stimuli are essential for the formation of pain sensations.

This model may also explain the synthetic heat discovered by Green. Synthetic heat sometimes occurred when the outer D2 (index) and D4 (ring) fingers were warmed and the central D3 (middle) finger was cooled [9]. There is still a problem with the temperature configuration in synthetic heat. Green reports that synthetic heat occurs only when the outer D2 and D4 are warmed and the central D3 is cooled, but not when the outer D2 and D4 are cooled and the central D3 is warmed. A possible reason is that enough spatiotemporal summation of the stimulus is required. In general, the spatiotemporal summation of warm stimuli is greater than that of cold stimuli [1,13,20,21,26]. Spatiotemporal summation of warm stimulus is required to inhibit the cold stimulus and furthermore makes the noxious component HPC-cool large. When the two outer fingers are warmed, the warmth of the two fingers is summated, making HPC-cool large enough to cause synthetic heat. On the other hand, when only the middle finger is warmed, the summation is not enough.

The surface of the skin is divided into areas called dermatomes. A dermatome is an area innervated by sensory nerves extending from a single spinal nerve root. In this study, we conducted two experiments on D3 (middle) finger. Since the entire D3 finger belongs to the same dermatome [12], it seems that the hot and cold signals in this study are integrated within the same dermatome. In other words, the gate control model proposed in this study is considered to be effective at least within the same dermatome. More study is required to investigate if our gate control model can also be effective among multiple dermatomes.

5.3   Relationship with Gate Control Theory of Pain

We find our model is similar to the gate control theory of pain mechanism [23,24]. In the theory of pain, the fiber terminal (SG) receives an excitatory effect from activity in large-diameter fibers and an inhibitory effect from activity in small-diameter fibers (Fig. 6). In our theory, there is a similar innocuous fiber terminal that receives an excitatory effect from activity in large-diameter $A\delta$ fibers and an inhibitory effect from activity in small-diameter C fibers (Fig. 5). In addition, both SG in Fig. 6 and cool cells in Fig. 5 are in the dorsal horn [5,6,23] and project toward higher-order neurons. This similarity suggests a more generalized mechanism "modulates sensory input from the skin before it evokes pain perception and response" in the human body. However, there are some differences between the two theories. First, our theory emphasizes the generation of nociception by innocuous temperature stimulus, while the theory of pain emphasizes pain relief by the tactile stimulus. Second, in our theory, the opening of the gate only determines the quality of the resulting sensation. Even if the gate is closed, the innocuous temperature input could still add each other to evoke a more intense sensation, although there is little nociception in the resulting sensation. Nevertheless, in pain theory, the closed gate blocks completely the projection toward T cells. Third, in pain theory, emotional activities, such as anxiety or excitement play the role of the "central control" part. However, in our theory, HPC responds to physical stimuli (heat, pinch, and cold). More study is required to investigate the emotional effect of HPC cells.

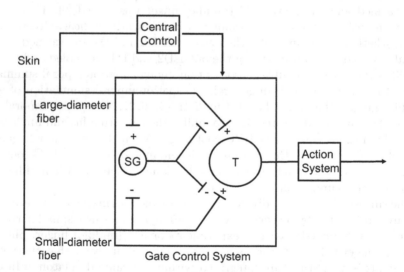

Fig. 6. Schematic diagram of the gate control theory of pain. The central control trigger is represented by a line running from the large-fiber input to the central control system. SG and T stand for substantia gelatinosa and transmission cells, respectively.

6   Conclusion

In this study, we summarized the transition of the spatiotemporal conditions among extrapolation of thermal sensation, paradoxical heat sensation, and thermal grill illusion and hypothesized that a common central mechanism exists. We tested whether the addition and the unmasking theory work for ETS. Percentage hot judgment was found to increase as the temperature difference of stimuli increases, suggesting that hot sensation at extrapolation site can be the result of an addition of non-noxious warm and cold signals. On the other hand, the cold threshold was found to decrease as the distance between warm and cold stimulus increases, suggesting that the unmasking process occurs at the cold site. Our findings suggested that unmasking and addition process involve in the temperature-tuning phenomenon at the site with and without physical stimulation. The co-work of two processes forms a gate control model of temperature.

References

1. Berg, S.L.: Magnitude estimates of spatial summation for conducted cool stimuli along with thermal fractionation and a case of secondary hyperalgesia. The Florida State University (1978)
2. Bouhassira, D., Kern, D., Rouaud, J., Pelle-Lancien, E., Morain, F.: Investigation of the paradoxical painful sensation ('illusion of pain') produced by a thermal grill. Pain **114**(1–2), 160–167 (2005)
3. Cataldo, A., Ferrè, E.R., Di Pellegrino, G., Haggard, P.: Thermal referral: evidence for a thermoceptive uniformity illusion without touch. Sci. Rep. **6**, 35286 (2016)
4. Craig, A.: Pain mechanisms: labeled lines versus convergence in central processing. Annu. Rev. Neurosci. **26**(1), 1–30 (2003)
5. Craig, A., Bushnell, M.: The thermal grill illusion: unmasking the burn of cold pain. Science **265**(5169), 252–255 (1994)
6. Craig, A., Krout, K., Andrew, D.: Quantitative response characteristics of thermoreceptive and nociceptive lamina i spinothalamic neurons in the cat. J. Neurophysiol. **86**(3), 1459–1480 (2001)
7. Craig, A., Reiman, E.M., Evans, A., Bushnell, M.C.: Functional imaging of an illusion of pain. Nature **384**(6606), 258–260 (1996)
8. Ferrè, E.R., Iannetti, G., van Dijk, J., Haggard, P.: Ineffectiveness of tactile gating shows cortical basis of nociceptive signaling in the thermal grill illusion. Sci. Rep. **8**(1), 1–7 (2018)
9. Green, B.G.: Localization of thermal sensation: an illusion and synthetic heat. Percept. Psychophys. **22**(4), 331–337 (1977)
10. Green, B.G.: Synthetic heat at mild temperatures. Somatosensory Motor Res. **19**(2), 130–138 (2002)
11. Green, B.G.: Temperature perception and nociception. J. Neurobiol. **61**(1), 13–29 (2004)
12. Greenberg, S.A.: The history of dermatome mapping. Arch. Neurol. **60**(1), 126–131 (2003)
13. Greenspan, J.D., Kenshalo, D.R.: The primate as a model for the human temperature-sensing system: 2. area of skin receiving thermal stimulation (spatial summation). Somatosensory Res. **2**(4), 315–324 (1985)

14. Greenspan, J.D., Taylor, D.J., McGillis, S.L.: Body site variation of cool perception thresholds, with observations on paradoxical heat. Somatosensory Motor Res. **10**(4), 467–474 (1993)
15. Hansen, C., Hopf, H., Treede, R.: Paradoxical heat sensation in patients with multiple sclerosis: evidence for a supraspinal integration of temperature sensation. Brain **119**(5), 1729–1736 (1996)
16. Harper, D.E., Hollins, M.: Coolness both underlies and protects against the painfulness of the thermal grill illusion. PAIN® **155**(4), 801–807 (2014)
17. Harper, D.E.: Psychophysical examination of the thermal grill illusion. Ph.D. thesis, The University of North Carolina at Chapel Hill (2014)
18. Ho, H.N., Watanabe, J., Ando, H., Kashino, M.: Mechanisms underlying referral of thermal sensations to sites of tactile stimulation. J. Neurosci. **31**(1), 208–213 (2011)
19. Hua, J., Furukawa, M., Maeda, T.: Extrapolation of thermal sensation and a neuron-like model based on distribution difference and interactions of thermoreceptors. In: 2021 IEEE World Haptics Conference (WHC), pp. 43–48. IEEE (2021)
20. Jones, L.A., Ho, H.N.: Warm or cool, large or small? The challenge of thermal displays. IEEE Trans. Haptics **1**(1), 53–70 (2008)
21. Kenshalo, D.R., Gallegos, E.: Multiple temperature-sensitive spots innervated by single nerve fibers. Science **158**(3804), 1064–1065 (1967)
22. Khasabov, S.G., Cain, D.M., Thong, D., Mantyh, P.W., Simone, D.A.: Enhanced responses of spinal dorsal horn neurons to heat and cold stimuli following mild freeze injury to the skin. J. Neurophysiol. **86**(2), 986–996 (2001)
23. Melzack, R., Wall, P.D.: Pain mechanisms: a new theory. Psychosoc. Process. Health Reader 112–131 (1994)
24. Moayedi, M., Davis, K.D.: Theories of pain: from specificity to gate control. J. Neurophysiol. **109**(1), 5–12 (2013)
25. Prescott, S.A., Ma, Q., De Koninck, Y.: Normal and abnormal coding of somatosensory stimuli causing pain. Nat. Neurosci. **17**(2), 183–191 (2014)
26. Stevens, J.C., Okulicz, W.C., Marks, L.E.: Temporal summation at the warmth threshold. Perception Psychophys. **14**(2), 307–312 (1973)
27. Susser, E., Sprecher, E., Yarnitsky, D.: Paradoxical heat sensation in healthy subjects: peripherally conducted by aδ or c fibres? Brain **122**(2), 239–246 (1999)
28. Yosipovitch, G., et al.: Paradoxical heat sensation in uremic polyneuropathy. Muscle Nerve Off. J. Am. Assoc. Electrodiagn. Med. **18**(7), 768–771 (1995)

Graphical Tactile Display Application: Design of Digital Braille Textbook and Initial Findings

Yang Jiao[1], Qixin Wang[2], and Yingqing Xu[1,2(✉)]

[1] The Future Laboratory, Tsinghua University, Beijing, China
{jiaoyang7,yqxu}@tsinghua.edu.cn
[2] Academy of Arts and Design, Tsinghua University, Beijing, China
wqx22@tsinghua.edu.cn

Abstract. According to WHO statistics in 2020, there were approximately 253 million visually impaired people worldwide, including 36 million blind individuals. Blind students learn the same knowledge as ordinary students do in their schools, but they lack a lot of graphical and image information as a learning aid. With the development of electronic graphical tactile display, in this paper, a digital version of Braille textbook is proposed and designed. It not only displays the paper-based Braille texts, but also includes related tactile images and illustrations, therefore the blind students can read texts and images in pair. A serial of initial design guidelines and principles for digital Braille textbook are discussed, followed by the five typical design examples. Twelve blind students in a primary school experienced five lessons of digital Braille textbook, and most of them showed positive responses. Our findings pave the way for future work on improving the user experience of tactile interface design that support the learning by digital Braille textbook.

Keywords: visually impaired people · graphical tactile display · digital Braille textbook · design guidelines

1 Introduction

According to the *World Report on Vision* released by the World Health Organization (WHO) in 2020, there were 253 million people with moderate to severe visual impairment in the world, including 36 million people who are totally blind [1]. In China, the *Disability Profile Report* released by China Disabled People's Federation in 2012 announced that the number of visually impaired people was 17.63 million [2]. Meanwhile, according to the *2019 Yearbook of the Ministry of Education of China*, only about 40,000 children with visual disabilities are covered by the national education system [3, 4] and able to enter schools and other institutions for the blind in the whole country. In blind schools, blind students learn the same knowledge as ordinary children do in their schools, including Chinese, mathematics, physics, chemistry, etc. It is known from a comparative study between Braille textbooks and ordinary ones, that texts are basically the same, but most illustrations disappear in Braille textbooks (Fig. 1). Moreover, for

D. Wang et al. (Eds.): AsiaHaptics 2022, LNCS 14063, pp. 121–134, 2023.
https://doi.org/10.1007/978-3-031-46839-1_10

some graphical knowledge involved in science, it would be reduced or even deleted directly, such as some geometric parts in mathematics and circuit parts in physics. Blind students lack a lot of graphical and image information as a learning aid. They need, but it is hard, to understand what sighted people are learning, which brings them serious challenges to the comprehensive knowledge learning.

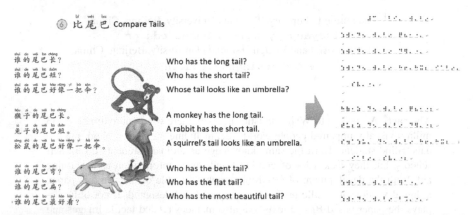

Fig. 1. Comparison of lesson *"Compare Tails"* in ordinary textbook and Braille textbook. Both textbooks are from China People's Education Press and are widely used for the first-grade primary school students.

Besides, apart from Braille reading, blind people can also make use of voice assistant or screen reader software for acquiring text knowledge. However, they extremely lack tools and equipment for learning and understanding graphical information. Typically, in blind schools or Braille libraries, images and pictures are usually handmade with shapeable paper, such as embossing, thermoplastic and braille dot printing, but these methods are expensive and time-consuming. This is one of the main reasons why lots of images and pictures disappear from the Braille textbooks.

In response to this problem, a digital refreshable tactile screen, where the pixels are replaced by tactile pins or dots, can greatly benefit information accessibility for blind people. Recently some graphical tactile display devices have been designed and developed, such as the devices made by Metec.AG, the American Printing House for the Blind and Orbit Research [5]. We also designed and developed a graphical tactile display prototype for the blind [6]. The tactile surface of our device consists of a matrix of 120 by 60 dots that can be raised and retracted dynamically. By controlling these dots through a built-in computing system, traditional pictures can be turned into tactile images. Blind users can read Braille texts and understand images by touching these raised dots (Fig. 2).

Therefore, with the recent development in electronic graphical tactile display devices, now is the time to consider adapting more learning contents, both texts and images to blind people, especially the Braille textbooks for the young blind students in primary and middle schools. We aim to digitize Braille textbooks, and put images and illustrations which are in the ordinary textbooks for sighted people back to blind people's learning contents. In this way, the blind students can read the Braille texts and tactile images

Fig. 2. The graphical tactile display prototype. It can display Braille text and tactile images.

in pair. "A picture is worth a thousand words", so we believe it can hugely improve information accessibility for these young blind students.

In our research, in order to digitize the Braille textbook and contain the images and illustrations, we made a serial of design principles and methods of Braille textbooks digitalization for a better user experience of Braille textbook learning, followed by several typical design examples of digital braille textbook in Chinese and Mathematics. Then twelve blind students in a primary school were invited to experience our braille textbook demonstrations. Our initial results with twelve participants have been very promising. In the rest of this paper, we present the background for our design research followed by design examples and user evaluations. We conclude the paper for guidelines for effective learning of digital Braille textbook with texts and images in pairs by the electronic tactile display device.

2   Related Work

There is a long history of research on the development of tactile displays as well as Braille and tactile images design as assistive technologies for visually impaired people (e.g., see reviews [5, 15]) that continues to the present day.

Braille is widely used to convey text information for blind people. There are two columns of three dots arranged longitudinally in a Braille cell, with a total of six dots. The distance between each dot is 2.5 mm, and the neighboring Braille cells are 3.5–4 mm apart in order to discriminate each cell. This different spacing standard between dots and cells is valid both in paper-based Braille books and Braille electric displays. However, most of the Braille displays can only show one line of Braille (typically 20 or 40 cells), so the blind can only read a single line of text at a time, which leads to low reading efficiency.

In terms of tactile images, it is urgently needed yet challenging in recognizing and understanding spatial information for blind people. Although the channel capacity of haptics is significantly smaller than that of sight (compared with the sighted people) [13], lots of progresses have been made to assist blind people learn graphical and two-dimensional spatial information [7, 16] summarized several factors affecting tactile images recognition in terms of tactile images design: image geometrical characteristics, image symmetry, image size and perspective. Meanwhile a serial of multi-level coding and quantification scheme criterion [7] was made to evaluate tactile images recognition performance.

In related to tactile interface design with combination of Braille texts and tactile images, one common idea is to keep the conventional interaction paradigm: Window-Icon-Menu-Pointer (WIMP) in graphical user interface (GUI). In this way, a transformation schema from GUI to tactile websites with scalable vector images was developed [8], opening a new way for browsing of web pages for blind people. Further studies begin to focus on the user experience and usability of tactile interface [9] defined four regions segmenting the tactile space to header, body, structure and detail region, while [10, 11] proposed six rectangular regions, allowing the user to perceive the given content at different modes of presentation and levels of detail.

These previous works laid the basis for designing better digital Braille textbook with texts and images in pairs in this paper. Based on the literature, we explored the tactile interface design of digital Braille textbook with the perspective of user experience.

3   Tactile Interface Design of Digital Braille Textbook

In order to achieve good user experience of digital Braille textbook learning, we spitted the design into three parts: typesetting design of Braille texts and tactile images, tactile images design and contextual knowledge learning design. Figure 3 shows the three parts that describe the tactile interface design.

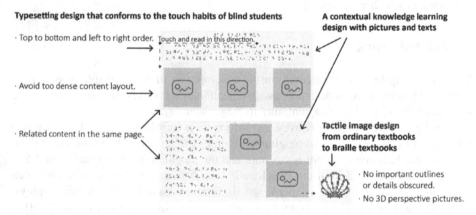

Fig. 3. The three parts that describe the tactile interface design of digital Braille textbook

3.1   Typesetting Design that Conforms to the Touch Habits of Blind Students

At present, the layout of Braille textbook used in blind school is basically the same as that of ordinary textbook. The order of content is both top to bottom and left to right. Such a convention should be considered for showing Braille on the tactile display for the blind.

In the tactile interface with Braille texts and images, several principles should be followed. Firstly, both texts and images should not be arranged too densely due to the much smaller channel capacity of haptics than vision, and the feature of tactile perception would be slow and discontinuous. The interaction design for the blind should be consistent with the concept, metaphors and paradigms of blind users. To make touch-reading easy, improve the accuracy of information expression and avoid causing difficulties or misunderstandings, the principles of Gestalt psychology [14] could be considered to simplify the tactile images in design.

Secondly, relevant content that needs to be read at the same time could be presented on the same page. The discontinuity of tactile perception affects blind people's touch-reading. Relevant content presented should not be separated, so that the reading and thinking will not be interrupted. For example, as the text *Comparing Tails* shows in the fourth example, the images of animals and related paragraphs are arranged on the same page in the Braille version design, so that we can ensure the consistency of the content and facilitates the association and understanding.

Finally, as same as sighted people, the cognitive process of blind people will also be affected by emotions. A touch-friendly layout can help blind people obtain correct information easily and reasonably, enhancing learning confidence and improving learning effect.

3.2 Tactile Image Design from Ordinary Textbooks to Braille Textbooks

To design a tactile image, several principles and methods should be considered to make images recognizable and easy to understand [7] have verified that the effect of tactile recognition can be affected by tactile images' features, including "lines omitted due to occlusion", "Perspective and Viewpoint", "Image Symmetry", "Image Geometrical Characteristic", as well as "Image Size". However, the last three features are about the characteristics of the tactile images themselves, which is difficult to improve the image recognition performance by Braille textbook design.

The other two features, "lines omitted due to occlusion" and "Perspective and Viewpoint", focus on the expression of tactile images, and can make images easy to understand. First, blind people are hard to distinguish the "foreground" and "background", so lines' occlusion affects recognition negatively. Second, their living and cognitive habits of blind people make them unable to understand the perspective relationship of objects well, perspective images would be very difficult to be recognized either.

Based on these two features, we summarized some suggestions on tactile image design:

- Do not obscure the important outlines or details. Keep a complete outline, display important details fully, and avoid confusing the foreground and background. For example, as the text *Understanding 1–5* in the second example shows, images with many animals obscuring each other have been adjusted to a non-overlapping arrangement to avoid misunderstanding.
- Do not use 3D perspective pictures. Parallel perspectives or sections at different angles are suitable ways to present three-dimensional objects. Both two lessons *Zhaozhou Bridge* and *Up and Down, Front and Back*, use single faces of objects to represent them, so that the tactile images would be easy to recognize and understand.

3.3 A Contextual Knowledge Learning Design with Pictures and Texts

Researches of cognitive psychology show that the content of text and images can complement each other, and help learners to integrate visual and language representations psychologically, thereby promoting good understanding of learners or the generation of meaningful learning. In other words, the combination of pictures and texts gives teaching advantages. For blind students, we believe textbooks with pictures and texts are easier to read, study and understand than text-only textbooks.

Whether putting the image before the text or after can both benefit learning, yet when combining images and texts in textbooks, it is also necessary to consider the specific connection of the context and arrange the order reasonably. Based on the viewpoint of simplicity to complexity from the elaboration theory of instruction [12], the order should be designed while combining with contextual content associations and factors such as the amount of image and text information, complexity and so on. Images put before text can help blind students to understand texts; while putting texts before can guide blind students to pay attention to the key information in the images.

In a word, tactile images should be fully contextualized, and simple images and textual information should be presented firstly, which can be helpful for Braille learners to understand their textbooks. As some examples in the fourth section show, *"The Story of 'Shell'"*, displays a paragraph of easy-to-understand text before an abstract picture about this Chinese character form evolution, so that the image could be much more understandable. *"Zhaozhou Bridge"* also has such a design purpose. Firstly, it shows a vivid picture of the bridge, with texts explaining more complex structural principles and functions after the image, blind students can therefore learn step by step.

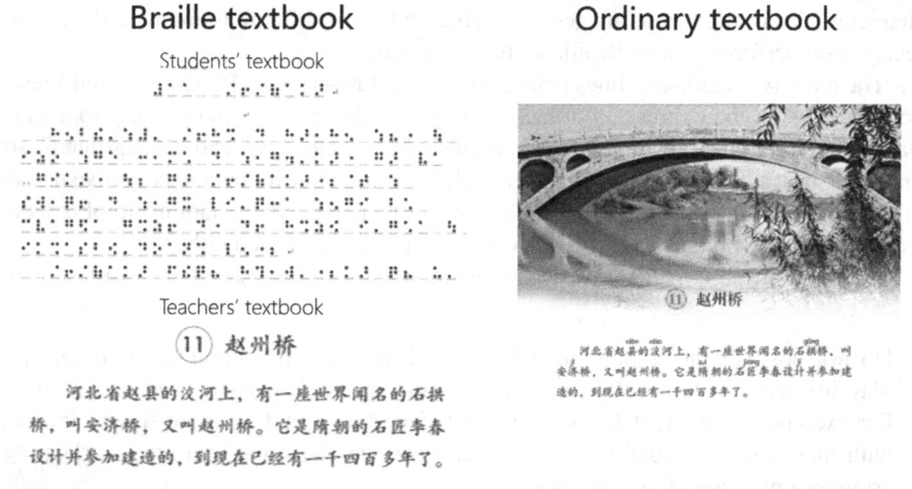
Braille textbook
Students' textbook
Teachers' textbook
11 赵州桥
河北省赵县的洨河上，有一座世界闻名的石拱桥，叫安济桥，又叫赵州桥。它是隋朝的石匠李春设计并参加建造的，到现在已经有一千四百多年了。
Ordinary textbook
⑪ 赵州桥

Fig. 4. Comparison of Texts *"Zhaozhou Bridge"* in Braille textbook and ordinary textbook

4 Typical Design Examples of Digital Braille Textbook

4.1 Lesson *"Zhaozhou Bridge"* in Chinese Textbook

As Fig. 4 shows, this lesson introduces the shape and design principles of Zhaozhou Bridge. In the ordinary textbook, a real photo of the bridge in three-dimensional space is displayed above the text, and the shape, location and water reflection of the bridge are presented. With the introduction in the text, sighted students can easily know the ingenious design of the Zhaozhou Bridge.

The question is, in the Braille textbook, only text description retains. Thinking about how complex the construction of the Zhaozhou Bridge is, blind students are not easy to imagine what the bridge looks like.

Our design adds a two-dimensional image to the screen (Fig. 5), allowing students to feel the shape of it. By reproducing the flat image of the bridge, this lesson is designed as follows:

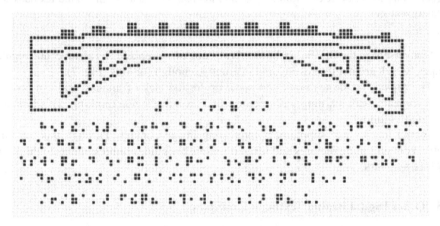

Fig. 5. Lesson *"Zhaozhou Bridge"* in digital Braille Textbook

With a tactile image about the structure of Zhaozhou Bridge that follows the principle of symmetry and no occlusion, the shape of the bridge can become clearer to blind students, and would make the abstract concepts described in the text easier to understand.

4.2 Lesson *"Know 1–5, Addition and Subtraction"* in Mathematics Textbook

As shown in the Fig. 6 is the text content of numbers 1–5 in math textbooks. In the ordinary textbook, a picture of the life scene is used for guiding students to recognize and distinguish numbers. Students learn the application of numbers by observing pictures, which also cultivates multi-angle thinking.

Fig. 6. Comparison of Texts *"Know 1–5, Addition and Subtraction"* in Braille textbook and ordinary textbook.

Conversely, in the Braille textbook, vivid pictures are replaced by abstract and regular shapes, which are not interesting and instructive enough for kids (Fig. 7).

The digital Braille textbook can make up for the lack of images, and can provide blind students math learning with pictures and texts that guide thinking. This lesson is designed as follow:

Tactile images can supplement interesting image content. Through this teaching method of combining pictures and texts, it reasonably guides blind students to think and explore numbers.

4.3 Other Digital Braille Textbook Examples

While studying different subjects, tactile images can guide blind students to associate text information and expand their imagination, helping them understand abstract concepts and recognize the world.

For example, the lesson *"The Story of 'Shell'"* adds tactile images to express the evolution of words. Blind students can learn about morphological changes by touching. In the same way, the addition of tactile images of animals in *"Compare Tails"* is also a kind of associative learning with images and texts.

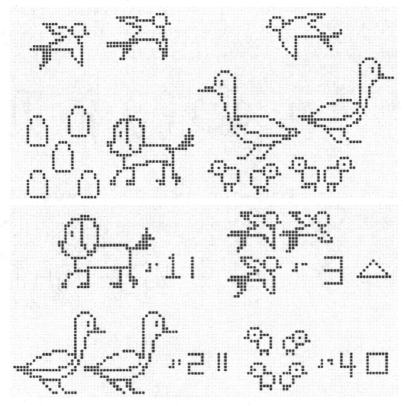

Fig. 7. Tactile images in Texts *"Know 1–5, Addition and Subtraction"*

For mathematics learning, tactile images can also help blind students recognize spatial locations and understand life scenes, and learn mathematics more interestingly (Fig. 8).

5 Evaluation and Discussion

A study with twelve blind students in a blind primary school was conducted, testing the usability of the digital Braille textbook in comparison with current paper-based textbook. Table 1 shows the demographic data of the participants.

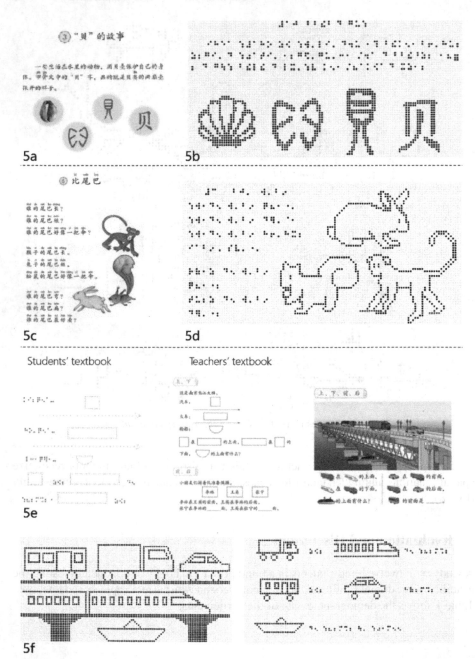

Fig. 8. a Lesson *"The Story of 'Shell'"* in ordinary textbook. **b** Digital Braille version of *"The Story of 'Shell'"*. **c** Lesson *"Compare Tails"* in ordinary textbook. **d** Digital Braille version of *"Compare Tails"*. **e** Comparison of lessons *"Up, Down, Front and Back"* in Braille textbook and ordinary textbook. **f** Digital Braille version of *"Up, Down, Front and Back"*.

Table 1. Demographic data of the participants

Participant	age / sex	Level of visual impairment	Grade in primary school
1	9	early blind	1
2	9	late blind	1
3	8	early blind	1
4	10	low vision	2
5	9	low vision	2
6	9	late blind	2
7	10	late blind	2
8	8	early blind	2
9	9	late blind	2
10	10	low vision	3
11	11	late blind	3
12	10	early blind	3

5.1 Method

Five lessons in the digital Braille textbook including three Chinese lessons ("*Zhaozhou Bridge*" "*The Story of 'Shell*'" and "*Compare Tails*"), and two Mathematical lessons ("*Know 1–5, Addition and Subtraction*" and "*Up, Down, Front and Back*") shown in Sect. 4 were displayed individually by our graphical tactile display prototype. Meanwhile, the current paper-based Braille textbook with the same five lessons was also prepared.

In the experiment, each participant spent around five minutes touching and reading one lesson of digital Braille Textbook or paper-based Braille textbook, and another five minutes doing the same task in another version of textbook in random sequence. Then the same procedure was followed for all five lessons. After all lessons were learned, the participant was required to answer several subjective questions with the score of 7 Likert-scale (see Table 2).

5.2 Results

Table 2 shows the score results of subjective questions by twelve participants.

From Table 2, Q1 is about the transfer barrier between paper textbook and digital one, and all the participants gave non-negative scores. Q2–4 asked about the usability of digital textbook, and 11 participants (not including P3) showed positive feedback. Q5–6 care about the future use, and all the participants were optimistic about the future promotion in terms of textbook learning.

Table 2. Score results of subjective questions by twelve participants. The scores represent: 1 = strongly disagree, 2 = disagree, 3 = slightly disagree, 4 = neutral, 5 = slightly agree, 6 = agree, 7 = strongly agree

Questions\Participants	1	2	3	4	5	6	7	8	9	10	11	12
Q1: There are no barriers to transfer from paper textbook to digital textbook	6	7	4	5	7	6	6	6	6	7	6	7
Q2: The digital Braille textbook is easier to read and understand than paper textbook	6	7	4	6	7	6	6	5	6	7	6	7
Q3: The digital Braille textbook conveys more knowledge than paper textbook	7	7	7	7	7	7	7	7	7	7	7	7
Q4: the tactile images in the digital Braille textbook are easy to understand	6	7	3	5	7	6	6	5	6	7	6	7
Q5: I would like to use digital Braille textbook for other Chinese and Mathematics lessons	7	7	5	6	7	7	6	6	7	7	7	7
Q6: I would like to recommend this learning tool to my friends	7	7	6	6	7	7	7	7	7	7	7	7

5.3 Discussion

Although most of the participants expressed their interests and positive feedback, there is one participant (P3) facing challenges for tactile image learning. "*I barely touched tactile images and it is always difficult for me to understand them*" said by P3, "*I can read Braille, but sometimes I cannot fully understand, nor imagine what it is. I know it is tough for blind people, so I get along with it*". That means tactile images are still a challenge for some blind people, but this is why they may need to be further educated to build up more space related abilities.

The other eleven participants are fond of digital version of textbook with Braille texts and tactile images in pairs. They feel that the tactile images include much more information as a nice addition of Braille texts. Moreover, P2, P5, P10–12 mentioned that Braille texts were abstract, while tactile images were concrete, and it was a perfect pair for knowledge learning. They would all like to have more classes with this digital textbook.

Last but not least, this experiment only includes five typical lessons which are related to graphical information. For other lessons, the inclusion of tactile image as illustration may need careful thinking. We suggest that the Braille text in a lesson should be fully kept and transferred to electric display as the main part, while leaving the choice of tactile images as a flexible feature. We believe with the help of the electric tactile display device and the digital Braille textbook, it would benefit blind students to study and live.

6   Concluding Remarks

The present study offers evidence to support the claim that a digital version of Braille textbook with Braille text and images in pair would be beneficial for the blinds' knowledge learning. With the development of electric refreshable tactile display, more spatial knowledge as tactile images and illustrations could be displayed and acquired by blind people.

In view of this, a serial of tactile interface design guidelines and principles for digital Braille textbook are discussed, including typesetting design, tactile image design and contextual knowledge learning design. With these guidelines, some typical design examples are proposed and explained, followed by a twelve participants' experiment. With the experience of five typical lessons, most of the blind students gave very positive responses. It is proved that there are nearly no barriers to transfer from paper textbook to digital one, and the content with Braille texts and tactile images is easier to read and understand. Our initial results with twelve participants have been very promising.

In the future, we will continue to improve the user experience of digital Braille textbook and haptic interactions. With the help of more amount of electric tactile displays, we hope that blind people can easily read both text and image, expand their knowledge and lead a better life.

References

1. World report on vision. Geneva: World Health Organization (2019). Licence: CC BY-NC-SA 3.0 IGO
2. China Disabled Persons' Federation: The total number of persons with disabilities and the number of persons with different types of disabilities at the end of 2010 [OL] (2022). https://www.cdpf.org.cn/zwgk/zccx/cjrgk/15e9ac67d7124f3fb4a23b7e2ac739aa.htm
3. Ministry of Education of the People's Republic of China: Basic information on special education schools [OL] (2020). http://www.moe.gov.cn/s78/A03/moe_560/jytjsj_2018/qg/201908/t20190812_394165.html
4. Ministry of Education of the People's Republic of China: Basic information on special education [OL] (2020). http://www.moe.gov.cn/s78/A03/moe_560/jytjsj_2018/qg/201908/t20190812_394169.html
5. Vidal-Verdu, F., Hafez, M.: Graphical tactile displays for visually-impaired people. IEEE Trans. Neural Syst. Rehabil. Eng. 15(1), 119–130 (2007). https://doi.org/10.1109/TNSRE.2007.891375
6. Jiao, Y., Gong, J., Xu, Y.: Graille: design research of graphical tactile display for the visually impaired. Zhuangshi 01(273), 094–096 (2016)
7. Gong, J., et al.: I can't name it, but I can perceive it" conceptual and operational design of "tactile accuracy" assisting tactile image cognition. In: The 22nd International ACM SIGACCESS Conference on Computers and Accessibility (ASSETS 2020). Association for Computing Machinery, New York, NY, USA, Article 18, pp. 1–12 (2020). https://doi.org/10.1145/3373625.3417015
8. Rotard, M., Knodler, S., Ertl, T.: A tactile web browser for the visually disabled. In: 2005 Proceedings of the Sixteenth ACM Conference on Hypertext and Hypermedia, pp 15–22 (2005)
9. Schiewe, M., Köhlmann, W., Nadig, O., Weber, G.: What you feel is what you get: mapping GUIs on planar tactile displays. In: Stephanidis, C. (ed.) Universal Access in Human-Computer Interaction. Intelligent and Ubiquitous Interaction Environments: 5th International Conference, UAHCI 2009, Held as Part of HCI International 2009, San Diego, CA, USA, July 19-24, 2009. Proceedings, Part II, pp. 564–573. Springer Berlin Heidelberg, Berlin, Heidelberg (2009). https://doi.org/10.1007/978-3-642-02710-9_63

10. Prescher, D., Weber, G., Spindler, M.: A tactile windowing system for blind users. In: ASSETS 2010 Proceedings of the 12th International ACM SIGACCESS Conference on Computers and Accessibility, pp.91–98 (2010)
11. Prescher, D., Bornschein, J., Köhlmann, W., et al.: Touching graphical applications: bimanual tactile interaction on the HyperBraille pin-matrix display. Univ. Access Inf. Soc. **17**, 391–409 (2018). https://doi.org/10.1007/s10209-017-0538-8
12. Reigeluth, C., Merrill, M., Wilson, B., Spiller, R.: The elaboration theory of instruction: a model for sequencing and synthesizing instruction. Instr. Sci. **9**, 195–219 (1980). https://doi.org/10.1007/BF00177327
13. Kokjer, K.J.: The Information capacity of the human fingertip. IEEE Trans. Syst. Man Cybern. **17**(1), 100–102 (1987)
14. Goldstein, E.B.: Sensation and Perception, 9th edn., pp. 5–11. Wadsworth, Belmont (2014)
15. Russomanno, A., O' Modhrain, S., et al.: Refreshing refreshable braille displays. IEEE Trans. Haptics **8**(3), 287–297 (2015)
16. Braille Authority of North America: Guidelines and Standards for Tactile Graphics. Braille Authority of North America, Baltimore (2010)
17. Cooper, A., Reimann, R., Cronin, D.: About Face 3: The Essentials of Interaction Design. Wiley, Indianapolis (2007)
18. Da-jung, K., Youn-kyung, L.: Handscope: enabling blind people to experience statistical graphics on websites through haptics. In: Proceedings of the ACM SIGCHI International Conference on Tactile & Haptics, pp.2039–2042 (2011)

DeltaFinger: A 3-DoF Wearable Haptic Display Enabling High-Fidelity Force Vector Presentation at a User Finger

Artem Lykov(✉) [iD], Aleksey Fedoseev [iD], and Dzmitry Tsetserukou [iD]

Skolkovo Institute of Science and Technology, Bol'shoy Bul'var, 30. 1, Moscow, Moscow Oblast 121205, Russia
{artem.lykov,aleksey.fedoseev,d.tsetserukou}@skoltech.ru

Abstract. This paper presents a novel haptic device, named DeltaFinger, designed to deliver the force of interaction with virtual objects by guiding the user's finger by a wearable delta mechanism.

DeltaFinger delivers a 3D force vector to the fingertip of the index finger of the user, allowing complex rendering of various virtual reality (VR) environments. The developed device is able to render linear forces up to 1.8 N in vertical projection and 0.9 N in horizontal projection without restricting the motion freedom of the remaining fingers.

The experimental results showed a sufficient precision in perception of force vector with DeltaFinger (mean angular error in the perceived force vector of 0.6 rad). The proposed device potentially can be applied to VR communications, medicine, and navigation for people with vision problems.

Keywords: Wearable Haptics · Haptic Interfaces · Inverted Delta Robot · Virtual Reality · Force Perception

1 Introduction

During the last decade, extensive research has been done in the field of wearable haptic interfaces for virtual reality (VR). Such interfaces allow their users a substantial benefit of the high mobility in VR environments and various modalities of interaction with virtual objects, thus, expanding the scope of applications with haptic feedback. For example, applications with wearable devices are beneficial in VR simulators for medical training, virtual CAD assembly, or remote control of robots through VR interfaces. The recent reviews of Pacchierotti et al. [18], Cao et al. [3], and See et al. [19] suggest that the majority of the developed devices are focused on providing kinesthetic feedback to the fingertips of users due to the large number of skin sensors located at this area.

The reported study was funded by RFBR and CNRS, project number 21-58-15006.

D. Wang et al. (Eds.): AsiaHaptics 2022, LNCS 14063, pp. 135–146, 2023.
https://doi.org/10.1007/978-3-031-46839-1_11

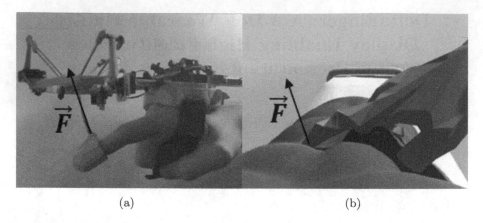

(a)   (b)

Fig. 1. (a) Kinesthetic feedback delivered by haptic display. (b) Force vector rendering in VR environment.

However, methods to generate kinesthetic haptic stimuli on human fingertips remain to be further investigated. While a high number of papers proposed solutions for realistic and intuitive perceptual clues of the force amplitude and distribution, there is a lack of means to provide the directional cues, supporting user exploration of the VR environment.

In this paper, we propose a novel wearable haptic device with kinesthetic haptic feedback delivered by a delta mechanism to render a force vector to be intuitive and recognizable by the user (Fig. 1). The developed interface delivers a linear force to the index finger of the user with a high range of force vector angles, allowing complex rendering of the VR environment.

2   Related Works

Humans fingers are most often used for probing, grasping, sliding and otherwise manipulating both with real and virtual surfaces. Therefore, there is a number of methods designed for rendering particular haptic experiences during manipulation with virtual objects through wearable interfaces.

Several works explored force vector rendering through the indentation of the moving tactors into the skin. For example, Gabardi et al. [8] proposed the Haptic Thimble display with two rotations and one translation degrees of freedom (DoF) to render local orientation of the virtual surface. The similar approach was implemented by Benko et al. [2] with the NormalTouch handheld controller rendering up to 45 deg surface tilt by a 3-DoF Stewart Platform. Another approach was introduced by Tsetserukou et al. [23] with the LinkTouch interface where kinesthetic feedback is delivered by an inverted five-bar mechanism. This concept was later extended by Ivanov et al. [12] in the LinkRing device able to render force at two contact points of the human fingertip independently. The mentioned above displays allow to render with high resolution the point of applied force.

However, the location of the actuators and the small area of the human finger-tip provide additional challenges for a human perception of the force direction. Moriyama et al. [16] proposed to combine the force vector direction feedback from an inverted five-bar mechanism located on the forearm of the user with vibrotactile feedback of force amplitude delivered to the fingers. This approach improves surface orientation perception by providing feedback to the larger area of the human forearm. However, its naturalness should be further investigated.

Normal and shearing force vector rendering with a belt placed in contact with the user's fingertip skin was proposed by Minamizawa et al. [15]. Pacchierotti et al. [17] suggested the hRing device aiming at realistic interaction without disturbance of hand tracking by locating belt on the proximal finger phalanx. The combination of shear force vector rendering with rotational platform and normal force vector rendering through electro-tactile display was introduced by Yem et al. [24] in FingAR interface. However, the mentioned above approaches are able to render only two horizontal directions of the haptic force aligned with the rotation direction of the actuators.

Exoskeletons mainly considered as heavy and cumbersome wearable haptic systems, with low naturalness and effectiveness of perceptual clues. However, a number of works are seeking a way to reduce the negative impact of exoskeleton designs. For example, Solazzi et al. [21] introduced finger exoskeleton for contact and orientation rendering. Agarwal et al. [1] proposed an exoskeleton delivering feedback at the index finger phalanx for post-stroke rehabilitation. Hernandez-Santos et al. [10] later suggested a finger exoskeleton able to provide haptic feedback to several phalanges, though only in 1-DoF. Li et al. [14] explored the restraints of index finger motion for an optimized rehabilitation exoskele-ton. Iqbal et al. [11] proposed a lightweight four-finger exoskeleton adjusting to variable hand sizes and other distinguishing features. More recently, Dragusanu et al. [4] developed a lightweight modular exoskeleton that apply bidirectional forces. This design, however, is limited in force orientation rendering. Fang et al. [6] proposed a novel Wireality design with force vector rendering through strings pulling user's fingers. The actuators are located on the user's shoulder, which allows the device to apply higher forces at a cost of limiting force vector angles. Sim et al. [20] developed a low-latency exoskeleton glove allowing the adduction and abduction motions of each finger.

3   System Overview

The system architecture of the developed haptic interface is shown in Fig. 2.

The DeltaFinger hardware consists of the haptic interface based on delta mechanism driven by three TGY-TS531A analog nano servo motors, Arduino Uno R3 WiFi microcontroller, and Oculus Quest 2 VR headset. The system software consists of the VR framework developed on Unity Engine, that estimates force amplitude and direction, and middleware, that calculates motor angles based on the high level commands from Unity. The motor angles are calculated by inverse kinematic algorithm discussed in Sect. 3.1.

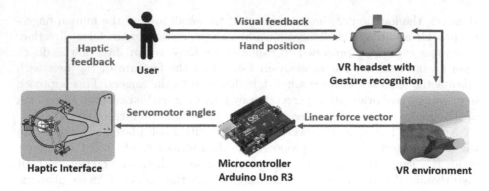

Fig. 2. System architecture. When user interacts with an object in the VR environment, the virtual framework calculates the position of their index finger with Oculus headset and renders the linear force vector at a point of a contact through the DeltaFinger wearable interface located above the user's index finger.

The operator is able to interact with virtual surfaces using the Oculus Quest 2 hand tracking interface. The virtual framework is developed to render the amplitude and direction of the linear force at the point of contact between users' hands and the surface of virtual object based on the approach proposed by Fedoseev et al. [7]. Thus, when the user interacts with objects in VR, a linear force vector is calculated at the point of their index finger collision with the object's surface. This vector is then delivered to the operator's hand via the DeltaFinger haptic interface.

3.1 DeltaFinger Kinematics

The DeltaFinger interface design is based on a delta mechanism proposed by Trinitatova et al. [22] for delivering haptic feedback to human palm. The advantages of the parallel structure are in high load capacity with respect to the total weight of the device, low inertia, relatively high rigidity, and high speed. These advantages are caused by the multiple kinematic chains linking the end-effector and the frame of the device. A three-revolute (3-RRR) parallel structure is developed with three RRR serial chains that join in a fixed base. Each RRR chain is a serial chain composed by three rotational joints. The solution of the inverse kinematic problem for 3-RRR parallel structure was developed based on the paper of Ouafae et al. [9].

The simulation in MATLAB Simulink was conducted to design the device with a working space that includes all points reachable by the motion of a human index finger, thus not restricting the mobility of the user's hand. The reachability of the three RRR chains and the resulting workspace of the DeltaFinger along with the motion space of the index finger is shown in Fig. 3.

The circuit consists of three consecutive RRR kinematic chains that connect it to a fixed base with a radius of 80 mm. Each RRR chain is a sequential

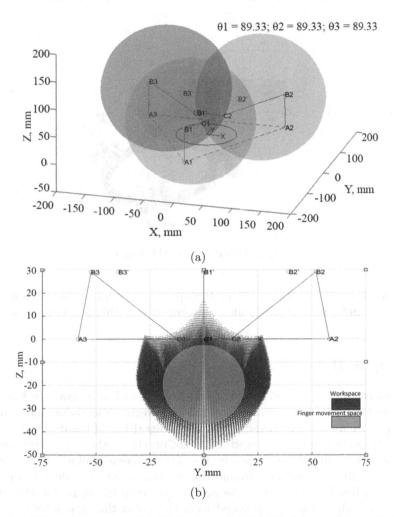

Fig. 3. DeltaFinger kinematics: (a) RRR chain plot. (b) Workspace of the end-effector.

structure with three rotational joints connected by the links with the sizes of 35 mm, 60 mm, and 10 mm starting from the base. The simulation results suggested that the DeltaFinger end-effector workspace is sufficient to cover an area with the radius of 25 mm, thus, allowing free motion of the user's finger in the YZ coordinate plane.

The CAD model of the proposed device was designed in SolidWorks 2020 (Fig. 4).

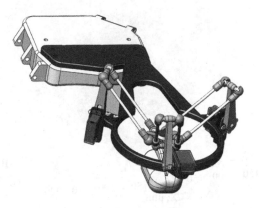

Fig. 4. DeltaFinger CAD design.

In addition, the base is fixed to the operator's hand by two flexible belts, and the output link is fixed to an index finger by a thimble with elastic inner surface.

4   Haptic Rendering

The performance of the force vector rendering algorithm is shown in Fig. 5.

To ensure the smooth transition of the force vector orientation and, thus, the stable performance of the inverse kinematics algorithm of the device, the direction of the surface normal was estimated not on the single point of collision but with the supporting plane defined by the three reference points at the "contact patch", i.e., 50 × 50 mm area around the collision point. To calculate the plane orientation, firstly, we calculate the normal vector to the surface at the contact point. Then, three rays are released from the point that was selected on this normal vector at 10 cm above the finger. The rays are faced towards the virtual surface at a 15 deg angle to the normal vector. The reference points are then obtained as the points of collision between the rays and the virtual surface. These points define the reference plane in 3D Cartesian space. Finally, the interaction force vector is defined as a normal vector to the reference plane. The amplitude of the force is proportional to the distance between the finger and the reference plane. The force is then transmitted to the Arduino microcontroller board and delivered to a user's finger by the developed haptic interface.

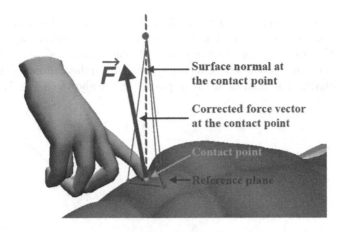

Fig. 5. Force vector rendering in virtual environment.

5   Experimental Evaluation

5.1   Force Vector Rendering Experiment

The experiment was carried out to estimate whether the maximal forces at the end-effector were adequate to render a virtual surface. For this, an experimental setup was assembled to evaluate the applied force by the Robotiq 6-DoF force/torque sensor [13]. The experimental setup is shown in Fig. 6.

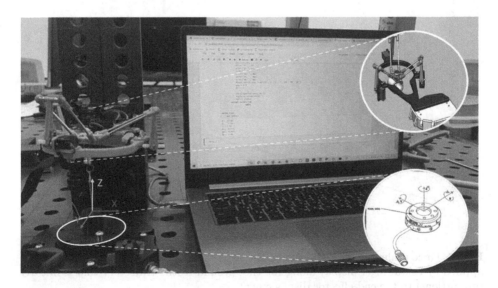

Fig. 6. Experimental setup for evaluation of the FigngerGuider applied forces with Robotiq 6-DoF force sensor.

To evaluate the performance of DeltaFinger, the end-effector was programmed to pass a set of circular trajectories with an increasing radius and distance to the force sensor. The experiment was conducted until the motors were not able to change the end-effector's position further, indicating the highest force feedback. The results of the experiment are shown in Fig. 7.

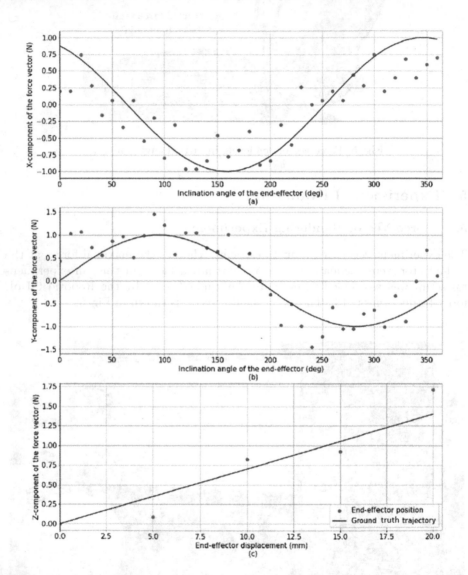

Fig. 7. Force evaluation experiment.(a) X-, (b) Y-, and (c) Z-components of the force applied by DeltaFinger display alongside the "ground truth" trajectory that is linearly proportional to the end-effector displacement.

With the end-effector rotating by the circle trajectory, the Y and X components of the force vector are defined as the outputs of a sine and a cosine wave functions. The graph shows that the interface performed the trajectory correctly with a maximal amplitude of 0.8 N in transverse plane. In the second experiment, the interface's ability to apply a force along Z axis was tested. The experiment showed that the interface correctly applied forces up to 1.8 N.

Experimental Results: The experimental results suggested that the interface renders the interaction force correctly. The direction and amplitude of the linear force were obtained with the following error (f is the ratio of the mean squares treatment to the mean squares error; p is the probability of error that corresponds to the f-statistic):

- The magnitudes of lateral forces (f_x and f_y) are kept relatively at the same level with the average standard deviation $\delta = 0.04$ (for normalized force values) and the mean magnitude of 1 N (for original force values).
- The deviation of lateral forces did not depend on the diameter of the rotation ($f = 0.11, p = 0.73$ for f_x, and $f = 0.43, p = 0.57$ for f_y).
- The normal force has a higher standard deviation δ of 0.16 and mean amplitude of 1.8 N.

5.2   Experiment on Direction Recognition of Linear Force Vector

We conducted a user study to evaluate the user's perception of a force vector.

Participants: We invited 10 volunteers (8 males, 2 females) aged from 21 to 25, right-handed, for the DeltaFinger evaluation. Three participants were familiar with haptic interfaces. Seven participants had never interacted with haptic displays before.

Procedure: All the participants were familiarized with the DeltaFinger force rendering approach prior to the experiment. A blinded experiment was then carried out based on the methodology proposed by Endo et al. [5]. The actuator was fixed in at 24 positions on a circle spaced $\pi/12$ rad apart, pulling user's index finger in each direction. The performed angles were first demonstrated and then shuffled to be presented in random order to each volunteer. The participant pointed out the perceived direction on the monitor with the patterns displayed on the 360 deg protractor. The main condition of the experiment was that the participant selects the answer based only on haptic feedback.

Experimental Results: The results of the experiment are shown in Fig. 8.

According to the one-way analysis of variance (ANOVA) with a 5% significance level, there is a statistically significant difference in user perception of different angles ($F = 10.22, p = 0.001 < 0.05$). The mean force vector error in

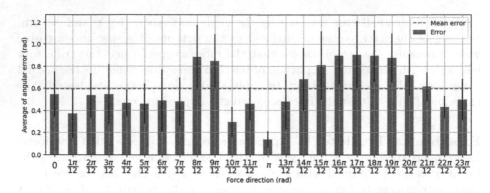

Fig. 8. Force vector direction recognition error by subjects.

user perception is of 0.6 rad. The results obtained suggest that the user perceives the force transmitted by the haptic interface with a high degree of accuracy. The error in degrees is comparable to the error in force vector perception evaluated in prior haptic research. The difference in error is dependent on the angle due to the peculiarities of tactile perception of the force vector with the index finger. This proves that with the haptic interface, the participants in the experiment were able to obtain high quality information about the direction of the transmitted force.

5.3   Conclusion

In this paper, the haptic interface for high-fidelity rendering of force vectors was presented. The distinctive feature of the DeltaFinger interface is the ability to deliver a force interaction experience in VR in nearly omnidirectional space by guiding the fingertip with the delta mechanism. The experimental results suggest that the display accurately renders force vectors with up to 1.8 N amplitude. The results of the user study revealed that users were able to perceive force vectors with a sufficient accuracy (mean error of 0.6 rad).

In future work, we plan to evaluate the ability of the DeltaFinger to render a force vector during contact with virtual surfaces that obtain non-linear stiffness properties. The minimal and maximal transferable stiffness is now also limited by the positional accuracy of the parallel mechanism and servo motor load. Therefore, we are planning to improve the design of the device to allow it to apply a higher range of force amplitudes while preserving the accuracy of the interface.

The DeltaFinger interface can be potentially applied in virtual scenarios for medical palpation simulators, precise teleoperation, and entertainment, e.g., VR musical applications. Additionally, the device may be potentially applied outside the VR scope for rehabilitation and guidance of people with vision problems.

Acknowledgements. The reported study was funded by RFBR and CNRS, project number 21-58-15006. The authors would like to thank Prof. Sergey Vorotnikov (BMSTU) and PhD Student Daria Trinitatova (Skoltech) for their support of the project.

References

1. Agarwal, P., Fox, J., Yun, Y., O'Malley, M.K., Deshpande, A.D.: An index finger exoskeleton with series elastic actuation for rehabilitation: design, control and performance characterization. Int. J. Robot. Res. **34**(14), 1747–1772 (2015). https://doi.org/10.1177/0278364915598388

2. Benko, H., Holz, C., Sinclair, M., Ofek, E.: NormalTouch and textureTouch: high-fidelity 3d haptic shape rendering on handheld virtual reality controllers. In: Proceedings of the 29th Annual Symposium on User Interface Software and Technology, pp. 717–728. UIST 2016, Association for Computing Machinery, New York, NY, USA (2016). https://doi.org/10.1145/2984511.2984526

3. Cao, S., Li, X., Yan, X., Jiang, D., Guo, Q.: Overview of wearable haptic force feedback devices and a further discussion on the actuation systems. In: 2018 IEEE 4th Information Technology and Mechatronics Engineering Conference (ITOEC), pp. 314–319 (2018). https://doi.org/10.1109/ITOEC.2018.8740410

4. Dragusanu, M., Troisi, D., Villani, A., Prattichizzo, D., Malvezzi, M.: Design and prototyping of an underactuated hand exoskeleton with fingers coupled by a gear-based differential. Front. Robot. AI **9**, 862340 (2022). https://doi.org/10.3389/frobt.2022.862340. www.frontiersin.org/article/10.3389/frobt.2022.862340

5. Endo, T., Kanno, T., Kobayashi, M., Kawasaki, H.: Human perception test of discontinuous force and a trial of skill transfer using a five-fingered haptic interface. J. Robot. **2010**, 1–14 (2010)

6. Fang, C., Zhang, Y., Dworman, M., Harrison, C.: Wireality: enabling complex tangible geometries in virtual reality with worn multi-string haptics, pp. 1–10. Association for Computing Machinery, New York, NY, USA (2020). https://doi.org/10.1145/3313831.3376470

7. Fedoseev, A., Chernyadev, N., Tsetserukou, D.: Development of mirrorShape: high fidelity large-scale shape rendering framework for virtual reality. In: 25th ACM Symposium on Virtual Reality Software and Technology. VRST 2019, Association for Computing Machinery, New York, NY, USA (2019). https://doi.org/10.1145/3359996.3365049

8. Gabardi, M., Solazzi, M., Leonardis, D., Frisoli, A.: A new wearable fingertip haptic interface for the rendering of virtual shapes and surface features. In: 2016 IEEE Haptics Symposium (HAPTICS), pp. 140–146 (2016). https://doi.org/10.1109/HAPTICS.2016.7463168

9. Hamdoun, O., El Bakkali, L., Fatima Zahra, B.: Analysis and optimum kinematic design of a parallel robot. Procedia Eng. **181**, 214–220 (2017). https://doi.org/10.1016/j.proeng.2017.02.374

10. Hernández-Santos, C., Davizón, Y.A., Said, A.R., Soto, R., Félix-Herrán, L., Vargas-Martínez, A.: Development of a wearable finger exoskeleton for rehabilitation. Appl. Sci. **11**(9), 4145 (2021). https://doi.org/10.3390/app11094145. https://www.mdpi.com/2076-3417/11/9/4145

11. Iqbal, J., Tsagarakis, N., Caldwell, D.: Four-fingered lightweight exoskeleton robotic device accommodating different hand sizes. Electron. Lett. **51**(12), 888–890 (2015). https://doi.org/10.1049/el.2015.0850

12. Ivanov, A., Trinitatova, D., Tsetserukou, D.: LinkRing: a wearable haptic display for delivering multi-contact and multi-modal stimuli at the finger pads. In: Nisky, I., Hartcher-O'Brien, J., Wiertlewski, M., Smeets, J. (eds.) EuroHaptics 2020. LNCS, vol. 12272, pp. 434–441. Springer, Cham (2020). https://doi.org/10.1007/978-3-030-58147-3_48
13. Kheddar, A., Gourishankar, V., Evrard, P.: A PHANTOM® device with 6DOF force feedback and sensing capabilities, vol. 5024, pp. 146–150 (2008). https://doi.org/10.1007/978-3-540-69057-3_16
14. Li, G., Cheng, L., Sun, N.: Design, manipulability analysis and optimization of an index finger exoskeleton for stroke rehabilitation. Mech. Mach. Theory **167**, 104526 (2022). https://doi.org/10.1016/j.mechmachtheory.2021.104526
15. Minamizawa, K., Fukamachi, S., Kajimoto, H., Kawakami, N., Tachi, S.: Gravity grabber: wearable haptic display to present virtual mass sensation. In: ACM SIGGRAPH 2007 Emerging Technologies, p. 8-es. SIGGRAPH 2007, Association for Computing Machinery, New York, NY, USA (2007). https://doi.org/10.1145/1278280.1278289
16. Moriyama, T., Kajimoto, H.: Wearable haptic device that presents the haptics sensation of the finger pad to the forearm and fingertip. In: Kajimoto, H., Lee, D., Kim, S.-Y., Konyo, M., Kyung, K.-U. (eds.) AsiaHaptics 2018. LNEE, vol. 535, pp. 158–161. Springer, Singapore (2019). https://doi.org/10.1007/978-981-13-3194-7_35
17. Pacchierotti, C., Salvietti, G., Hussain, I., Meli, L., Prattichizzo, D.: The hRing: a wearable haptic device to avoid occlusions in hand tracking. In: 2016 IEEE Haptics Symposium (HAPTICS), pp. 134–139 (2016). https://doi.org/10.1109/HAPTICS.2016.7463167
18. Pacchierotti, C., Sinclair, S., Solazzi, M., Frisoli, A., Hayward, V., Prattichizzo, D.: Wearable haptic systems for the fingertip and the hand: taxonomy, review, and perspectives. IEEE Trans. Haptics **10**(4), 580–600 (2017). https://doi.org/10.1109/TOH.2017.2689006
19. See, A.R., Choco, J.A.G., Chandramohan, K.: Touch, texture and haptic feedback: a review on how we feel the world around us. Appl. Sci. **12**(9), 4686 (2022). https://doi.org/10.3390/app12094686. https://www.mdpi.com/2076-3417/12/9/4686
20. Sim, D., Baek, Y., Cho, M., Park, S., Sagar, A.S.M.S., Kim, H.S.: Low-latency haptic open glove for immersive virtual reality interaction. Sensors **21**(11), 3682 (2021). https://doi.org/10.3390/s21113682. https://www.mdpi.com/1424-8220/21/11/3682
21. Solazzi, M., Frisoli, A., Bergamasco, M.: Design of a novel finger haptic interface for contact and orientation display. In: 2010 IEEE Haptics Symposium, pp. 129–132 (2010). https://doi.org/10.1109/HAPTIC.2010.5444667
22. Trinitatova, D., Tsetserukou, D.: DeltaTouch: a 3D haptic display for delivering multimodal tactile stimuli at the palm. In: 2019 IEEE World Haptics Conference (WHC), pp. 73–78 (2019). https://doi.org/10.1109/WHC.2019.8816136
23. Tsetserukou, D., Hosokawa, S., Terashima, K.: LinkTouch: a wearable haptic device with five-bar linkage mechanism for presentation of two-DOF force feedback at the fingerpad. In: 2014 IEEE Haptics Symposium (HAPTICS), pp. 307–312 (2014). https://doi.org/10.1109/HAPTICS.2014.6775473
24. Yem, V., Okazaki, R., Kajimoto, H.: FinGAR: combination of electrical and mechanical stimulation for high-fidelity tactile presentation. In: ACM SIGGRAPH 2016 Emerging Technologies. SIGGRAPH 2016, Association for Computing Machinery, New York, NY, USA (2016). https://doi.org/10.1145/2929464.2929474

Improvement of Discrimination of Haptic Motion Experience by Reproducing Multi-point Spatial Distribution of Propagated Vibrations at the Wrist

Kosuke Yamaguchi, Masamune Waga, Masashi Konyo$^{(\boxtimes)}$ (ID), and Satoshi Tadokoro (ID)

Tohoku University, Sendai 980-8579, Japan
konyo@rm.is.tohoku.ac.jp

Abstract. In recent years, there has been a growing demand for technology to deliver haptic experiences related to skills remotely. This study attempts to reproduce the spatial pattern of vibrations generated at the wrist using a bracelet-type device equipped with multiple sensors and vibrators to convey haptic experiences of tool motions. First, we measured the frequency response characteristics of the propagation of vibrations applied to the fingertips to the wrist and confirmed that high frequencies above 1000 Hz could propagate to the wrist position. Then, we measured the tool and the wrist vibration at multiple points during multiple haptic movements. The relationship between the ability to discriminate between different haptic-related movements and spatial distribution reproduction is investigated by comparing the case of spatial reproduction at the wrist with a conventional tool-mounted device. The effect of the ISM method, which can modulate the waveform to a lower frequency while maintaining the original sensation, is also investigated. Results of discrimination experiments indicate that reproduction of the spatial distribution by vibration stimulation of multiple points on the wrist improves discrimination of different rotational directions and that ISM further improves discrimination of rotational directions compared to the raw signal.

Keywords: Spatial reproduction of vibration · Propagated vibrations · Bracelet-type device

1 Introduction

The Pandemic of COVID-19 in the early 2020 s has led to a growing demand for assistive technologies for remote communication. One technological challenge is realizing haptic sensory transmission concerning skills that cannot be delivered by audio or vision. Such haptic communication is expected to be useful for teaching skills of physical sensation, such as changes in contact force synchronized with

This paper is based on results obtained from a project, JPNP21004, commissioned by the New Energy and Industrial Technology Development Organization (NEDO).

motion. This paper focuses on an approach to measuring and transmitting vibrations propagated from the hand to the wrist as a potential transmission method for conveying haptic experiences of various tasks. Measuring at the wrist has the advantage of not blocking the fingertips or hand.

High-frequency vibrations of several hundred Hz or higher have been reported to be effective in reproducing the tactile sensations to discriminate material [8, 15] or tapping hardness [5] and friction [7] during collisions with an object. Some studies also tried to enhance audiovisual experiences in motion with vibrotactile stimuli [3,4,9,10]. The authors have proposed a vibrotactile signal conversion method called the Intensity Segment Modulation (ISM) [19] that converts high-frequency vibrations, including in the auditory range, into sensory equivalent signals of about 200 Hz. This technology makes it possible to reproduce the sensation of high-frequency vibration above several hundred Hz, which has not received much attention until now, even with small transducers. This study aims to use this technology to reproduce high-frequency vibrations generated at the wrist position.

Another necessary aspect of remote haptic transmission is the measurement-based reproduction of vibrations. It is known that a simple method of amplifying vibrations acquired by a microphone to drive a transducer can provide a good haptic experience, such as the feeling of a ball rolling in a cup or a racket shot [13]. A method of transmitting tactile sensations by presenting vibrations measured by acceleration sensors attached to tools has also been proposed [12] and applied to a surgical robot [6]. A similar approach has been reported for attaching a vibration sensor to a construction robot to transmit collisions of the robot arm [14]. This research also aims to perform such measurement-based haptic transmission with the human hand.

In this study, we focus on reproducing the spatial spread of vibrations propagated to the hand and wrist. It has been verified that by attaching numerous acceleration sensors to the skin, vibrations at the fingertips are transmitted throughout the hand [18]. Neurophysiological simulations have shown that the Pacinian corpuscle far from the contact point can perceive propagated vibrations [16]. However, it is not yet clear how the spatial distribution of vibrations propagating from these contact points is involved in identifying haptic experiences.

The objective of this study is to investigate whether measuring vibrations propagating from the fingertip to the wrist at multiple points and reproducing their spatial distribution contributes to the discrimination of haptic motion experience. First, we investigate the propagation of vibrations to the wrist position, including more than 1 kHz, which has not been reported before. Spatial differences in propagation at different measurement points are also confirmed. Next, we measure the vibration of the wrist while performing a task with a tool that generates high-frequency vibration in different directions of motion, and compare the effect of reproducing the spatial distribution of the vibrations. Here, we also verify the effectiveness of the ISM, a high-frequency vibration conversion technology proposed by the authors.

2   Measurement of Vibration Transmitted from the Fingertip to Wrist

The present study focuses on high-frequency vibration, including more than 1 kHz. This section investigates the frequency response characteristics of propagated vibrations at the wrist from the fingertip, which has not been reported before. Spatial propagation differences at different measurement points at the wrist are also confirmed.

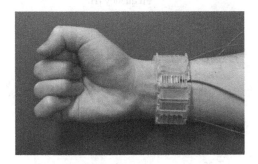

Fig. 1. The bracelet-type device that measures vibration with four piezoelectric sensors.

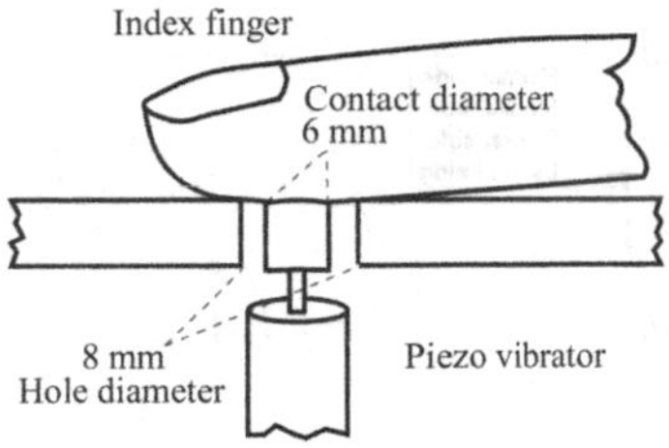

Fig. 2. Contact condition of vibrations applied.

2.1   Method

For sensing vibration on the skin, a piezoelectric sensor (TOKIN, VS-BV203) was used. This sensor is suitable for measuring minute high-frequency vibrations due to its high signal-to-noise ratio and high responsiveness with an almost flat frequency response from above 20 Hz to 10 kHz. Figure 1 shows a bracelet-type sensing device that measures four sides; palmar, medial, dorsal, and lateral sides of the wrist. The length of the belt was adjusted to ensure that the four vibration sensors stick to the skin.

Vibrations were applied by a vibrator to the finger pad of the five fingers of the right hand individually. A stack-type piezoelectric actuator (Matsusada Precision, PZ12-112) was used as the vibrator. Its push and pull forces were 800 N and 50 N, respectively, which were enough to deform the skin. The subject's finger contacted the actuator through an 8-mm diameter hole in the plate; the diameter of the contact part is 6 mm, as shown in Fig. 2. The subject was trained to maintain the pressing force on the vibrator at 1.0 N in advance. Applied frequencies were 100, 150, 200, 250, 300, 400, 600, 1000, and 1600[Hz]. The amplitudes of the applied vibration were 17.8 μm for 100–600 [Hz], 15.9 μm for 1000 Hz, and 9.44 μm for 1600 Hz, which were ensured by the measurement with a laser displacement sensor in advance. Note that the applied vibrations tried to be set to the same amount, but the amplitude decreased at higher frequencies, so they were selected to the extent available .

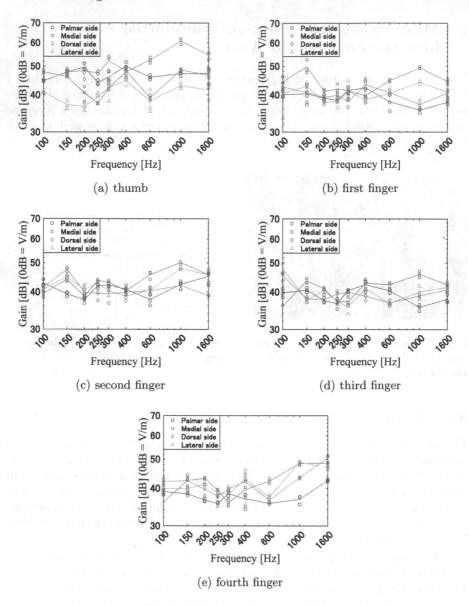

Fig. 3. Gain diagrams of vibration transmitted to each finger.

Vibrations are measured at a sampling rate of 50 kHz. Electrical noise was removed by a low-pass filter cut off at 2.5 kHz. The peak-to-peak amplitude of the wrist vibration is calculated to determine the vibration amplitude. To ensure synchronization with the applied frequencies, histograms of the intervals of the measured vibrations at each frequency were checked, and amplitudes with intervals outside the standard deviation were excluded. The gain was calculated with the input as the amplitude [m] of the actuator and the output as the output voltage of the sensor [V]. The average value was representative of the gain.

2.2   Results and Discussion

The gain diagrams on each contacted finger are shown in Fig. 3. For any finger contact, the gain characteristics of the vibration measured at the wrist position showed that it propagated at more than 600 Hz without decreasing with the site. In general, it was expected that the higher the frequency, the lower the gain, but in this measurement, vibrations were transmitted without attenuation even at the wrist position.

In addition, differences can be seen in the measurement site of the vibration. Although it is impossible to show a general trend, the area of increased gain appears to vary depending on the finger contacted.

The limitation of this result is that there is only one subject. We have already confirmed the gain characteristics for the thumb contact cases of two other subjects, and we have confirmed that the high-frequency vibrations propagate to the wrist position without attenuation in the other two subjects as well. We need to conduct further experiments in the future, including individual differences and characteristics of the measuring site.

3   Spatial Vibration Representation During Haptic Motions

In this section, we measure and present the vibration at the wrist position for several haptic motions with different contact directions when the tool is grasped and attempt to reproduce the spatial distribution of the vibrations. Measurement is also performed when a sensor is directly attached to the tool. The effect of presenting the vibration at the wrist position and the vibration conversion method ISM proposed by the authors are also verified.

3.1   Overview of Intensity Segment Modulation: ISM

As confirmed in the previous section, high-frequency vibrations above 1 kHz could propagate well at the wrist position. However, if the measured vibration is presented directly, there is an issue with the frequency response of the vibration transducer. Generally, the frequency response of vibrators is not uniform, and the amplitude of vibrations in the high-frequency range is insufficient. Another problem is that presenting high-frequency vibration generates audible noise. This paper attempts to use ISM, a method proposed by the authors to convert high-frequency vibrations, to solve the above problems.

The ISM (Intensity Segment Modulation) is a technology that converts vibrations into AM-modulated waves with arbitrary carrier frequencies while maintaining the original tactile sensation [19]. The ISM considers two human perceptual characteristics of high-frequency vibrations, the perception of the intensity of high-frequency vibrations and the perception of envelope information. It performs the conversion based on the following two policies:

1. Keep the perceived intensity equal to the original at any time.
2. Maintain the intensity fluctuation less than 100 Hz, but no more than that.

The perceived intensity can be determined by a psychophysical model [1] to characterize the intensive information of vibratory stimuli represented by the total intensity I_{total} that is a summation of the intensity $I(f)$ at frequency f as follows:

$$I_{total} = \sum I(f) = \sum \left[\left(\frac{A(f)}{A_T(f)} \right)^2 \right]^{\alpha(f)}, \tag{1}$$

where $A(f)$ is the amplitude of the vibration at f, $A_T(f)$ is the threshold amplitude at f, and $\alpha(f)$ is the exponent for weighing the frequency dependence of the Pacinian system.

To maintain the number of fluctuations, the ISM divides the original signal into time segments of a fixed period (10 ms or less) and calculates the intensity of each segment. This is based on the envelope perception characteristics that humans can easily distinguish the envelope of the AM vibration if the envelope frequency is less than 50 Hz; this becomes difficult if the frequency exceeds 80 – 125 [Hz] [2]. Then, ISM outputs the amplitude-modulated vibration at the frequency of a single carrier wave (Typically 200 Hz) with the same intensity for each segment.

The ISM performs conversion for high-frequency vibrations above 100 Hz and outputs the waveform as it is at frequencies below that. Therefore, ISM eliminates the influence of the frequency response of the transducer because the carrier frequency is fixed at 200 Hz for vibrations above 100 Hz.

3.2 Vibration Measurements of Haptic Motions

We measured several haptic motions with different contact directions when the tool was grasped. In this study, the haptic motion to be measured is the motion of stirring in a bowl with a whisk in various directions. Specifically, the following four types of motions were targeted as shown in Fig. 4:

A) Clockwise horizontal circular stirring action.
B) Counterclockwise horizontal circular stirring action.
C) Vertical circular stirring motion (arcing in the air to hit the ball).

A) CW rotation   B) CCW rotation   C) Vertical   D) Linear horizontal

Fig. 4. Four types of haptic motion for discrimination.

D) Horizontal linear reciprocating stirring motion.

Wrist vibration is measured using the sensing device described in the previous section as shown in Fig. 1. Vibrations were measured at a sampling rate of 50 kHz using a data logger. The low-frequency vibrations derived from human arm movements are then removed through a 10 Hz high-pass filter, and resampled to 48 kHz, the standard used in audio signals.

Figure 5 shows a tool-mounted device used for comparison with a wrist vibration measurement. A fixture fabricated by a 3D printer is used to hold the vibration sensor and a vibrator at the handle of the whisk. The same piezoelectric vibration sensor used in the wrist vibration measurement is attached to the underside of the handle in the figure. The vibrator is also attached to the upper surface of the handle for the vibration presentation described in the next section. The vibrator is an LRA-type transducer (Alps Alpine, Haptic Reactor). It can operate over a relatively wide frequency range by designing resonance frequencies at two locations, 160 Hz and 320 Hz.

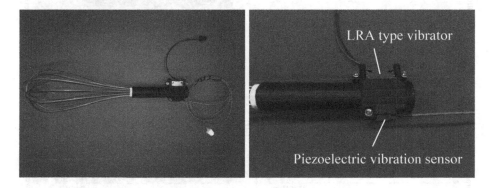

Fig. 5. Tool attachment device.

Examples of the measured vibrations and FFT results on each condition are shown in Fig. 6. Each left figure shows the vibration measured at the tool, and palmar, medial, dorsal, and lateral sides of the wrist, from top to bottom. The amplitude of the vibration tended to increase at the timing when the whisk and bowl collided. In addition, the existence of spatial distribution information at the wrist, such as different amplitude magnitudes depending on the sensor position at the wrist, was confirmed. Each right figure shows the FFT analysis for each of the same waveforms. The power spectra indicate that high-frequency vibrations in the band far above 500 Hz are also generated during collisions in all conditions. In the tool vibration, resonance-like vibration components appear in the high-frequency band after the collision, but these components seem to be attenuated in the measurement at the wrist position. However, it can still be seen that high-frequency vibration power appears sufficiently at the wrist position.

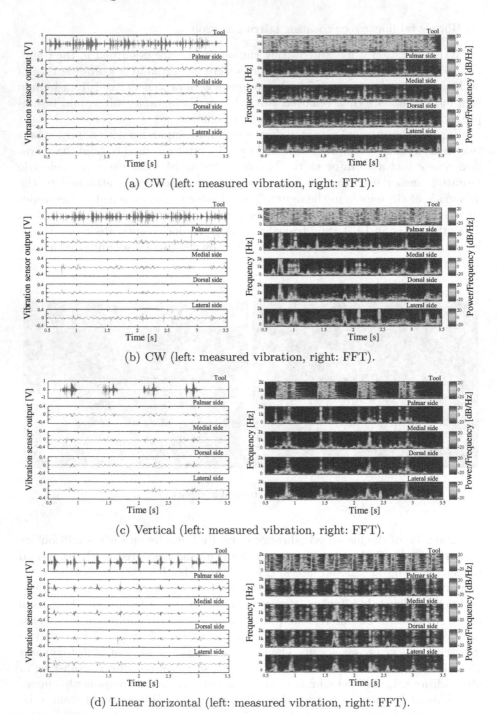

(a) CW (left: measured vibration, right: FFT).

(b) CW (left: measured vibration, right: FFT).

(c) Vertical (left: measured vibration, right: FFT).

(d) Linear horizontal (left: measured vibration, right: FFT).

Fig. 6. Measured vibrations and FFT results on each condition.

3.3 Discrimination Experiment of Haptic Motion

Multi-point Vibrotactile Display. A multi-point vibration display for wrist stimulation is shown in Fig. 7. Four vibrators are fixed with a belt. The position of the vibrators can be adjusted by sliding them on the belt. The vibrator was fabricated using an audio exciter (Tectonic Elements, TEAX13C02-8), a voice coil type transducer. As shown in the figure, the center of the exciter contacts the skin, and the outside of it is surrounded by a 3D printed part to prevent excessive pushing.

The vibration stimulus outputs waveforms via a multi-channel USB audio interface and drives four exciters with amplifiers.

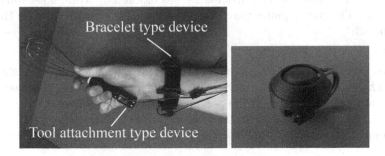

Fig. 7. Bracelet-type devices attached to the wrist. The tool mount-type device is also held in hand. The right image shows the skin contact side of the vibrator fabricated with an exciter.

Experimental Conditions. Haptic motion discrimination experiments are performed for each of the four combinations of vibration measurement and presentation devices as shown in Table 1 for two signals: the raw measurement waveform and the converted waveform by the ISM. In the multi-point wrist stimulation condition (ii) and (iv) and the tool–tool condition (i), the vibrators corresponding to the measured positions were driven. In contrast, when the tool measured vibration was stimulated at multiple points at the wrist uniformly (iii), the same single waveform measured at the tool was used to drive the four vibrators by adjusting the magnitude of the perceived vibration. The carrier frequency of the ISM conversion was set to 200 Hz, a band easily perceived by humans.

Procedure. In all conditions, the participants are initially presented with the stimuli until they memorize the four haptic motion types. After sufficient memorization, the participants respond to the test stimuli by keyboard input. Each test stimulus could be presented as many times as needed, and participants were allowed to fully examine the stimulus before responding. Subjects were given

Table 1. Combinations of experimental conditions.

	Measured location	Displayed location
(i)	Tool	Tool
(ii)	Wrist (Multi)	Wrist (Multi)
(iii)	Tool	Wrist (Uniform)
(iv)	Tool + Wrist(Multi)	Tool + Wrist (Multi)

correction feedback on their responses to correct for mislearning of the reference stimulus. Three test stimuli were prepared for each motion, with 12 trials per condition. The hearing of the participants was blocked by white noise during the experiment. The participants were ten males and ten females between the ages of 22 and 43.

Results. A confusion matrix summarizing the experiment results is shown in Fig. 8. The numbers in the graph indicate the percentage of responses, with the diagonal component being the percentage of correct responses. The order of the graphs corresponds to the order of Table 1. The left graphs present the raw measurement waveforms, while the right graphs show the results when ISM is applied.

In Condition (i), experiencing the vibration waveform as it is in the tool resulted in the highest percentage of correct responses; the trend was similar to that of the raw waveform, although the percentage of correct responses was slightly lower in the case of the ISM.

In Condition (ii), this is the case of reproducing the spatial distribution of the wrist, which showed that the discrimination between clockwise and counterclockwise motions of stimuli A and B tended to be better discriminated for the multi-point stimuli than for the other conditions. In particular, the discrimination rate was highest when the ISM was applied.

In Condition (iii), The response rate was almost the same when the vibration was produced at the tool position and when a uniform stimulus was produced at the wrist vibrators. In this case, the discrimination performance for the direction of rotation was the worst.

In Condition (iv), this condition is where all tools and wrists are reproduced, but the performance was not particularly better than in other conditions.

As an overall trend, relatively high discrimination rates were observed for the longitudinal and front-back movements of stimuli C and D in all conditions. In all conditions, no responses fell below the chance level of 25%.

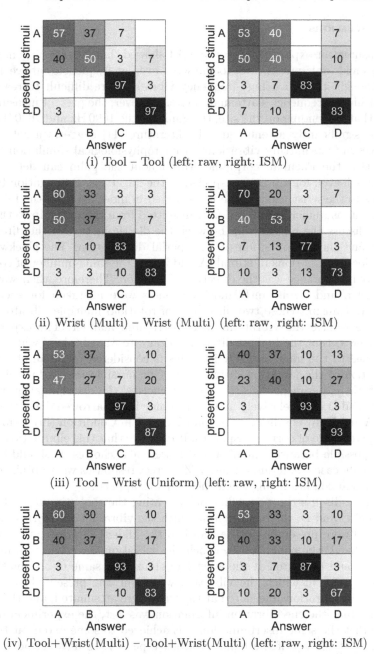

(i) Tool – Tool (left: raw, right: ISM)

(ii) Wrist (Multi) – Wrist (Multi) (left: raw, right: ISM)

(iii) Tool – Wrist (Uniform) (left: raw, right: ISM)

(iv) Tool+Wrist(Multi) – Tool+Wrist(Multi) (left: raw, right: ISM)

Fig. 8. Results of the experiment (measured position – presented position). The numbers represent percentages of subjects' answers.

3.4   Discussions

The measurement experiments on the wrist showed that vibrations generated at fingertips and tools propagated to the wrist even at frequencies above 1000 Hz. It was thought that such high-frequency vibrations are difficult to reach there and that higher frequencies attenuate more. However, the present measurements showed that, depending on the site, the gains for the 1000 Hz and 1600 Hz inputs were not significantly attenuated. The literature [11] suggests a role for surface waves in transmitting vibrations. A neurophysiological simulation [16] also reports that the Pacinian corpuscles throughout the palm can detect propagated stimuli even for vibrations applied to the fingertips. Propagation from the fingertips to the wrist needs to be investigated in more detail in the future.

In the measurement of vibration transmitted from the fingertip to the wrist, first, we discuss the relationship between the discrimination of the direction of rotation and the reproduction of the spatial distribution. The clockwise and counterclockwise motions of stimuli A and B had the same number of collisions, and the only difference was the direction of rotation. Therefore, their waveforms were similar, and significantly more responses were mistaken for each other. In order to transmit these two directions of rotation, multiple vibrators would need to reproduce the vibrations in a distributed manner. The experimental results showed that the highest discrimination rate was obtained when the ISM was applied to the multi-point wrist. This is considered to be an effect of the reproduction of the vibration distribution. One possible reason for this is that although the experiment consisted of four choices, the discrimination rates for stimuli C and D were relatively high, which may have narrowed down the choices to two, A and B, by elimination. Stimuli C and D in Condition (iii) seem to have a lower percentage of correct responses. It could be that this elimination method was not possible because stimuli A and B were also choices. It should be noted that the only case where more than 50% correct responses were obtained for all stimuli was in condition (iii) when the ISM was applied.

Next, we discuss the possibility of presenting the tool stimuli at the wrist. For stimuli C and D, the condition in which the vibration waveforms measured by the tool were presented on the tool had the highest discrimination rate. On the other hand, the condition in which the vibration waveform was measured by the tool and presented at the wrist had almost the same discrimination rate as the condition in which the vibration waveform was presented at the tool. Although the vibrations measured at the wrist were attenuated, and there was a possibility that the cue vibration information was lost, the experimental results indicate that the same discrimination was achieved to some extent at the wrist position as at the tip of the hand. Bracelet-type devices have an advantage in that they can be used universally, whereas tool-mounted devices are dedicated devices and can be installed only in limited locations. The results suggest that a general-purpose bracelet-type device can be used as a vibration presentation device and still maintain a practical level of discrimination rate.

Note that Condition (iv) had the highest number of stimulus points and was expected to give the best results, but the experimental results showed that the discrimination rate was not particularly high. The tool was good at discriminating C and D stimuli, and the multi-point wrist was good at discriminating A and D stimuli, but the combination of the two may have been influenced by the lower discrimination rate of each.

We also discuss the effects of ISM. The measured vibration contained a wide range of frequency components, including high frequencies, but high frequencies are generally considered to be easily attenuated. However, the results were the same or slightly lower than expected under the present conditions. The vibrators employed in this experiment were an acoustic exciter and an LRA with a relatively wide frequency bandwidth and good response in the high-frequency range, so it is considered that the raw measured waveforms were sufficient to present a satisfying sensory experience. Smaller LRAs with narrower frequency bandwidths have lower discrimination performance in presenting raw waveforms. For transducers with limited performance, ISM is expected to be more effective. Note that ISM has the advantage of not generating acoustic noise compared to measured waveforms because it is a method of converting high-frequency components to low-frequency ones.

Finally, we discuss why the reproduction of stimuli at multiple points on the body is necessary. It might not be required to reproduce vibration propagation if the same vibration intensity as the vibration source can be presented to the hand. However, it is difficult to attach a large vibrator to the hand that provides such a strong stimulus. Furthermore, to reproduce a variety of contact points and directions, the number of vibrators would eventually have to be increased. Therefore, the multiple-point stimulation approach is useful for wearable devices with small vibrators. For example, it has been reported that the realism of a tennis shot can be improved by reproducing the waveform propagated by stimulating multiple points on the forearm, including the elbow [17]. This paper suggests that even a four-point stimulus at the wrist can help distinguish between different movements and that the experience from vibration propagation may also involve a high-frequency vibration component above 1 kHz.

4 Conclusion

This study tried to reproduce the spatial pattern of vibrations generated at the wrist using a bracelet-type device equipped with multiple sensors and vibrators to convey haptic experiences of contact motions. First, we measured the frequency response characteristics of the propagation of vibrations applied to the fingertips to the wrist. We confirmed that high frequencies above 1000 Hz could propagate to the wrist position. Then, we measured the tool and the wrist vibration at multiple points during multiple haptic motions of stirring in a bowl with a whisk in various directions. The relationship between the ability to discriminate between different haptic motions and spatial distribution reproduction is investigated by comparing the case of spatial reproduction at the wrist with a conventional tool-mounted device. Results of discrimination experiments indicate that reproducing the spatial distribution by vibration stimulation of multiple points on the wrist improves discrimination of different rotational directions.

The effect of the ISM method, which can modulate the waveform to a lower frequency while maintaining the original sensation, is also investigated. ISM further improved the discrimination of rotational directions compared to the raw signal.

References

1. Bensmaia, S., Hollis, M., Yau, J.: Vibrotactile intensity and frequency information in the Pacinian system: a psychophysical model. Percept. Psychophysics **67**, 828–841 (2005). https://doi.org/10.3758/bf03193536
2. Cao, N., Konyo, M., Nagano, H., Tadokoro, S.: Dependence of the perceptual discrimination of high-frequency vibrations on the envelope and intensity of waveforms. IEEE Access **7**, 20840–20849 (2019). https://doi.org/10.1109/ACCESS.2019.2898029
3. Gongora, D., Konyo, M., Nagano, H., Tadokoro, S.: Haptic exploration during fast video playback: vibrotactile support for event search in robot operation videos. IEEE Trans. Haptics **13**(2), 436–447 (2019). https://doi.org/10.1109/TOH.2019.2957792
4. Gongora, D., Nagano, H., Konyo, M., Tadokoro, S.: Vibrotactile rendering of camera motion for bimanual experience of first-person view videos. In: 2017 IEEE World Haptics Conference (WHC), pp. 454–459. IEEE (2017). https://doi.org/10.1109/WHC.2017.7989944
5. Higashi, K., Okamoto, S., Yamada, Y., Nagano, H., Konyo, M.: Hardness perception based on dynamic stiffness in tapping. Front. Psychol. **9**, 2654 (2019). https://doi.org/10.3389/fpsyg.2018.02654
6. Koehn, J.K., Kuchenbecker, K.J.: Surgeons and non-surgeons prefer haptic feedback of instrument vibrations during robotic surgery. Surg. Endosc. **29**(10), 2970–2983 (2015). https://doi.org/10.1007/S00464-014-4030-8
7. Konyo, M., Yamada, H., Okamoto, S., Tadokoro, S.: Alternative display of friction represented by tactile stimulation without tangential force. In: Ferre, M. (ed.) Haptics: Perception, Devices and Scenarios. EuroHaptics 2008, Lecture Notes in Computer Science, vol. 5024, pp. 619–629. Springer, Berlin Heidelberg, Berlin, Heidelberg (jun (2008). https://doi.org/10.1007/978-3-540-69057-3_79
8. Kuchenbecker, K., Fiene, J., Niemeyer, G.: Improving contact realism through event-based haptic feedback. IEEE Trans. Visual Comput. Graphics **12**(2), 219–230 (2006). https://doi.org/10.1109/TVCG.2006.32
9. Lee, J., Choi, S.: Real-time perception-level translation from audio signals to vibrotactile effects. In: Proceedings of the SIGCHI Conference on Human Factors in Computing Systems, pp. 2567–2576 (2013). https://doi.org/10.1145/2470654.2481354
10. Lim, J.M., Lee, J.U., Kyung, K.U., Ryou, J.C.: An audio-haptic feedbacks for enhancing user experience in mobile devices. In: 2013 IEEE International Conference on Consumer Electronics (ICCE), pp. 49–50 (2013). https://doi.org/10.1109/ICCE.2013.6486790
11. Manfredi, L.R., et al.: The effect of surface wave propagation on neural responses to vibration in primate glabrous skin. PLoS ONE **7**(2), e31203 (2012). https://doi.org/10.1371/JOURNAL.PONE.0031203

12. McMahan, W., Kuchenbecker, K.J.: Haptic display of realistic tool contact via dynamically compensated control of a dedicated actuator. In: 2009 IEEE/RSJ International Conference on Intelligent Robots and Systems, IROS 2009, pp. 3170–3177 (2009). https://doi.org/10.1109/IROS.2009.5354607
13. Minamizawa, K., Kakehi, Y., Nakatani, M., Mihara, S., Tachi, S.: Techtile toolkit: A prototyping tool for designing haptic media. In: ACM SIGGRAPH 2012 Emerging Technologies, SIGGRAPH 2012, pp. 387–392 (2012). https://doi.org/10.1145/2343456.2343478
14. Nagano, H., Takenouchi, H., Cao, N., Konyo, M., Tadokoro, S.: Tactile feedback system of high-frequency vibration signals for supporting delicate teleoperation of construction robots. Adv. Robot. **34**(11), 730–743 (2020). https://doi.org/10.1080/01691864.2020.1769725
15. Okamura, A., Cutkosky, M., Dennerlein, J.: Reality-based models for vibration feedback in virtual environments. IEEE/ASME Trans. Mechatron. **6**(3), 245–252 (2001). https://doi.org/10.1109/3516.951362
16. Saal, H.P., Delhaye, B.P., Rayhaun, B.C., Bensmaia, S.J.: Simulating tactile signals from the whole hand with millisecond precision. Proc. Natl. Acad. Sci. USA. **114**, E5693–E5702 (2017). https://doi.org/10.1073/PNAS.1704856114
17. Sakata, S., Nagano, H., Konyo, M., Tadokoro, S.: Multipoint vibrotactile stimuli based on vibration propagation enhance collision sensation. In: EuroHaptics 2016: Haptics: Perception, Devices, Control, and Applications, Lecture Notes in Computer Science, vol. 9775, pp. 65–74. Springer International Publishing (2016). https://doi.org/10.1007/978-3-319-42324-1
18. Shao, Y., Hayward, V., Visell, Y.: Spatial patterns of cutaneous vibration during whole-hand haptic interactions. Proc. Natl. Acad. Sci. USA. **113**, 4188–4193 (2016). https://doi.org/10.1073/PNAS.1520866113
19. Yamaguchi, K., Konyo, M., Tadokoro, S.: Sensory equivalence conversion of high-frequency vibrotactile signals using intensity segment modulation method for enhancing audiovisual experience. In: 2021 IEEE World Haptics Conference (WHC), pp. 674–679 (2021). https://doi.org/10.1109/WHC49131.2021.9517147

Peripersonal Space Tele-Operation in Virtual Reality: The Role of Tactile - Force Feedback

Yiru Liu[1,2], Nicholas Katzakis[3], Frank Steinicke[3], and Lihan Chen[1,2,4](✉)

[1] School of Psychological and Cognitive Sciences and Beijing Key Laboratory of Behavior and Mental Health, Peking University, Beijing 100871, China
CLH@pku.edu.cn
[2] Key Laboratory of Machine Perception (Ministry of Education), Peking University, Beijing 100871, China
[3] Department of Informatics, Universität Hamburg, Hamburg, Germany
[4] National Engineering Laboratory for Big Data Analysis and Applications, Peking University, Beijing 100871, China

Abstract. In tele-operated human-robot collaboration, a human operator typically engages with a distant physical environment through a robotic system equipped with multiple sensors and actuators, allowing for haptic-based precise manipulation. Although these technical systems have been in use for years, the connection between multisensory perception and action in peripersonal space during tele-operations remains less understood. To delve deeper into this relationship, we examined distance perception in virtual peripersonal space. Participants wore an HTC Vive head-mounted display (HMD) featuring integrated eye-tracking (SMI) and moved a comparison object (a yellow ball) towards a target object (a blue ball) using a Geomagic Touch haptic device stylus, receiving either force feedback ('closed-loop') or no force feedback ('open loop') during the operation. They were instructed to focus on fixation points while performing the task, with SMI eye-tracking monitoring their gaze. The spatial positions of the comparison and target objects were arranged in four layouts: (i) center-to-center, (ii) center-to-peripheral (20 degrees in visual eccentricity), (iii) peripheral-to-center, and (iv) peripheral-to-peripheral. We employed seven distance levels between the objects in Experiment 1 and five distance levels in Experiment 2, using consistent methods of stimuli presentation. The findings revealed that estimation errors were significantly influenced by force feedback, spatial arrangement, and distance. Crucially, the visibility of the movement trajectory enhanced the effectiveness of tactile force feedback. Overall, this study proposes a potential guideline for human-computer ergonomic design, emphasizing the importance of force feedback for accurate targeting.

Keywords: tele-operation · multisensory · virtual reality · peripersonal space · eye-tracking · tactile feedback

1 Introduction

Efficient and skillful human-robot collaboration necessitates a comprehension of how vast amounts of sensory data (e.g., visual, tactile, proprioceptive, and kinaesthetic) are combined and how the connection between perception, action planning, execution, and

D. Wang et al. (Eds.): AsiaHaptics 2022, LNCS 14063, pp. 162–175, 2023.
https://doi.org/10.1007/978-3-031-46839-1_13

learning is addressed [1–3]. This collaboration has recently seen significant advancements in teleoperation, where a distant robot is controlled remotely by a human operator. Typically, the operational scenario is simulated in virtual environments (VEs) to facilitate the manipulation of experimental variables [4–9]. However, this presents considerable challenges for empirical perceptual research. For instance, sensory feedback (including force-feedback) is diminished in VEs. The field of view and access to visual cues are significantly limited in VEs. In earlier studies, researchers discovered that users could accurately perceive the position of virtual objects, with a precision of approximately 1 mm in augmented reality (AR) environments. By utilizing consistent proprioception and corrective visual feedback, operators could achieve better matching accuracy [10, 11]. A haptic system integrated with a virtual environment engine was designed to simulate delicate multi-finger manipulation. Throughout the interaction, the most relevant associations between physiological and physical parameters involved in manipulation were well maintained in virtual operations, with fidelity largely reliant on the quality of perceived force feedback [12].

Prior research has analyzed the impact of haptic feedback and visual indicators (like stereo cues) on motor skills tasks (such as basic target selection) in simulated environments, revealing the enhancing effects of force feedback under low task difficulty scenarios [11, 13], as well as the characteristics of force-feedback and spatial references (e.g., egocentric-based operations) [14]. This line of research implies that combining sensory cues can improve human-computer interaction, but the benefits depend on functional priorities and specific task demands (like movement trajectories). Consequently, an empirical study is needed to determine how these sensory cues are combined and prioritized. Furthermore, there is limited knowledge about how visuomotor coordination is achieved when interactions primarily occur in the visual periphery, which is often the case when focusing on a primary task while simultaneously performing a secondary task, such as grabbing an object or moving an item without directly looking at the peripheral location. Previous research has explored the impact of force-feedback and target size on reaction time and movement trajectories, but these studies did not investigate the relationship between initial operation positions and final targeting, nor did they accurately record perceptual errors in spatial arrangements [15, 16]. Numerous studies have demonstrated that perception is impaired at greater visual eccentricities (i.e., peripheral conditions) [17–21]. Importantly, an accurate perception of space and a thorough understanding of actions within the given peripersonal space (including restricted vision conditions) are crucial for effectively operating remote robotic systems [5, 22–24].

Considering these outstanding issues and research objectives, our current study investigates users' depth perception during actions in peripersonal space with or without force feedback (Experiment 1). We also examine if and how visual-tactile interactions can compensate for and potentially enhance performance when reaching for target depths in virtual environments (Experiment 2).

2 Methods

2.1 Participants

Thirteen college students (with mean age of 22.3, 7 females) attended in this experiment. The experiment was performed in compliance with the institutional guidelines set by the Academic Affairs Committee, School of Psychological and Cognitive Sciences, Peking University. The protocol was approved by the Committee for Protecting Human and Animal Subjects, School of Psychological and Cognitive Sciences, Peking University. All participants gave written informed consent in accordance with the Declaration of Helsinki, and were paid for their time on a basis of 50 CNY/hour.

2.2 Stimuli and Apparatus

We composed three balls (with radius of 0.1 in Unity 3D scale) to show the correspondence between standard (target) stimulus and comparison stimulus in a given trial. The red ball indicated the manipulating hand/effector for a participant. The yellow ball showed the initial position of comparison stimulus and the blue ball was the target stimulus. Participants were encouraged to move the red ball to the position of the yellow one until both balls were overlapping (at this time point instantly the red ball disappeared), and then performed the moving task as described in the following 'procedure' section.

The yellow ball, as a comparison, was located either in the center (near the participants hand-homing position), or left periphery ($20°$ to fovea) or right periphery ($20°$ to fovea). The blue ball, as a target was placed in mirror positions to the yellow ball but was farther way from the participant. The (vertical) distance between the yellow ball (standard stimulus) and the blue one (target) was defined and picked from one of the seven levels (for the nearest to the farthest from the observers' perspective): -1.9, -1.2, -0.5, 0.2, 0.9, 1.6, 2.3 (relative to calibrated homing point "0" in the Unity3D design environment, i.e., the middle point of 70 mm for the motion range in Z-axis for Geomagic Touch), with fully randomization and counterbalance across trials. The visual stimuli were presented in virtual reality with Unity 3D program (Unity3d.com, 2015). Participants wore a HTC Vive head-mounted display (HMD) (with a refresh rate of 90 Hz), with integrated SMI eye-tracking components. The HMD was interfaced with a LCD display (with resolution of 2160×1200). The force feedback, if presented, was given by Geomagic Touch device (3D systems, USA). The haptic device has 6 degrees of freedom. Its workspace is within the range of $160 \times 120 \times 70$ mm. The maximum output force is about 1N. The moving trajectory of 'yellow' ball (comparison) was invisible during the trajectory towards the 'blue' ball (target).

The parameters for force feedback was designed as follows:

$$Force = startZCallback(dis * 25.0f, -target.transform.position.z * 25.0f) \quad (1)$$

In Formula (1), the *startZCallback* is a customized function. *Dis*25* indicates the magnitude of force behaves as a function of discrepancy between the Z- axis depths between comparison and target. *-target.transform.position.z* shows the force in negative direction with reference to the center point of the 'blue' ball (target) in diameter.

2.3 Experimental Design and Procedure

We adopted within-participants $2 \times 4 \times 7$ factorial design. The first independent variable is the force-feedback (no force vs. force-present). The second one is the spatial correspondence between the standard stimulus ('yellow ball') and comparison ('blue ball'): center-to-center (i.e., C-C), center-to-periphery (C-P), periphery-to-center (P-C) and periphery-to-periphery (P-P). The third one is the distance (depth) between the standard stimulus (target: blue ball) and comparison stimulus (yellow ball). During the experiment, participants were encouraged to use the stylus of Geomagic Touch device and move the standard stimulus (yellow ball) with the stylus of Touch device to the position of comparison stimulus (blue ball). In the force-feedback trial, when they approached the comparison within three radii of the target, they perceived incremental force on the end of the thumb and forefinger. However, when they moved out of the range (three radii of the target), the force (intensity) was decreased and finally disappeared. Throughout the experiment, participants fixed their eyes on the central fixation point (a red cross with 2°) and was monitored by the integrated SMI eyetracking sensors. To initiate a valid trial, the participants' eye-gaze range should be within 3° around the fixation point and maintain above 200 ms. Otherwise, the same trial would restart. We implemented eight blocks with rests in between. Each block included 112 trials (2 repetitions × 8 locations of standard vs. comparison stimuli × 7 levels of distances). The open-loop (no force-feedback) and closed-loop (force-present) conditions were arranged in blocks. However, within each block, the sub-conditions of the distance and position were fully randomized. Between blocks, participants could take a rest up to 5 min (Fig. 1).

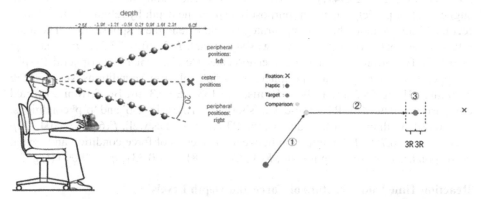

Fig. 1. Paradigm and schema for the present experiment. (A) Participants controlled the stylus of Geomagic Touch by moving the comparison to the target (location). (B) The view in head mounted display. The red ball indicates the current position of moving (right) hand. The yellow ball was the comparison and the blue one was the target. (C) The sample moving trajectory and experimental procedure. Participants initially moved the red ball to the position of yellow one, and both became invisible. Then they moved the comparison (yellow ball) to the target (blue ball). During this process, they had to fixate upon the fixation point.

Before the formal test, participants received a practice in which the conditions and trials were reduced. It included 32 trials in which we manipulated the depth (4 levels:

−2.2, −0.7,0.8 and 2.3), the correspondence of locations between comparison and the target (4 levels) and the visibility of the red ball (visible vs. invisible). In the first part of practice (16 trials), participants got familiar with the sensation of force-feedback along the trajectory of moving red ball (being visible). In the second part of the practice (another 16 trials), participants were requested to fixate on the central fixation point and the red ball was invisible. After issuing each response, participants obtained feedback of either 'correct', 'underestimation' or 'overestimation' by the text message that lasted about 1 s on the screen. However, during the formal test no feedback was given. The response time window for a given trial was three seconds.

2.4   Results for Experiment 1

The deviation of estimated depths from the physically target positions and the reaction times were obtained. We then performed repeated measures analysis of variance (ANOVA). Moreover, we used MATLAB *grpstats* function to sort out the data by averaging the of reaction time and deviation for the depth judgments, and their associated errors of means. We obtained the proportions of 'overestimation' and then used SPSS 16.0 (Chicago, SPSS Inc.) to conduct repeated measures ANOVA. We also sorted out the reaction times under each experimental condition and did repeated measures ANOVA.

Reaction Time Under Force and Spatial Correspondence Factors
The repeated measures of ANOVA showed that the reaction time under force-feedback condition was longer (1370 ± 61.5 ms) than the one under no-force condition (1243 ± 59.4 ms), $F(1,12) = 23.441, p < 0.01, \eta^2 = 0.054$. The finding was counterintuitive but suggested that participants might purposely exploit the depth by relying on the 'force-feedback' information, this waiting strategy could extend the response time. The main effect of the spatial correspondences was significant, $F(3,36) = 23.212, p < 0.01, \eta^2 = 0.145$. The mean RTs for the center-to-center ('c-c'), center-to-peripheral ('c-p'), peripheral to center ('p-c') and peripheral to peripheral ('p-p') conditions were 1272 ± 56.6 ms, 1317 ± 55.2 ms, 1299 ± 59 ms, and 1335 ± 60.3 ms. Bonferroni-corrected comparisons showed the RT for 'c-c' was shorter than those in 'c-p' and 'p-p' conditions, ps < 0.001. With the increased depths, the RTs increased as well, $F(6,72) = 204.751p < 0.01, \eta^2 = 0.750$. The interaction between the factors of force condition and spatial correspondences was not significant, $F(3,36) = 1.181, p = 0.331, \eta^2 = 0.090$ (Fig. 2).

Reaction Time Under Factors of Force and Depth Levels
The repeated measures of ANOVA showed that the reaction time under force-feedback condition was longer (1370 ± 61.5 ms) than the one under no-force condition (1243 ± 59.4 ms), $F(1,12) = 11.272, p < 0.001, \eta^2 = 0.484$. The main effect of the depth was significant, $F(6,72) = 61.749, p < 0.001, \eta^2 = 0.837$. The mean RTs for the seven depths (from near to far, labeled as 'D1' to'D7') were 1060 ± 52.3 ms, 1176 ± 53.4 ms, 1250 ± 57 ms, 1329 ± 58.8 ms, 1392 ± 64.2 ms and 1501 ± 67.7 ms. Bonferroni-corrected comparisons showed except for the comparisons between D2 and D3 ($p = 0.115$) and between D5 and D6 (p $= 0.392$), the other cohorts for comparisons were significant, ps < 0.05. The two-way interaction between force and depth conditions was significant, $F(6,72) = 7.074, p < 0.001, \eta^2 = 0.371$. Further simple effects analysis indicated that

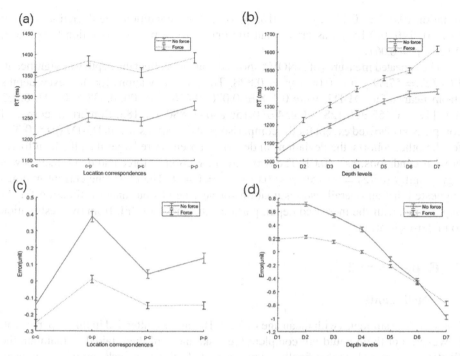

Fig. 2. Results for Experiment 1. (a) Reaction Time as function of the four types of location correspondences; (b) Reaction Time as a function of the seven levels of depths; (c) The Error (deviation) as a function of the location correspondences; (d) Error (deviation) as a function of the seven levels of depths. Error bars denoted the standard errors.

except for D1, the RTs in D2-D7 were longer for force-feedback conditions than those for force-absent conditions, $ps < 0.05$.

Deviation Analysis in Experiment 1
The deviation (error) was defined as the difference between the recorded depth estimation and the given depth. The positive deviation indicated over-estimation while the negative one under-estimation. We implemented repeated measures of ANOVA on the deviation. The repeated measures of ANOVA showed that the deviation under force-feedback condition was nearly the same (0.107 ± 0.150) as the one under no-force condition (-0.131 ± 0.108), $F(1,12) = 3.312$, $p = 0.094$, $\eta^2 = 0.216$. The main effect of the spatial correspondences was significant, $F(3,36) = 27.288$, $p < 0.001$, $\eta^2 = 0.695$. The mean deviations for the 'c-c', 'c-p', 'p-c' and 'p-p' conditions were -0.197 ± 0.109, 0.2 ± 0.126, -0.05 ± 0.103 and -0.001 ± 0.126. Bonferroni-corrected comparisons showed the deviation for 'c-c' was smaller than the ones in 'c-p', 'p-c' and 'p-p', $ps < 0.05$. Moreover, the deviation in 'c-p' was larger than the one in 'p-c', $ps < 0.001$. There were no differences of deviations in 'p-c' and 'p-p'. The two-way interaction between force condition and spatial correspondences was significant, $F(3,36) = 13.593$, $p < 0.001$, $\eta^2 = 0.531$. Further simple effects analysis indicated that in 'c-p' condition, the deviation without force (0.387 ± 0.166) was larger than the one in force-present

situation (0.013 ± 0.114), $p = 0.016$. Also, in 'p-p' condition, the deviation without force (0.140 ± 0.157) was larger than the one in force-present condition (-0.143 ± 0.128), p $= 0.061$.

The repeated measures of ANOVA showed that main effect the depth was significant, $F(6,72) = 57.897$, $p < 0.001$, $\eta^2 = 0.828$. The mean deviations for the seven depths (from near to far, D1-D7) were 0.448 ± 0.076, 0.466 ± 0.106, 0.338 ± 0.107, 0.162 ± 0.118, -0.165 ± 0.128, -0.454 ± 0.156 and -0.880 ± 0.183. Bonferroni-corrected comparisons showed except for the comparisons of deviations within D5-D7 ($ps > 0.37$), for the other cohorts, the deviations under force-absent were larger than those in force-present conditions, $ps < 0.01$. The two-way interaction of force and depth factors was significant, $F(6,72) = 11.256$, $p < 0.001$, $\eta^2 = 0.484$. Therefore, the current findings suggested that an overall over-estimation for near depths but under-estimation for far depths, i.e., with the increased depth, participants tended to shift from over-estimation to under-estimation.

3 Experiment 2

3.1 Participants

Forty college students (with mean age of 22.2, 18 females) attended in this experi-ment, however, 4 of them could not complete the task, and 6 of them failed to maintain the fixation as required, so that finally 30 participants fulfilled the task and their data were valid for subsequent analysis. All the participants had normal or corrected-to-normal vision. The experiment was performed in compliance with the institutional guidelines set by the Academic Affairs Committee, School of Psychological and Cognitive Sciences, Peking University.

3.2 Experimental Design and Procedure

The general design was similar to that in Experiment 1 but we made the moving trajectory visible. To balance the effectiveness of the depths as well as to reduce the number of trials (preventing fatigue), in Experiment 2 we reduced the depths as 5 levels: $-1.9f$, $-0.85f$, $0.2f$, $1.25f$, $2.3f$. The spatial correspondences were the same as in Experiment 1 and the periphery area was defined as $20°$ eccentricity. The side length for fixation was given by the following formula:

$$fixationRange\_length = 2 * ((fixationRange.transform.position.z - camera\_z)$$
$$* (float)Math.Tan((float)Math.PI/(180/fixationAngle)))$$

(2)

in which *fixationRange_length* represents the size length of the fixation, *fixationRange.transform.position.z* shows the depth where the fixation point lies. *Camera_z* indicates the position of HTC_Vive in the Unity virtual environment. *(float)Math.Tan((float)Math.PI/(180/fixationAngle))* was equal to size corresponding to tan20° (with the default 20° of fixationAngle). The fixation cross had a size of 2° and was located at a distance of 6.0f in Unity environment. After the practice, participants received formal test with 8 blocks, in which 4 blocks with force-feedback and 4 with-out force-feedback. For the force-absent condition, each sub-condition had 4 trials (5 depth levels and 4 spatial correspondences), totally 80 trials were included. For the force-present condition, in addition to the 80 trials with congruent visual-tactile moving information (i.e., the maximum force was coincident with the contact of blue/target ball), we inserted randomly 20 trials as fillers in which the maximum force was given beyond the 0.5f of the very depth for the blue ball:

$$startZCallback(dis * 25.0f, -target.transform.position.z * 25.0f + 0.5f) \qquad (3)$$

In formula (3) the *startZCallback* is customized function to regulate the magnitude of force. '*-target.transform.position.z * 25.0f + 0.5f*' indicates that the (max) force is given when the stylus has been moved to the point of 0.5f further away from the blue ball. The parameters of a multiply (*25.0f*) means that the distance has been transformed to meet the counterpart distance in real space.

Participants could start a trial when they met two mandatory requirements: the gaze duration upon the fixation should be above 300 ms and the response time should be within 4 s. If they failed to meet one of the two constraints, they had to redo the current trial. Before the formal test, we calibrated the eye-tracking equipment with the established 5-point protocol. After the calibration, they received a practice session of 40 trials, one half with force-feedback and the other without force. We defined the 'overestimation' as the deviation from the produced depth to the exact depth was above one radius of the blue ball and 'underestimation' as the deviation was below one radius. Participants received due verbal feedback appearing the screen, immediately after the issued the response. The response modes were the same as in Experiment 1 except that the moving trajectory was visible throughout the experiment.

3.3 Results for Experiment 2

Reaction Time
Contrary to the finding in Experiment 1, the repeated measures of ANOVA showed that the reaction time under force-feedback condition was shorter (1793 ± 82.1 ms) than the one under no-force condition (1979 ± 74.5 ms), $F(1,29) = 23.462, p < 0.001, \eta^2 = 0.447$. This suggests that with the visual feedback, the inputs from the force (tactile) facilitated the depth discrimination in virtual space. The main effect of the spatial correspondences was not significant, $F(3,87) = 1.921, p = 0.132, \eta^2 = 0.062$. The mean RTs for the 'c-c', 'c-p', 'p-c' and 'p-p' conditions were 1853 ± 75 ms, 1893 ± 80.1 ms, 1896 ± 73.8 ms, and 1902 ± 79.9 ms. The interaction between force condition and spatial correspondences was significant, $F(3,87) = 4.929, p = 0.003, \eta^2 = 0.145$. Further simple effects analysis indicated that for each spatial layout, the RTs in force-feedback condition were faster than those in force-absent condition, $ps < 0.01$. On the other hand, for no-force condition, the RTs were statistically not different among the four spatial correspondence; while for force-present condition, the RT in 'c-c' condition was the shortest, $ps < 0.05$.

As shown above, the main effect of force factor was significant, $F(1,29) = 23.462$, $p < 0.001, \eta^2 = 0.447$. The main effect of depth was significant, $F(4,116) = 176.909$,

$p < 0.001$, $\eta^2 = 0.859$. The RT increased linearly as a function of the depth. The RTs were 1544 ± 68.8 ms, 1764 ± 73.4 ms, 1909 ± 78.8 ms, 2039 ± 82.3 ms and 2174 ± 84.4 ms for D1-D5 respectively. However, the two-way interaction between force and depth factors was not significant, $F(4,116) = 2.214, p = 0.272, \eta^2 = 0.071$.

Results of Deviations for Experiment 2

The main effect of the force factor was significant, $F(1,29) = 48.277, p < 0.001, \eta^2 = 0.625$. The deviation in no-force condition (0.230 ± 0.034) was larger than the one with force-feedback (0.042 ± 0.028). The main effect of spatial correspondences was significant, $F(3,87) = 25.995, p < 0.001, \eta^2 = 0.473$. The mean deviations for the 'c-c', 'c-p', 'p-c' and 'p-p' conditions were -0.021 ± 0.009, 0.328 ± 0.047, 0.118 ± 0.024 and 0.116 ± 0.051 respectively. Bonferroni-corrected comparisons indicated that except for the cohort of 'c-c' and 'p-p' ($p = 0.059$), the cohort of 'p-c' and 'p-p' ($p = 1$), the other cohorts were significantly different, $ps < 0.001$. The interaction between force and spatial correspondences was significant, $F(3,87) = 17.175, p < 0.001, \eta^2 = 0.372$. Further simple effects analysis indicated that on each spatial layout, the deviations in no-force were larger than those in force-feedback conditions, $ps < 0.001$. However, on the other hand, for 'no-force' condition, the comparison between deviations in 'p-c' and 'p-p' was not significant, $p = 1$, the comparisons in other cohorts were significant, $ps < 0.01$. For 'force-present' condition, the comparison between 'c-c' and 'p-p', and the comparison between 'p-c' and 'p-p' were not significant, $ps = 1$. The other cohorts were significantly differed in the deviations, $ps < 0.001$.

The main effect of depth was significant, $F(4,116) = 38.501, p < 0.001, \eta^2 = 0.570$. The mean deviations across D1-D5 were 0.126 ± 0.018, 0.238 ± 0.032, 0.241 ± 0.034, 0.139 ± 0.037 and -0.066 ± 0.040 respectively. Bonferroni-corrected comparison indicated that except that there was no statistical difference between the deviations in D1 and D4 ($p = 1$), there remained significant differences in other cohorts, $ps < 0.05$. Typically, the deviations were larger with mid-range of depths. The two-way interaction between the factors of force and depth was significant, $F(4,116) = 22.595, p < 0.001, \eta^2 = 0.438$. Further simple effects analysis indicated that across each depth level, the deviation in no-force condition was larger than the one with force-feedback, $ps < 0.05$. On the other hand, in the no-force dimension, the comparisons between D1 and D4 ($p = 0.875$), between D2 and D3 ($p = 1$), between D2 and D4 ($p = 0.106$) were not significant, while the other cohorts were significantly different in the deviations, $ps < 0.001$. For the force-present condition, except that there were no differences in the cohorts of D1 vs. D3 ($p = 0.872$), D2 vs. D3 ($p = 1$), the comparisons in other cohorts showed significantly differences, $ps < 0.05$ (Fig. 3).

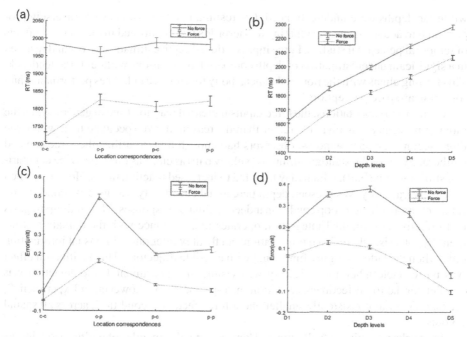

Fig. 3. Results for Experiment 2. (a) Reaction Time as function of the four types of location correspondences; (b) Reaction Time as a function of the seven levels of depths; (c) The Error (deviation) as a function of the location correspondences; (d) Error (deviation) as a function of the seven levels of depths.

4 Discussion

In this study, we explored 3D depth comparison in a desktop virtual reality system, focusing on the interaction between two essential sensory inputs: visual stimulation and force feedback. In the first experiment, we utilized force feedback while keeping the visual trajectory hidden. The second experiment involved a cross-modal design, where depth discrimination was enhanced by force feedback in conjunction with visible moving balls (specifically, the "yellow" ball used for comparison). In both experiments, we assessed participants' depth perception performance in virtual peripersonal space, using reaction time and deviation indices for depth perceptual judgments, and analyzing the differences between the two experiments' critical manipulations.

We discovered that estimation errors were significantly influenced by force feedback, spatial arrangement, and depth. Both deviation analysis and (over)estimation proportion analysis revealed that the smallest estimation errors occurred in the closed-loop condition (with appropriate force feedback) and congruent spatial layouts (center-to-center and peripheral-to-peripheral). Estimation errors were larger in the open-loop condition (without force feedback), incongruent spatial layouts (c-p and p-c), and the peripheral condition (p-p).

Overall, we observed an overestimation of depth perception, with participants overestimating the target's depth (indicated by the blue ball). Short depths were overestimated, while far depths were underestimated. Overestimation proportions were inversely proportional to actual distances, adhering to Vierordt's law as outlined in the contrast effects of temporal perceptual studies. Force inputs reduced depth estimation errors and resulted in a significant underestimation of depth compared to conditions without force feedback. This finding aligns with the notion that near-body touch/force enhances performance and fosters near-space perception.

Contrary to expectations, the force inputs increased reaction time in general when the moving trajectory was invisible rather than decreasing it. We speculate that, within the three-second response window, observers had enough time to utilize the force cue and deliberately move the standard stimulus (yellow ball) as close as possible to the comparison stimulus (blue ball), which may have led to increased reaction times. However, when the visual trajectory was present, depth perceptual uncertainty was greatly reduced, and force inputs as a closed-loop condition indeed facilitated responses. This finding suggests that effective cross-modal integration operates in accordance with the domain recruitment hypothesis, where force information can flexibly integrate with visual information only when the latter is highly functional with a visible trajectory. This facilitation effect was more stable when the trajectory was visible. In Experiment 1, the deviation was smaller for the force-feedback condition in "c-p" and "p-p"; however, in Experiment 2, the deviation was consistently smaller under force-feedback conditions across all spatial layouts.

In conclusion, this study illuminated key perceptual principles of multisensory inputs (i.e., force feedback) in enhancing teleoperation in peripersonal space using depth perception and manual operation in virtual reality (VR), as well as the limiting factors of spatial correspondence and distances between effectors/controllers and targets in depth perception and precise designated actions (e.g., pointing). A significant implication from this study is that observers may assign different weights to the estimation of physical distances in virtual environments based on the construal level theory. For example, due to the immediate and direct interaction nature of the tactile modality, people may rely more on force feedback under uncertain visual conditions and form a general schema for depth estimation in those situations (including Vierordt's law). Moreover, when visual information was more reliable (with visible trajectory), force cues maximized their role in enhancing target-reaching accuracy, and potential contamination from response strategy (such as purposefully exploiting force inputs) was largely reduced. These findings offer valuable insights for designing perceptually-inspired visuo-haptic interactions in areas related to redirected touching, haptic retargeting, and passive haptic feedback in visually disrupted environments. These results have important implications for the development of more effective virtual reality systems and applications. By understanding how multisensory inputs, particularly force feedback, can enhance depth perception and accuracy in teleoperation, we can create more immersive and realistic virtual experiences. This knowledge can be applied to various fields, such as remote surgery, telepresence robotics, training simulations, and entertainment.

Moreover, our findings suggest that the integration of force feedback with visual cues should be carefully considered and optimized to maximize its benefits. In situations where visual information is less reliable, the use of force feedback can be crucial for enhancing depth perception accuracy. On the other hand, when visual information is more reliable (e.g., with visible trajectories), force feedback can still play an important role in improving the user's overall performance.

Lastly, it is essential to consider the spatial correspondence and distances between effectors/controllers and targets in the design of VR systems, as these factors can significantly impact depth perception and the accuracy of designated actions. By addressing these constraints and leveraging the insights gained from our study, developers can create more efficient and user-friendly virtual environments that facilitate accurate depth perception and interaction.

In summary, this research contributes valuable knowledge to the field of virtual reality and visuo-haptic interactions. It highlights the importance of multisensory inputs, particularly force feedback, and the need to carefully integrate these elements within virtual environments to maximize user performance and the overall VR experience.

Acknowledgements. This study was funded by STI2030-Major Projects 2021ZD0202600 and Sino-German Crossmodal Learning Project from Natural Science Foundation of China (Grant No. 62061136001).

References

1. Ernst, M.O., Banks, M.S.: Humans integrate visual and haptic information in a statistically optimal fashion. Nature **415**(6870), 429–433 (2002)
2. Hillis, J.M., Ernst, M.O., Banks, M.S., Landy, M.S.: Combining sensory information: mandatory fusion within, but not between, senses. Science **298**(5598), 1627–1630 (2002)
3. Kording, K.P., Wolpert, D.M.: Bayesian integration in sensorimotor learning. Nature **427**(6971), 244–247 (2004)
4. Popescu, V.G., Burdea, G.C., Bouzit, M., Hentz, V.R.: A virtual-reality-based telerehabilitation system with force feedback. IEEE Trans. Inf Technol. Biomed. **4**(1), 45–51 (2000)
5. Pacchierotti, C., Tirmizi, A., Bianchini, G., Prattichizzo, D.: Enhancing the performance of passive teleoperation systems via cutaneous feedback. IEEE Trans. Haptics **8**(4), 397–409 (2015)
6. Neupert, C., Matich, S., Scherping, N., Kupnik, M., Werthschützky, R., Hatzfeld, C.: Pseudo-haptic feedback in teleoperation. IEEE Trans. Haptics **9**(3), 397–408 (2016)
7. Panzirsch, M., Balachandran, R., Weber, B., Ferre, M., Artigas, J.: Haptic augmentation for teleoperation through virtual grasping points. IEEE Trans. Haptics **11**(3), 400–416 (2018)
8. Bugdadi, A., et al.: Is virtual reality surgical performance influenced by force feedback device utilized? J. Surg. Educ. **76**(1), 262–273 (2019)
9. Wang, Z., Sun, Y., Liang, B.: Synchronization control for bilateral teleoperation system with position error constraints: a fixed-time approach. ISA Trans. **93**, 125–136 (2019)
10. Swan, J., Singh, G., Ellis, S.: Matching and reaching depth judgments with real and augmented reality targets. IEEE Trans. Visual Comput. Graphics **21**(11), 1289–1298 (2015)
11. Wall, S.A., Harwerth, R.S.: Quantification of the effects of haptic feedback during a motor skills task in a simulated environment. In: Proceedings at Phantom User Research Symposium, Zurich, Switserland, pp. 61–69 (2000)
12. Bergamasco, M., Avizzano, C.A., Frisoli, A., Ruffaldi, E., Marcheschi, S.: (2006) Design and validation of a complete haptic system for manipulative tasks. Adv. Robot. **20**(3), 367–389 (2006)

13. Wall, S.A., Paynter, K., Shillito, A.M., Wright, M., Scali, S.: The effect of haptic feedback and stereo graphics in a 3D target acquisition task. In: Proceedings of Eurohaptics, Edinburgh, UK, pp. 23–29 (2002)
14. Pawar, V.M., Steed, A.: Evaluating the influence of haptic force-feedback on 3D selection tasks using natural egocentric gestures. In: IEEE Virtual Reality, Lafayette, Louisiana, USA, pp. 11–18 (2009)
15. Pawar, V.M., Steed, A.: Profiling the behaviour of 3D selection tasks on movement time when using natural haptic pointing gestures. In: Proceedings of the 16th ACM Symposium on Virtual Reality Software and Technology, New York, United States, pp. 79–82 (2009)
16. Pawar, V.M., Steed, A.: Poster: the effect of target size and force feedback on 3D selection within a co-located visual-haptic immersive virtual environment. In: 2013 IEEE Symposium on 3D User Interfaces (3DUI) 2013, Orlando, FL, USA, pp. 169–170 (2013)
17. Xing, J., Heeger, D.J.: Center-surround interactions in foveal and peripheral vision. Vision. Res. 40(22), 3065–3072 (2000)
18. Latham, K., Whitaker, D.: Relative roles of resolution and spatial interference in foveal and peripheral vision. Ophthalmic Physiol. Opt. 16(1), 49–57 (1996)
19. Siderov, J., Harwerth, R.S.: Stereopsis, spatial frequency and retinal eccentricity. Vision. Res. 35(16), 2329–2337 (1995)
20. Thibos, L.N., Walsh, D.J., Cheney, F.E.: Vision beyond the resolution limit: aliasing in the periphery. Vision. Res. 27(12), 2193–2197 (1987)
21. Katzakis, N., Chen, L., Ariza, O., Teather, R.J., Steinicke, F.: Evaluation of 3D pointing accuracy in the fovea and periphery in immersive head-mounted display environments. IEEE Trans. Visual Comput. Graphics 27(3), 1929–1936 (2021)
22. de Haan, A.M., Smit, M., Van der Stigchel, S., Dijkerman, H.C.: Approaching threat modulates visuotactile interactions in peripersonal space. Exp. Brain Res. 234, 1875–1884 (2016)
23. Chen, Y.C., Maurer, D., Lewis, T.L., Spence, C., Shore, D.I.: Central–peripheral differences in audiovisual and visuotactile event perception. Atten. Percept. Psychophys. 79, 2552–2563 (2017)
24. Grechuta, K., Guga, J., Maffei, G., Rubio Ballester, B., Verschure, P.F.M.J.: Visuotactile integration modulates motor performance in a perceptual decision-making task. Sci. Reports 7(1), 3333 (2017)
25. Foley, A.J., Michaluk, L.M., Thomas, D.G.: Pace alteration and estimation of time intervals. Percept. Mot. Skills 98(1), 291–298 (2004)
26. Rammsayer, T., Wittkowski, K.M.: Time order error and position effect of a standardized stimulus in discrimination of short time duration. Arch. Psychol. (Frankf) 142(2), 81–89 (1990)
27. Roy, M.M., Christenfeld, N.J.: Effect of task length on remembered and predicted duration. Psychon. Bull. Rev. 15(1), 202–207 (2008)
28. Ryan, L.J., Havens, A.: Responses contribute to context effects on ratio-setting timing tasks. Perception 42(5), 537–550 (2013)
29. Schiffman, H.R., Bobko, D.J.: The role of number and familiarity of stimuli in the perception of brief temporal intervals. Am. J. Psychol. 90(1), 85–93 (1977)
30. Vatakis, A., Ulrich, R.: Temporal processing within and across senses. Acta Physiol. (Oxf) 147, 1 (2014)
31. Serino, A., Haggard, P.: Touch and the body. Neurosci. Biobehav. Rev. 34(2), 224–236 (2010)
32. Hara, M., et al.: Voluntary self-touch increases body ownership. Front. Psychol. 6, 1509 (2015)
33. Michalka, S.W., Kong, L., Rosen, M.L., Shinn-Cunningham, B.G., Somers, D.C.: Short-term memory for space and time flexibly recruit complementary sensory-biased frontal lobe attention networks. Neuron 87(4), 882–892 (2015)

34. Rim, S., Uleman, J.S., Trope, Y.: Spontaneous trait inference and construal level theory: psychological distance increases nonconscious trait thinking. J. Exp. Soc. Psychol. **45**(5), 1088–1097 (2009)
35. Trope, Y., Liberman, N.: Construal-level theory of psychological distance. Psychol. Rev. **117**(2), 440–463 (2010)
36. Trautmann, S.T., van de Kuilen, G.: Prospect theory or construal level theory? Diminishing sensitivity vs. psychological distance in risky decisions. Acta Psychol. **139**(1), 254–260 (2012)

CobotTouch: AR-Based Interface with Fingertip-Worn Tactile Display for Immersive Control of Collaborative Robots

Oleg Sautenkov, Miguel Altamirano Cabrera$^{(\boxtimes)}$, Viktor Rakhmatulin, and Dzmitry Tsetserukou

Center for Digital Engineering, Skolkovo Institute of Science and Technology (Skoltech), Bolshoy Boulevard 30, bld. 1, 121205 Moscow, Russia
{oleg.sautenkov,miguel.altamirano,viktor.rakhmatulin, d.tsetserukou}@skoltech.ru

Abstract. Complex robotic tasks require human collaboration to benefit from their high dexterity. Frequent human-robot interaction is mentally demanding and time-consuming. Intuitive and easy-to-use robot control interfaces reduce the negative influence on workers, especially inexperienced users. In this paper, we present CobotTouch, a novel intuitive robot control interface with fingertip haptic feedback. The proposed interface consists of a projected Graphical User Interface (GUI) on the robotic arm to control the position of the robot end-effector based on gesture recognition and a wearable haptic interface to deliver tactile feedback on the user's fingertips. We evaluated the user's perception of the designed tactile patterns presented by the haptic interface and the intuitiveness of the proposed system for robot control in a case study. The results revealed a high average recognition rate of 75.25% for tactile patterns. The average NASA Task Load Index (TLX) indicated small mental and temporal demands, indicating a high level of intuitiveness of CobotTouch for interaction with collaborative robots.

Keywords: Human-Robot Interaction · Haptic Interfaces · Augmented Reality

1 Introduction

Industrial collaborative robots are becoming increasingly important in modern manufacturing industries. Collaborative robots perform routine and repeatable tasks, whereas workers focus on dexterous operations. Robot operations are complex and require expert knowledge of the robotics domain. Moreover, changes in the production of Small and Medium Enterprises (SMEs) are frequent and lead to an increase in the time workers spend interacting with robotic systems [12]. Intuitive and efficient control interfaces significantly decrease the number of errors produced by the operators [9].

D. Wang et al. (Eds.): AsiaHaptics 2022, LNCS 14063, pp. 176–188, 2023.
https://doi.org/10.1007/978-3-031-46839-1_14

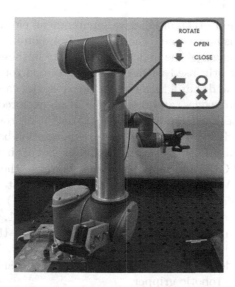

Fig. 1. Projected Graphical User Interface on the robotic arm with DNN-based hand gesture recognition to control the position of a collaborative robot UR10 by Cobot-Touch.

Virtual Reality (VR) technology is widely used in entertainment, education, and other business applications. Augmented Reality (AR) and VR provide alternative robot control interfaces to traditional methods, such as teaching pendants and joysticks. These technologies are aimed at supporting efficient and low-cognitively demanding human-robot interaction [8]. For example, Charão dos Santos et al. [15] designed a 3D environment to teach children to program robots using a head-mounted display (HMD). VR technologies can be used to share tasks between workers and industrial robots naturally and intuitively, as presented by Beibei et al. [16]. However, VR devices have numerous limitations, such as restricted field of view and motion sickness [19].

AR enriches the surrounding environment using virtual layers, providing the user with the required information and enabling interactive interfaces. AR has found a variety of applications in Human-Robot Interaction (HRI). A complete setup for safe and efficient HRI was presented by Papanastasiou et al. [11]. Smart glasses provide an AR interface to visualize safety zones. However, the projection mapping approach overcomes the limitations of restricted field of view and motion sickness. Projected GUIs allow interaction with a virtual control panel at almost any type of surface, as shown in [10]. Hartmann et al. [6] presented a combined system with a head-mounted projector and a Hololens AR headset that allows multi-user collaboration and shared use of the projected interface.

VR and AR-based technologies rely mostly on visual modality, while in cases with limited or absent visual feedback, tactile sense could complement HRI and make it more intuitive. Wearable haptic interfaces deliver a sense of grasping for solid and deformable bodies, as presented in [3] and [2], slippage of manipulated virtual objects [5], and other interactive environment parameters that are not identifiable by the visual channel. Tactile stimuli are often applied on the palm [1][?] or fingertips because of the high skin sensitivity in these areas, and because they are more frequently used to interact with the surrounding environment. Gabardi et al. [4] showed that a finger-worn haptic device can successfully render the texture, curvature, edges, and orientation of an explored virtual surface.

We present CobotTouch, a novel AR robot control interface that consists of a camera projector module (CPM), hand gesture recognition based on Deep Neural Network (DNN), and a fingertip-worn tactile display. CobotTouch inherits the benefits of projected GUIs and tactile feedback; however, there are no drawbacks typically caused by VR helmets. The CPM is mounted statically on the body of the robot and projects a Graphical User Interface (GUI) to control the robot interacting with the manipulator surface, as shown in Fig. 1. Gesture recognition captures the position of the hand while interacting with the GUI, and allows dexterous manipulation of the end effector of the robot. Two fingertip-worn tactile interfaces guide the user during the control of the end effector, rendering the orientation of the robotic gripper.

The remainder of this paper is organized as follows. In Sect. 2, a detailed overview of the proposed system is presented. In Sect. 3, a tactile pattern perception experiment is conducted to evaluate users' responses to the fingertip-worn tactile interface. Section 4 describes a robot control use case, in which users evaluate the convenience and intuitiveness of the developed system. In the last section, the obtained results are discussed and further work is proposed.

2 System Overview

CobotTouch is a novel HRI system that implements AR projector-based spatial displays, which generates an interactive projected GUI on the links of a collaborative robot UR10. The system tracks the position of the user's hand using DNN-based gesture recognition. This allows users to interact with the projected GUI and intuitively control the robot's position. The projector-camera module is statically mounted on the shoulder of the robot. Two fingertip-worn tactile interfaces, introduced in [7], guide the user during the control of the end effector, rendering the orientation of the robotic gripper.

The CobotTouch hardware system consists of a pocket pico pocket projector Optoma PK301, a Logitech HD Webcam C930e, a 6 DoF collaborative robot from Universal Robots UR10 [14], a two-finger gripper from Robotiq 2f-85 [13], two fingertip-worn tactile interfaces, and a laptop.

Three computational modules are responsible for data processing and robot control: a) gesture recognition based on DNN, b) image processing through the OpenCV library for the projection, and c) fingertip-worn tactile interface control. The system architecture is shown in Fig. 2, and the system overview is shown in Fig. 3. The software architecture is based on the ROS Melodic framework.

The DNN-based algorithm detects the user's hand gestures. This allows users to interact with any type of GUI projection and control the robot's position

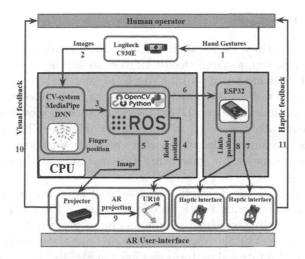

Fig. 2. System architecture of CobotTouch.

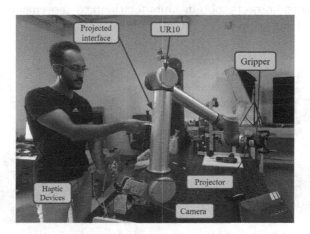

Fig. 3. The user controls the UR10 collaborative robot through the projected interface from an ultra-compact mobile projector and an HD Webcam C930e mounted on the joint of the UR10 robot.

more intuitively. The CPM was mounted on the UR10 robot to provide a more extensive projection area and to avoid shadows in the projection. Simultaneously, the Computer Vision (CV) algorithm processes the webcam image using the hand tracking module. It estimates the position of fingers in a specific area and defines it as a "press button" command. The central program defined the required robotic action as a result of the gesture recognition process. CobotTouch can present different GUIs with buttons to interact with the robotic parts, e.g., users can visualize the inner structure of the robot by projecting on it without disassembling it.

2.1   Haptic Interface

We used two fingertip-worn tactile interfaces, which consist of an inverted five-bar linkage mechanism, as tactile feedback modules on the thumb and index fin-gertips. The devices are based on LinkTouch [17] and LinkRing [7] technologies. The device consists of a 3D-printed PLA body, a 3D-printed flexible material finger cap holder, links, and two DSM44 servo motors, as shown in Fig. 4a. Two ESP32 microcontrollers are used to operate the interface. The program sends a signal to the microcontrollers of the devices when a trigger occurs, and the haptic devices become active, generating a normal force at the desired position on the fingertips.

The fingertip-worn tactile interfaces allow the user to interact more efficiently with the robot by receiving haptic feedback support. The configuration of the inverted five bar-linkage mechanisms allows one to perceive the position of the dynamic contact point on the fingertips. By combining the two LinkRing devices, we have generated rotational patterns as shown in Fig. 4b. By wearing two tactile interfaces, the operator can understand the direction of the robot's rotation while grasping the objects, obtain hints for the next movement, or experience the direction of the gripper.

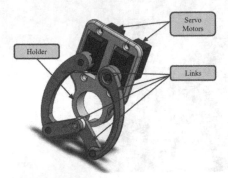

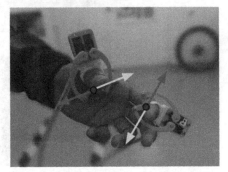

(a) 3D CAD model of wearable tactile display LinkRing.

(b) Example of rotational patterns. The purple arrows correspond to the coun-terclockwise pattern and the yellow ar-rows correspond to the clockwise pat-tern.

Fig. 4. Wearable tactile display LinkRing, used to provide tactile feedback on the thumb and index fingertips.

2.2   DNN-Based Gesture Recognition

The DNN-based gesture recognition module was implemented based on the Mediapipe framework [20]. It provides high-fidelity hand tracking by employing machine learning (ML) to infer 21 3D landmarks of a human hand per frame.

The DNN algorithm was trained to recognize eight gestures. Two gestures were chosen to perform the pressing buttons task: one with the open fingers ("Palm") and the second with only the index finger pointing ("One").

If the index finger coordinates are located on the button's area, and the gesture has been changed from "Palm" to "One", the corresponding button will be activated. The algorithm sends the number of active buttons to the robot control system using the ROS framework. The control system modifies the position of the robot end-effector during the time that the button has been pressed, and the projected GUI changes the color of the pressed button to inform the user that the action is in progress.

3   Experiment on Tactile Perception

This evaluation is centered on the analysis of human perception of tactile patterns on the fingertips. Eight tactile patterns were designed to evaluate the human perception when the thumb and index fingertips were stimulated simultaneously or once at a time. The contact points of the fingertip-worn tactile interfaces slide on the fingertips in different directions according to the patterns shown in Fig. 5a.

Seven right-handed participants (two females) aged 22 to 32 years volunteered to complete the evaluation. None of the users reported any deficiencies in the sensorimotor function.

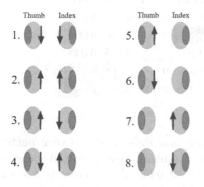

(a) Set of tactile patterns represented on the thumb and index fingertips. The arrows represent the sliding direction of the LinkRing contact points.

(b) Experimental setup for study on tactile pattern perception.

Fig. 5. Experiment on tactile perception.

Before the experiment, the device was calibrated, and a training session was performed. During the training session, the experimenter explained the purpose of the fingertip-worn tactile interfaces to each participant and demonstrated the tactile patterns at least three times. During the experiment, the user was asked to sit in front of a desk and to wear the haptic display on the left thumb and index fingers as shown in Fig. 5b. A visual barrier was located between the left hand and the user. All the possible patterns were displayed on the screen during the experiment. The users were asked to tell the perceived pattern to the experimenter, who recorded the pattern number and time. Each pattern was presented five times blindly in random order, thus, 40 patterns were provided to each participant in each evaluation.

3.1 Experimental Results of Tactile Perception

The results of the recognition of tactile patterns shown in Fig. 5a, are summarized in the confusion matrix presented in Table 1.

Table 1. Confusion Matrix for Actual and Perceived Pattern Recognition Across All Subjects.

%		*Answers (Predicted Class)*							
		1	2	3	4	5	6	7	8
Patterns	1	0.700	0.100	0.150	0.050	0.000	0.000	0.000	0.00
	2	0.050	0.825	0.050	0.000	0.000	0.025	0.025	0.025
	3	0.075	0.075	0.550	0.275	0.025	0.000	0.000	0.000
	4	0.025	0.050	0.100	0.750	0.075	0.000	0.000	0.000
	5	0.025	0.000	0.000	0.025	0.800	0.125	0.025	0.000
	6	0.025	0.000	0.000	0.000	0.100	0.725	0.125	0.025
	7	0.050	0.000	0.000	0.000	0.000	0.000	0.775	0.175
	8	0.025	0.000	0.000	0.000	0.000	0.000	0.100	0.875

In order to evaluate the statistically significant differences between pattern perceptions, we analyzed the results using a single-factor repeated-measures ANOVA with a chosen significance level of $\alpha < 0.05$. The open-source statistical package Pingouin [18] was used for statistical analysis. The sphericity and normality assumptions were examined, and no violations were detected. According to the ANOVA results, there was a statistically significant difference in the pattern recognition $F(7, 48) = 2.077, p = 0.064$. The ANOVA results showed that the pattern influenced the percentage of correct responses. The average pattern recognition rate was 75%.

The paired t-tests showed statistically significant differences between patterns 1 and 3 ($p = 0.037 < 0.05$), 2 and 3 ($p = 0.001 < 0.05$), 3 and 5 ($p = 0.028 < 0.05$), 3 and 7 ($p = 0.015 < 0.05$), and 3 and 8 ($p = 0.026 < 0.05$).

4   User Study Experiment

The principal approach of this study is to design a new AR control interface with fingertip-worn tactile display. We conducted a user study to investigate the advantages and disadvantages of the proposed system according to the NASA Task Load Index (TLX) rating.

4.1   Experimental Design

The GUI implemented to control the UR10 robot using the CobotTouch system is shown in Fig. 6. The robot end-effector moved along the three axes by pressing on the projected buttons. The user could use six different movement control buttons to guide the robot. The button "close" closes the gripper, the button "open" opens it. To rotate the end effector and overturn the container, users must press the button "rotate". When the gripper rotates, the CPU constantly sends a rotational pattern to the fingertip-worn tactile interfaces, as shown in Fig. 4b according to the directions represented in Fig. 8.

The subject can simultaneously use only one button. During the experiment, the user was able to correct the robot trajectory each time.

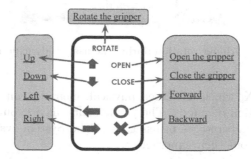

Fig. 6. CobotTouch control interface. The interface contains nine buttons. The gesture recognition system detects the pressed button and moves the robot in the desired direction or perform pre-defined action.

We located one empty plastic box and two containers filled with white Styrofoam pieces on the experimental table, as shown in Fig. 4b. The participants were asked to put the contents of the two containers into the box by controlling the robot with the CobotTouch interface.

Before starting the experiment, the participants performed a training session in which each participant familiarized themselves with the interface and tested it. After the training session, the UR10 robot returned to the predetermined initial position and the experiment was started.

Eight volunteer participants (two females) aged 22 to 32 years participated in the test. After the trial, each participant completed a questionnaire based

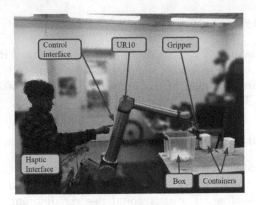

Fig. 7. Setup for the user study experiment

Fig. 8. Gripper rotation during the user study experiment.

on the NASA TLX, which measured physical, mental, temporal, performance, effort, and frustration demands. The participants filled it out to determine the advantages and disadvantages of using the CobotSystem system and provided some comments about their experiences.

5   Experimental Results

5.1   Average Score of NASA TLX Rating

The average results of the NASA TLX ratings are shown in Table 2. It can be observed that physical demand had the highest value of 2.08. One of the participants noticed that the performance of this task through the CobotTouch interface was ongoing with a constantly raised hand, as shown in Fig. 7, which could affect the evaluation of the physical demand (Fig. 9).

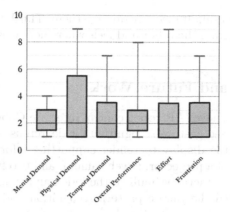

Fig. 9. NASA TLX rating results for the six sub-clases during the operation of the robot by the CobotTouch interface.

Table 2. Average NASA TLX Rating

	CobotTouch system
Mental Demand	1.33
Physical Demand	2.08
Temporal Demand	1.58
Performance	1.67
Effort	1.75
Frustration	0.92
General TLX Score	13

Results also showed that participants had the lowest frustration level of 0.92 compared to other criteria. Several participants noticed that it was simple to observe the controlling interface and the robotic end-effector simultaneously.

5.2   Post-Experience Questionnaire

Generally, the users were very inspired by the CobotTouch system. Some participants noticed that they could push the robot only with the finger in a desirable direction. The comments are as follows: "I liked the projector interface (Cobot-Touch), it felt like I was pushing the robotic arm, and it was moving". "I like how easy the robot can be guided by hand. However, my arm was tired at the end of the experiment; for me, it would be comfortable to control the robot by both hands". "The haptic feedback helped me to understand better when the rotation of the end effector started and to stop it at the right time".

The main advantage of CobotTouch interface is that a person can move the robot with one hand, and the second hand is free to feel haptic feedback. Second, it is not obligatory to constantly switch the view from the interface to the end effector. A person can simultaneously observe them. Third, the operator receives kinesthetic feedback from the robot and feels where he/she is moving the robotic arm.

6   Conclusion and Future Work

We have developed a novel AR robot control interface CobotTouch with a projected GUI, DNN-based gesture recognition for dexterous cobot operation, and a fingertip-worn tactile display to render supporting information to the user. Our system consists of a projector, a web camera, and two fingertip-worn tactile interfaces that provide tactile stimuli to the index and thumb fingertips.

We have evaluated the tactile pattern recognition and the intuitiveness of the interface in the robot control task. The results revealed that the haptic display demonstrates a high average recognition rate of 75% for the eight tactile patterns. CobotTouch interface achieved a low NASA TLX rating of 13 scores on average.

In future work, more tactile patterns will be studied during the operation of the robot using the proposed system, and a study to compare it with other interfaces will be conducted.

The proposed robot control interface could potentially improve industrial and collaborative robot learning through demonstration programming. An intuitive and immersive interface coupled with highly sensitive tactile feedback could support the worker during complicated tasks, such as pegging in a hole, where the visual channel does not provide sufficient information. For future work, we consider extending the functionality of the projected interface by adding new virtual buttons for speed regulation. In addition, we plan to study the control actions that should be carried out by gestures and by interaction with the panel.

Acknowledgments. The reported study was funded by RFBR and CNRS, project number 21-58-15006.

References

1. Cabrera, M.A., Tsetserukou, D.: LinkGlide: a wearable haptic display with inverted five-bar linkages for delivering multi-contact and multi-modal tactile stimuli. In: Kajimoto, H., Lee, D., Kim, S.-Y., Konyo, M., Kyung, K.-U. (eds.) AsiaHaptics 2018. LNEE, vol. 535, pp. 149–154. Springer, Singapore (2019). https://doi.org/10.1007/978-981-13-3194-7_33
2. Bakker, T., Verlinden, J., Abbink, D., van Deventer, R.: Development of a haptic device with tactile and proprioceptive feedback for spatial design tasks. In: 2017 IEEE International Symposium on Mixed and Augmented Reality (ISMAR-Adjunct), pp. 223–228 (2017). https://doi.org/10.1109/ISMAR-Adjunct.2017.74
3. Choi, I., Culbertson, H., Miller, M.R., Olwal, A., Follmer, S.: Grabity: a wearable haptic interface for simulating weight and grasping in virtual reality. In: Proceedings of the 30th Annual ACM Symposium on User Interface Software and Technology. UIST 2017, New York, NY, USA, pp. 119–130. Association for Computing Machinery (2017). https://doi.org/10.1145/3126594.3126599

4. Gabardi, M., Solazzi, M., Leonardis, D., Frisoli, A.: A new wearable fingertip haptic interface for the rendering of virtual shapes and surface features. In: 2016 IEEE Haptics Symposium (HAPTICS), pp. 140–146 (2016). https://doi.org/10.1109/HAPTICS.2016.7463168

5. Gleeson, B.T., Horschel, S.K., Provancher, W.R.: Design of a fingertip-mounted tactile display with tangential skin displacement feedback. IEEE Trans. Haptics 3(4), 297–301 (2010). https://doi.org/10.1109/TOH.2010.8

6. Hartmann, J., Yeh, Y.T., Vogel, D.: Aar: augmenting a wearable augmented reality display with an actuated head-mounted projector. In: Proceedings of the 33rd Annual ACM Symposium on User Interface Software and Technology. UIST 2020, New York, NY, USA, pp. 445–458. Association for Computing Machinery (2020). https://doi.org/10.1145/3379337.3415849

7. Ivanov, A., Trinitatova, D., Tsetserukou, D.: LinkRing: a wearable haptic display for delivering multi-contact and multi-modal stimuli at the finger pads. In: Nisky, I., Hartcher-O'Brien, J., Wiertlewski, M., Smeets, J. (eds.) EuroHaptics 2020. LNCS, vol. 12272, pp. 434–441. Springer, Cham (2020). https://doi.org/10.1007/978-3-030-58147-3_48

8. Kagermann, H., Wahlster, W., Helbig, J.: Recommendations for implementing the strategic initiative industrie 4.0 - securing the future of german manufacturing industry. Final report of the industrie 4.0 working group, acatech - National Academy of Science and Engineering, München (2013)

9. Malý, I., Sedláček, D., Leitão, P.: Augmented reality experiments with industrial robot in industry 4.0 environment. In: 2016 IEEE 14th International Conference on Industrial Informatics (INDIN), pp. 176–181 (2016). https://doi.org/10.1109/INDIN.2016.7819154

10. Mistry, P., Maes, P.: Sixthsense: a wearable gestural interface. In: ACM SIGGRAPH ASIA 2009 Sketches. SIGGRAPH ASIA 2009, Association for Computing Machinery (2009). https://doi.org/10.1145/1667146.1667160

11. Papanastasiou, S., et al.: Towards seamless human robot collaboration: integrating multimodal interaction. Int. J. Adv. Manuf. Technol. 105(9), 3881–3897 (2019). https://doi.org/10.1007/s00170-019-03790-3

12. Perzylo, A., et al.: Smerobotics: smart robots for flexible manufacturing. IEEE Robot. Autom. Mag. 26(1), 78–90 (2019). https://doi.org/10.1109/MRA.2018.2879747

13. Robotiq: 2f85 140 Adaptive Robot Gripper. https://robotiq.com/products/2f85-140-adaptive-robot-gripper. Accessed 06 Nov 2021

14. Robots, U.: Universal Robots UR10. https://www.universal-robots.com/products/ur10-robot/. Accessed 06 Nov 2021

15. Charão dos Santos, M.C., Sangalli, V.A., Pinho, M.S.: Evaluating the use of virtual reality on professional robotics education. In: 2017 IEEE 41st Annual Computer Software and Applications Conference (COMPSAC), vol. 1, pp. 448–455 (2017). https://doi.org/10.1109/COMPSAC.2017.121

16. Shu, B., Sziebig, G., Pieskä, S.: Human-robot collaboration: task sharing through virtual reality. In: IECON 2018–44th Annual Conference of the IEEE Industrial Electronics Society, pp. 6040–6044 (2018). https://doi.org/10.1109/IECON.2018.8591102

17. Tsetserukou, D., Hosokawa, S., Terashima, K.: Linktouch: a wearable haptic device with five-bar linkage mechanism for presentation of two-DOF force feedback at the fingerpad. In: 2014 IEEE Haptics Symposium (HAPTICS), pp. 307–312 (2014). https://doi.org/10.1109/HAPTICS.2014.6775473

18. Vallat, R.: Pingouin: statistics in python. J. Open Source Softw. **3**, 1026 (2018)
19. Zhang, C.: Investigation on motion sickness in virtual reality environment from the perspective of user experience. In: 2020 IEEE 3rd International Conference on Information Systems and Computer Aided Education (ICISCAE), pp. 393–396 (2020). https://doi.org/10.1109/ICISCAE51034.2020.9236907
20. Zhang, F., et al.: Mediapipe hands: on-device real-time hand tracking (2020)

Multi-modal Sensing-Based Interactive Glove System for Teleoperation and VR/AR

Xinwei Yao[1], Ming Chen[1], Chuan Cao[2], Lei Zhang[2], Wenzhen Yang[2(✉)], Mukherjee Mithun[3], and Hujun Bao[4]

[1] Faculty of Mechanical Engineering and Automation, Zhejiang Sci-Tech University, Hangzhou 310018, China
[2] Research Center for Humanoid Sensing, Zhejiang Lab, Hangzhou 311121, China
ccao@zhejianglab.com, ywz@zhejianglab.edu.cn
[3] School of Artificial Intelligence, Nanjing University of Information Science and Technology, Nanjing 210044, China
m.mukherjee@ieee.org
[4] The State Key Laboratory of CAD & CG, Zhejiang University, Hangzhou 310027, China
bao@cad.zju.edu.cn

Abstract. Haptic interaction is a fundamental approach to our perception surrounding people; at this stage, haptic interaction is mainly used in virtual reality (VR) and remote medical procedures (teleoperation). The traditional large volume, complex operation seriously affects the function of immersive. This paper develops a multi-modal sensing interactive glove system for teleoperation and VR/AR. The device is small in size and convenient to wear; we integrate temperature sensing and tactile sensing into our glove system and deliver real-time and accurate environmental signals to the wearer through the acquisition and processing of information and program-controlled regulation to better realize the fusion of virtual and real. This paper first introduces the structure and working principle of the system and analyzes its performance. Then a sensory experiment based on human hand skin was designed, and volunteers were selected to experience it.

Keywords: Teleoperation · VR/AR · Vibration · Temperature

1 Introduction

As one of the five senses for perceiving properties and motion, touch plays a vital role in our interaction with the world around us. In the past 30 years, with the development of computing platforms, haptic human-computer interaction has gone through three stages: desktop haptic, surface haptic, and wearable haptic. Representative products include Phantom force feedback devices, iPad, and Haptx Gloves [1].

This paper is supported by the National Key Research and Development Program of China (2021YFF0600203); the Zhejiang Provincial Natural Science Foundation (LY20F020019, LQ19F020012, LQ20F020001); the Zhejiang Basic Public Welfare Research Project (LGF19E050005); the Major Scientific Research Project of the Zhejiang Laboratory (2019MC0AD01, 2022MG0AC04).

© The Author(s), under exclusive license to Springer Nature Switzerland AG 2023
D. Wang et al. (Eds.): AsiaHaptics 2022, LNCS 14063, pp. 189–207, 2023.
https://doi.org/10.1007/978-3-031-46839-1_15

At present, VR/AR technology mainly simulates the process of actual operation and operating vision from vision and hearing, but it seldom introduces other channels such as touch and smell, which also reduces the experience of human-computer interaction. According to ergonomics, the most commonly used sensory media are visual (80%) and auditory (14%), followed by tactile and other channels (6%). Therefore, to improve the immersion and interaction in VR/AR technology, many researchers are trying to introduce other sensory channels such as touch, smell, and taste into the virtual world [2, 3], by analyzing the intrinsic advantages of immersion, interaction, and imagination of virtual reality system, and combining with the idea of engineering cybernetics, the human-computer interaction mechanism of multi-mode organic fusion of audio-visual and tactile for human intelligence enhancement is proposed.

Generally, a teleoperation system is a system that controls remote equipment to complete complex operations in an environment far from the operator under the control and participation of human beings. The operator plays a significant role in teleoperation. For teleoperating systems, tactile feedback devices are generally required for the auxiliary operation, mainly applied in extreme, hard-to-reach environments such as high temperature, high pressure, intense radiation, and suffocation [4]. Teleoperation technology is widely used to control and perceive intelligent devices in dangerous environments. The operator must fully communicate with the remote working environment to give full play to people's subjective initiative in teleoperation. Therefore, appropriate teleoperation equipment is crucial for safe operation [5].

Therefore, haptic feedback with human perception properties must be considered when telemanipulating in VR/AR applications. The operators can realize effective humanized interaction with the help of equipment to reduce or even avoid interaction delay, thereby improving the operability of the proposed system.

2   Related Work

The tactile sense plays a crucial role in perceiving the environment around humans. Current research and design have realized temperature, humidity, and vibration feedback from different levels in VR/AR and teleoperation systems.

For the design of the temperature haptic reproduction device, Tamura Y [6] made a semiconductor cooling piece into a temperature-sensing device close to the palm, which was used as a thermal display in the virtual reality system in large scenes to perceive heat distribution. Suppose only the temperature effect of temperature tactile reproduction is considered. In that case, the tactile feedback devices studied are usually bulky and inflexible, making them difficult to use in unique interactive scenes. Therefore, more researchers prefer a single finger's temperature tactile reproduction scheme. Hsin-Ni H [7] constructed a thermal model of fingers touching objects according to the temperature characteristics of human skin in 2006, which was used to predict the temperature response and heat flow exchange between skin and material surfaces when fingers are touching objects. Gallo S [8] designed a temperature display device that could present four independently controllable temperature displays at users' fingertips and proved that the temperature gradient of the device could be sensed. Fuimihiro [9] designed a one-finger tactile glove based on the tactile primary color theory [10]. The glove's binding force, vibration, and temperature can present the feeling from touch to deep pressure. Gabardi [11] designed a fingertip temperature rendering device that can move directionally around the fingertip, which can be used for transient thermal rendering in a virtual environment. In 2017, MurakamiT [12] developed a small fingertip tactile display integrating haptics and temperature feedback forces. The device is small in size and weighs less than 50 g. It is connected to a PC via a USB cable and can be used with VR or AR devices such as HoloLens, Oculus, and Leap Motion.

For the design of vibration tactile reproduction equipment, vibration-based tactile feedback is the most common reproduction way, through the vibration of different intensities and vibration of different frequencies to feedback the sense of touch. This vibration feedback method is generally arranged in data gloves, such as CyberTouch and VRTRIX data gloves are available on the market. Many small vibration sensors are placed on the finger or palm of the glove. Each vibration sensor can send out a single frequency or continuous vibration of different intensities. And each small vibration sensor is independent of the other. Tactile feedback based on the ultrasonic pulse is formed using ultrasonic touch or changing the ultrasonic frequency in different tactile feedback, even can simulate the shape of a virtual object because ultrasonic pressure will produce deformation and simulate a kind of pressure; the pressure is known as the "acoustic emission force," make the skin stimulates the sense of touch is the force and can vary the intensity of the ultrasound to create a different understanding of touch. For example, T Watanable [13]. Used ultrasound to generate the sense of touch, which can sense the roughness of the surface of an object.

In terms of the design of teleoperation equipment, cutting-edge technologies were applied in space teleoperation. In 1986, the German Aerospace Center launched the Roboter Technology Experiment program [14], and the robot system developed included a slave end manipulator, manipulator, and slave end auxiliary camera. By the ground space center, teleoperation control and complete the grasp, capture, and other tests. However, in some extreme environments, the current teleoperation equipment can not timely transmit the environmental information of the manipulator in the universe to the operator on the ground, resulting in failure that can not be repaired in time and causing certain economic losses. This system provides some ideas and schemes to solve these problems.

So far, the research work has achieved single tactile feedback in different situations, but there are still some shortcomings in the realization of teleoperation and the authenticity of VR/AR tactile feedback. Because there are many action areas of the actuator, researchers didn't discuss the perceived characteristics of the action area with the actuator, so it is difficult to establish a clear mapping relationship between the action of the actuator and skin perception resolution. These deficiencies limit the further application of multi-tactile feedback devices.

Combined with the research work on tactile feedback in the process of human-computer interaction, this paper analyzes the advantages and disadvantages of existing tactile reproduction devices and interaction methods and innovatively designs a multi-mode sensor interaction glove system, which can adapt to virtual scenes and remote control in VR equipment, operating system and verify the practicability of the overall system. According to the test results, the system designed in this paper shows good performance and effectively improves the 3I indicators of human-computer interaction.

The master-slave operation space of the system is matched to realize the tactile reproduction of the slave end, which improves the realism of the virtual scene and the safety and feasibility of remote control operation. It has made certain contributions to the integration of virtual reality technology and tactile perception and the integration of interactive devices and tactile reproduction devices.

3   Implementation of the Proposed Glove System

3.1   Overall Design

The design of the system with temperature and vibration feedback haptic gloves for VR/AR virtual reality and teleoperation intelligent perception is mainly divided into six functional modules: main controller module, actuators module, power module, Bluetooth wireless communication module, temperature detection module, and temperature display module. The central controller module and Bluetooth wireless communication module are in the communication module, and the actuators module and temperature detection and display module are in the feedback module to achieve the function of information reproduction and feedback. Virtual scene and optical fiber sensing gloves as two sets of systems and the reappearance glove is connected to accomplish the program download, wireless communication, temperature collection, and actuator driver functions. Figure 1 illustrates the block diagram of the system.

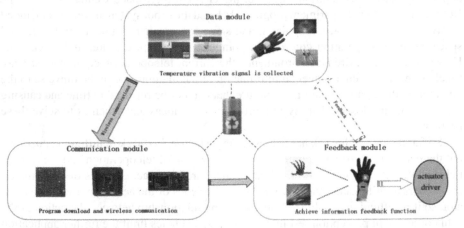

Fig. 1. Block diagram of the proposed system. The data, communication, and feedback modules comprise the system.

3.2   VR/AR System Design

The software platform of this system uses Unity3D to model virtual equipment such as beakers, glass bottles, glass rods, and other experimental environments such as tables, giving the operator an immersive feeling. We equipped various bionic functions of the scene in the virtual location. We used its particle system to simulate phenomena that would occur in the actual experimental setting, such as special effects of concentrated sulfuric acid liquid, aqueous solution, and the water vapor generated by heat release in the dilution process of concentrated sulfuric acid. Through C# script editing, the operator can complete the operation in the virtual scene according to their actual actions and strive to give the operator a more flexible and fully functional VR virtual scene platform. The Unity3D virtual scene system is shown in Fig. 2.

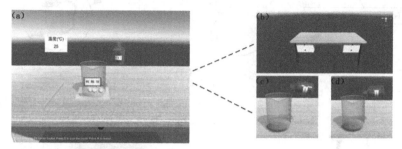

Fig. 2. Virtual scene system diagram. (a) Overall view of the system scenario. (b) Table diagram in the virtual scene. (c) and (d) Solution dumping effect diagram.

This system uses the reappearance glove to simulate temperature and vibration, and touch. The integrated circuit board of the central controller is designed, which mainly includes a power supply voltage stabilizer/buck circuit, microcontroller module, actuator driver circuit, and so on. Six interfaces (L1-L6) are arranged on the integrated circuit board, corresponding to the five finger-ends of the right hand (R1-R5) and the temperature module R6, respectively, used to connect the vibration motor and the Peltier component. The thermistor is placed on the contact area between the pay band and the back of the hand to ensure that it can accurately measure real-time temperature changes. The MicroUSB interface on the circuit board connects a small power battery to power the system while downloading the program. The OLED temperature display and integrated circuit control panel are placed in a housing on the back of the hand. Solidworks modeling diagram and physical diagram of gloves are shown in Fig. 3. This simple and small design can realize the stable operation of the components and ensure that we can carry out convenient maintenance in time when the details are damaged. Its small size allows it to be placed entirely on the arm, making it flexible to wear and adding to the manipulation experience.

3.3 Design of the Remote Operating System

The teleoperation system of augmented perception in virtual reality systems mainly includes the simulation of hand behavior and the perceptual feedback in the simulation process.

In the system, first of all, we need to collect the sensing data of the sensing gloves by the sensing equipment. In the glove system, the dynamic data of the environment can be obtained by the optical fiber sensing glove. In the optical fiber sensing glove, two kinds of

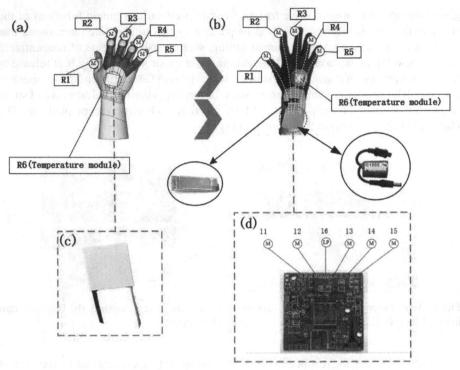

Fig. 3. Reappearance glove model and part drawings. (a) Solidworks modeling diagram. (b) The physical picture of gloves. (c) Peltier installation position diagram. (d) Biological illustration of the integrated circuit control board.

data can be obtained: temperature change data and pressure change data. We can get the actual change of the object touched by the current operator through real data, optical fiber passes through the pressure change in perception glove can produce a different intensity of electrical signals, then processing into a corresponding level data and sent via BLE Bluetooth to the vibration sensors on the reappearance glove, vibration sensors generate vibration feedback of varying intensity according to the grade data. The thermocouple temperature sensor in the sensing glove senses the change of the temperature signal of the object being touched, which is sent to the Peltier temperature sensor arranged on the reappearance glove through BLE Bluetooth, and the Peltier generates real-time temperature feedback according to different temperature signals. Before sending data from the sensing glove to the reappearance glove execution, we need to package the obtained data and then convert it into the reappearance glove execution instruction so that the glove execution element can work and feedback real-time temperature and vibration information.

The physical connection of the teleoperated glove system is shown in Fig. 4. Two fixed optical fibers are installed on both ends of the forefinger and thumb of the sensing glove, corresponding to the temperature and vibration module of the reappearance glove, respectively.

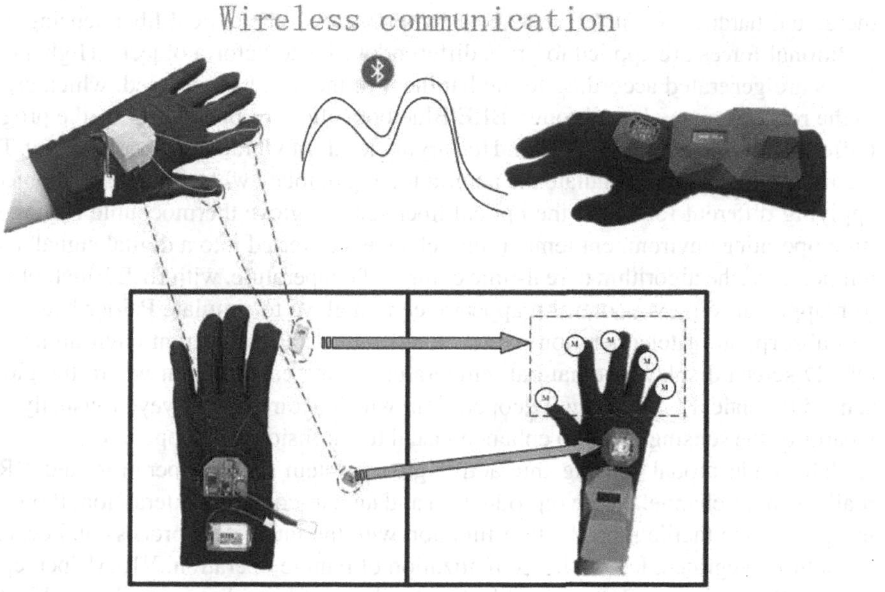

Fig. 4. Physical picture of teleoperation system. The one on the left is an optical fiber sensing glove, and the one on the right is a reappearance glove wireless connection via Bluetooth.

3.4 Working Principle of the System

The multi-modal sensing interactive glove system for teleoperation and VR/AR designed in this paper is applied to the system shown in Fig. 4, which is divided into VR/AR virtual scene platform multi-modal sensing and teleoperation platform sense.

VR/AR multi-modal sensing system can be divided into two parts: PC virtual scene platform and reappearance glove. We created the virtual scene in Unity3D and wrote the temperature and vibration functions generated during the virtual scene's virtual operation in the Script. Users by operating in our virtual scene, communication data wireless transmission from the PC serial port to reappear the glove, glove on the main controller integrated circuit decoding data, corresponding to different frequencies of vibration and vibration control motor control Peltier produce temperature changes, temperature changes reflect the temperature corresponding to the virtual scene, the feeling of being in cold or fever, enhance immersion in VR operations. The central controller integrated circuit temperature sensor module on the detected Peltier to stick on the surface of the module temperature and the temperature of the analog signal through the circuit transmission to the central controller; the main controller converts analog signals into digital signals and displays the surface temperature of the Peltier module through the temperature display module (OLED screen).

The teleoperation platform's sensing system is combined with the optical fiber sensing glove and the reappearance glove, which are integrated into one procedure to realize the feedback of vibration and temperature information. The optical fiber of the fiber sensing glove will produce different deformations under different forces of different sizes and directions. We convert various deformations into other electrical signals to simulate the actual hardness of different objects. When wearing the optical fiber sensing glove, additional forces are applied to press different objects to deform objects. High and low levels are generated according to the hardness of the objects contacted, which are sent to the reappearance glove through BLE Bluetooth after pre-processing by the program. Different levels of forces correspond to varying levels of vibration motor intensity. There are five levels (I–V) to simulate the natural feeling of touch when operating an object by applying different forces. In the optical fiber sensing glove thermocouple feeling real-time operating environment temperature change, converted into a digital signal and set temperature, the algorithm to real-time control of temperature, with BLE Bluetooth, sent to reappearance glove, control reappearance in a glove to simulate Peltier heat release and absorption of teleoperation natural temperature under different environment. The OLED screen displays the natural temperature of the environment where the glove is sensed by optical fiber during teleoperation, which is directly conveyed visually to the wearer of the sensing glove to enhance visual touch fusion in teleoperation.

The multi-modal sensing interactive glove system for teleoperation and VR/AR realizes multi-channel tactile reproduction and human-computer interaction. It proposes integrating the tactile reproduction function with the interactive process and designs a miniature integrated device. In the realization of remote operation, VR/AR perception, and intelligent fusion. We set the different hardness of virtual scene and real object as a tactile representation of varying stimulus intensity, feedback and control different real-time temperature, realize master-slave glove and virtual scene collocation to ensure that the tactile information imposed on users can express different meanings clearly. The system framework is shown in Fig. 5.

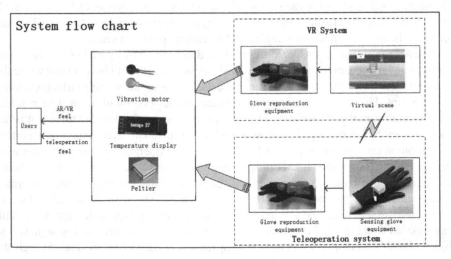

Fig. 5. Glove system framework

4 Functional Module Design for the VR/AR Glove System

4.1 Power Supply Module

The multi-modal sensing interactive glove system for teleoperation and VR/AR uses an independent power supply for main functional components such as BLE Bluetooth, central controller integrated circuit board, OLED temperature display, vibration element, and Peltier. The power supply uses a rechargeable polymer lithium battery (37 * 21 * 16 mm), capacity 1000 mAh, a rated voltage of 4.2–5.0 V, its maximum operating current is 1000 mA, and a voltage stabilizer/step-down circuit is designed on the integrated circuit board of the central controller, which can stably output 5 V and 3.3 V voltage. Available for BLE Bluetooth, OLED temperature display, vibration components, and Peltier. Calculate teleoperation and virtual scene duration, and mobile power supply can provide 1 h.

4.2 Reproducing the Glove Actuator Module

In this system, the vibration motor and the Peltier are controlled by adjusting the output voltage of the microcontroller. The glove system uses Pulse Width Modulation (PWM) method to adjust the output voltage of the microcontroller. The I/O port voltage of the microcontroller is 5 V, and the output PWM signal frequency is about 500 Hz.

4.2.1 Micro-vibrating Elements

The 0827 vibration motor is adopted for miniature vibration components. The specific structure is shown in Fig. 6, with an outer diameter of 8MM and a thickness of 2.7 mm. In Figures (a) and (b), the vibration components are installed inside and outside the finger end, and (c) is the three-dimensional modeling diagram of the structure of the vibration element. The small volume of these vibration components makes it convenient for us to fix it in the reproduction glove through sewing. It is distributed in the five-finger ends of the glove (R1-R5) and does not affect the wearer's experience to make it light. The vibration intensity experienced by the installation method of (b) is more comprehensive, and it is easier to sew it inside the finger sleeve of the glove. Therefore, the vibration components are installed fixedly (b) in the glove system. The micro-vibration motor can produce different vibration intensities according to the different voltage we input, which can be divided into (I-V) 5 vibration levels to feedback VR/AR virtual scene system and remote operating system finger end stress.

After the vibration motor is energized, the coil is torqued by the ampere force in the magnetic field generated by the permanent magnet, which drives the rotor with an eccentric counterweight to rotate in the magnetic field. Due to the rotor structure's uneven mass distribution, the rotor's center of gravity is constantly changing in the rotation process, resulting in exciting force and continuous vibration externally. Changing the current's direction can change the rotor's rotation direction. When the element is in direct current, the excitation force that can be generated is:

$$F = m \cdot r \cdot \omega^2 \tag{1}$$

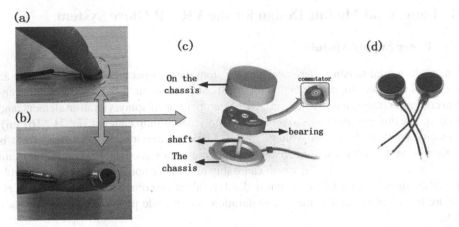

Fig. 6. Structure diagram of miniature Vibration components. (a), (b) position of vibration element. (c) structural modeling diagram of vibration element. (d) physical diagram of vibration element.

where m is the mass of eccentric counterweight, r is the rotational eccentricity, and ω is the rotational angular velocity.

The optical fiber sensing glove system uses an embedded STM32 microcontroller as the development platform, and the haptic reappearance glove system uses an embedded Arduino microcontroller as our development platform. The fiber optic and 0827 vibration motors are respectively arranged on two different integrated circuit boards. Wireless communication between the two integrated circuit boards is carried out through the self-made BLE Bluetooth module to separate the two parts of the haptic feedback system, and the haptic reappearance glove can be connected to the virtual scene on the PC side. The glove system is powered by a mobile power supply and can move freely.

Micro nanofiber is used to access the integrated circuit board for the fiber pressure sensing module. When a force of different sizes and directions is applied to the fiber, the fiber will bend in various degrees, corresponding to electrical signals of multiple degrees. We calibrated them into (1–5) levels and sent them to the haptic playback glove via BLE Bluetooth, corresponding to 5 levels of different vibration intensities of the flat vibration motor (I-V).

For the pressure reproduction module, we connected the flat vibration motor to the analog port of the integrated circuit board with Arduino chip as the central controller, deployed the vibration motor driving circuit, and then connected the integrated circuit board with BLE Bluetooth, through which the pressure signal of a virtual scene or the pressure signal of optical fiber glove could be obtained. The received data is checked first, and if the total length of the information is wrong, it is discarded. The sampling frequency we take is low, and the lost, useless data has little impact. When the data is mapped to the corresponding analog voltage, the vibration motor will produce different vibration intensity according to the change of the input analog quantity. The value of analog signal port input ranges from 0 to 255. We divide 0 to 255 into (I-V) five levels of different vibration intensity, that is, the pressure data of (1–5) levels in the corresponding VR/AR system and teleoperation system. The grades I, II, III, IV, and V intensity correspond to the five values 51, 102, 153, 204, and 255 written in the analog signal port, respectively. After our test, we can experience different vibration sensations.

4.2.2 Peltier Temperature Sensing Components

A semiconductor refrigeration sheet, also known as Peltier, is used in the haptic reappearance glove system. When the device has a current through, one side will heat up, and the other side will cool down, mainly caused by the thermoelectric effect of the conductor. Common thermoelectric effects are the See beck effect, Peltier effect, and Thomson effect, which belong to the conversion of electric energy and heat energy, simultaneous generation, and reversible process; in addition, the Joule effect and Fourier law belong to the two irreversible effect network of thermoelectric effect. We use the Peltier effect for cooling and heating, and the principle is shown in Fig. 7.

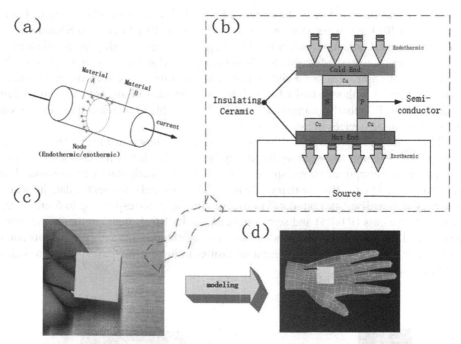

Fig. 7. Peltier schematic diagram. (a) Schematic diagram of Peltier effect, (d) working principle diagram, (c) Physical Peltier diagram, (d) Modeling diagram of Peltier in hand position.

In this glove system, Pulse Width Modulation (PWM) is used to control the work of the Peltier. PWM is a very compelling technology to control the analog circuit by using the digital output of the microprocessor. It can adjust the duty cycle, that is, the pulse width. When the duty ratio of the PWM signal increases, the driver controls the average voltage at both ends of the semiconductor, and the power of the semiconductor refrigeration chip increases. Conversely, when the duty ratio of the PWM signal decreases, the average voltage at both ends of the semiconductor refrigeration chip decreases, and its refrigeration power also decreases.

In the VR/AR operating system, Peltier can receive the virtual temperature signal generated when the virtual scene changes and adjust the working power of Peltier through the fixed duty cycle so that the Peltier module of the haptic reproduction glove hand back can generate the actual temperature matching the virtual scene.

In the teleoperation system, the thermocouple temperature sensor on the optical fiber sensing glove senses the real-time temperature change data and sends the temperature signal to the tactile reappearance glove through BLE Bluetooth. The temperature signal is adjusted to different pulse widths in the reappearance glove integrated circuit board, and the power of the Peltier is controlled to produce different degrees of cold and hot sensation.

4.3 Design of Bluetooth Communication Module

The communication module of the system adopts Mesh Bluetooth networking technology born in 2014 and Bluetooth low power technology (BLE) based on Bluetooth 4.0 protocol standard, which is widely used in wearable devices, intelligent mobile terminals, and other devices. Mesh Bluetooth networking technology is commonly used in the Internet of Things, featuring high scalability, reliability, robust security, and connectivity. Compared with standard Bluetooth transparent transmission, it can also realize many-to-many Bluetooth communication, which is suitable for wireless communication between multiple devices in many scenarios.

The system adopts the BLE Bluetooth module, as shown in Fig. 8. The working voltage is 3.3 V, and the working frequency is 2.4 GHZ. It has the characteristics of low power consumption, strong signal, small size, and stable data transmission. The data transmitted by the Bluetooth module is hexadecimal and contains the data information header. Usually, "start bit+data" means sending data corresponding to 5 miniature vibration elements (R1-R5) and semiconductor cooler R6 arranged in the haptic reappearance glove. Realize the independent action of the components and generate vibration and temperature stimulation of different intensities following the sensory characteristics of human skin.

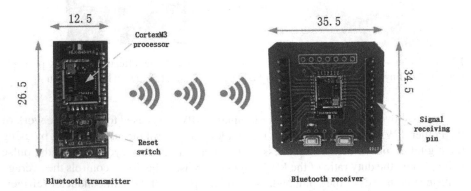

Fig. 8. Physical picture of BLE Bluetooth

The coding part of the Arduino program is completed on the PC side, which is divided into two stages. First, the input String data is encoded, and then the encoded data is converted into hexadecimal for BLE Bluetooth module transmission. The coding part will format the control data transmitted from the PC end to the integrated circuit control board, and the standard data format of the whole protocol is as follows (Table 1):

Starting Indicator+Peltier working grade+Peltier cooling/heating+AAAAA.

Table 1. Control data information

Data Type	Value or range
Start Indicator	==9
Peltier working grade	0–5
Peltier Working mode	0–2
Vibration components working grade	0–5

Among them, the Peltier work grade is divided into 1–5 steps, from low to high, representing the speed of temperature change: Peltier cooling/heating data format is set as 1 and 2, mode 1 is a cooling mode, mode 2 is heating mode; AAAAA can be 1–5 grades, namely 11111–55555, from low to high, representing different vibration intensity stimulation, corresponding to VR scenes and different object hardness in teleoperation.

4.4 Temperature Detection and Temperature Display Module

In the multi-modal sensing interactive glove system, the Peltier is placed on the back of the hand. To prevent damage to the skin caused by heating and cooling processes, we need to add a temperature detection module to measure the surface temperature of the Peltier on the skin side. According to the characteristics of the temperature sensor, we adopt a contact thermal resistance sensor. Among them, the thermal resistance sensor is divided into positive and negative temperature coefficients; the resistance value of the former increases with the increase of temperature, and the negative temperature coefficient means that the resistance decreases with the rise of temperature. The Temperature measuring module of the glove system adopts a Negative Temperature Coefficient (NTC) thermistor. Its measurement range is $-40\ °C$ to $300\ °C$ temperature value, resistance accuracy $\pm 1\%$, rated power 45 mW, meets the temperature requirements of Peltier.

The temperature display module adopts 0.91-in. Organic Light-emitting Diode (OLED) screen. Compared with the traditional LED and LCD, the thickness of THE OLED display module can be designed to be less than 1 mm. Moreover, OLED has a luminous field of $170°$.

5 System Effect Verification

5.1 Temperature Change Effect

To better measure the heating or cooling performance of pars, one side of the pars is coated with cooling silicon grease, and the heat sink is installed. Working under rated conditions, we record the temperature change of the surface of Peltier every 5 s. Here is the Peltier cooling curve in the cooling mode, as shown in Fig. 9, while the heating curve is the opposite. Due to the working principle of Peltier, the temperature of Peltier will rise to some extent with the increase of time. We took the temperature drop in the first 60 s as the cooling period and adopted the PID algorithm to control the temperature. At the same time, the difference in temperature change produced by the Peltier module under different duty cycles was tested, and the temperature data was automatically recorded every 5 s. See Fig. 10. We find that the temperature change is most apparent when the duty cycle is 255.

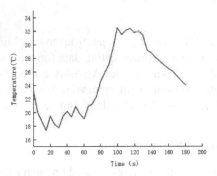

Fig. 9. Temperature curve variation figure

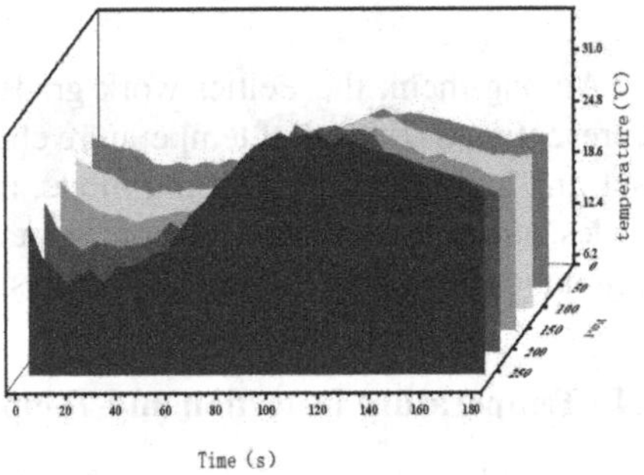

Fig. 10. Temperature change diagram at different duty ratios

5.2 Vibration Change Effect

In order to better measure the vibration performance of the vibration element, we designed the vibration element test experiment. In the experiment, an acceleration sensor is used to collect vibration acceleration data of the miniature vibration element when the output voltage duty ratio is 100% (255), as shown in Fig. 11. It can be seen that the excitation force generated by the eccentric structure can be used to deliver different vibration sensations. We artificially divided the vibration grade into five grades (I-V). The experimenter wore a gloved system to experience vibration at different levels and told the experimenter about the vibration levels experienced. Under the condition of teleoperation and VR/AR scene, we designed five kinds of object hardness, soft, a little soft, medium, a little hard, and hard (20%, 40%, 60%, 80%, 100%), corresponding to the vibration element (I-V) 5 grades. At the beginning of the teleoperation experiment, we applied different forces to the optical fiber end of the fiber sensing glove to simulate five approximate hardness, and the wearer would tell the corresponding vibration level after the glove felt vibration. At the beginning of the VR/AR virtual scene experiment, we set conditions in the virtual environment to simulate five approximate hardness, the wearer operates the keyboard buttons themselves, and tell the corresponding vibration level conveyed by different approximate hardness. The experimental results are shown in Fig. 12.

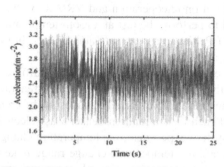

Fig. 11. Duty cycle change of 100% acceleration data change

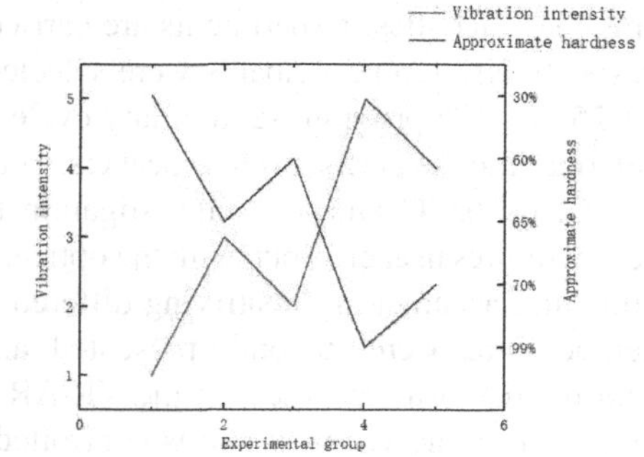

Fig. 12. Vibration effect experience results

6   User Experience and Experimental Conclusions

Different intensities of stimuli represent different information, so correctly distinguishing vibration and temperature stimuli of varying intensity is essential. The experiment of temperature perception and tactile perception using the tactile reproduction glove interactive system can analyze the sensitivity of the device, and explore the judgment ability of the human hand skin to vibration, touch, and temperature stimuli and the feasibility of the device. We used the glove interactive system to conduct the perceptual discrimination experiment of temperature stimulus and vibration stimulus, respectively. The experimental process is shown in Fig. 13 below.

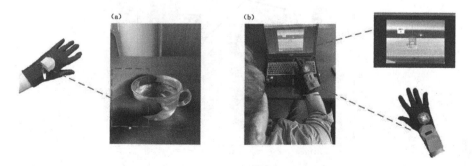

Fig. 13. Experimental operation scene diagram

6.1 Remote Operation and VR/AR System Temperature and Vibration Sensing Experiments

The remote operation module of the glove system designs a temperature sensor on the back of the hand, which displays the real-time perceived temperature on the OLED screen. This experiment was designed to detect the accuracy of signals and the sensitivity of temperature in teleoperation transmission and to study the skin temperature sensing characteristics. Experiments are carried out on teleoperation and VR/AR systems, respectively. Ten participants were selected to perform the test at a room temperature of 25 °C. The program set the duty cycle of Peltier to a constant value of 255. In the teleoperation experiment, five beakers were placed respectively at 5 °C, 20 °C, 35 °C, 50 °C, and 65 °C. During the investigation, the experimenter held the beakers of different temperatures in each group with the optical fiber sensing glove and recorded the reaction time and accuracy of identifying different temperature levels. The grades of different temperatures were randomly presented, and each time a random beaker was selected, and the data was recorded. In the VR/AR system experiment, the temperature change imposed on the virtual scene is controlled, and the temperature change range is kept within 5 °C; 20 °C, 35 °C, 50 °C, and 65 °C. Wear the reappearance glove to operate in the virtual environment, and the corresponding temperature values appear step by step. The response time and accuracy of different temperature levels were recorded when the temperature data of the virtual scene was recorded. The rise and fall of temperature is a gradual process with a slow time. When the temperature reaches equilibrium, the test is repeated, and the stimulus maintenance time is in the 30 s. Each test should be conducted at an interval of 1 min to dissipate the residual temperature in the glove and avoid affecting the perception of the second temperature measurement. Experimental data are shown in Fig. 14.

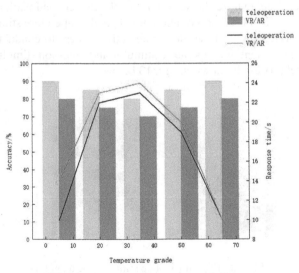

Fig. 14. Temperature experimental diagram

The experimental results are roughly identical in the teleoperation and VR/AR systems. Temperature stimuli at 5 °C and 65 °C showed the shortest recognition time and the highest accuracy, and the errors mainly occurred at 20 °C–50 °C, which indicated that subjects were most sensitive to the change of extreme temperature but not to the intermediate temperature. The experimental results show that the operator's discrimination of temperature is more accurate, which also proves that the teleoperation and VR/AR system work normally, but there are some problems such as slow reaction time and individual temperature perception errors, so for most people, the temperature reproduction effect is accurate.

This glove system has designed five vibration sensing sources in five fingers. To detect the real-time accuracy of telemanipulation in VR/AR systems, we selected 10 participants to experiment without experience. In the remote operation experiment, the recorder wore the optical fiber sensing glove on his left hand, and the subject wore the reappearance glove on his right hand. The recorder controls the optical fiber sensing glove to emit different pressures, if the reappearance glove can feel the different vibration intensity, the subject tells the corresponding intensity to the recorder, who records the subject's response. In the VR/AR system, the force applied (essential duration) in the virtual scene is controlled and divided into (I-V) vibration levels like in the remote operation experiment. Wearing the reappearance glove is operated in the virtual environment, the corresponding vibration intensity value appears step by step, and the reaction time and accuracy of different vibration intensity experiences are recorded. Six experiments were performed for each stimulus, and each subject performed 30 experiments in each round, and these 30 stimuli were presented in random order. The experimental data are shown in Fig. 15.

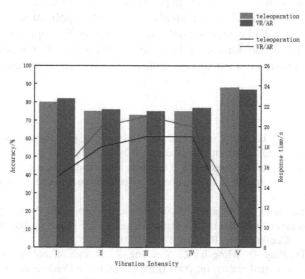

Fig. 15. Vibration experiment diagram

Analysis of the experimental results shows that the subjects' response time and accuracy rate are higher for low-intensity and high-intensity vibration stimuli, and the intermediate intensity discrimination accuracy rate is the lowest. This result is similar to the temperature stimulation experiment, indicating that the extreme vibration intensity is easier to distinguish, and the response time and accuracy are significantly higher than that of the temperature experiment. Therefore, in our system, when the vibration intensity changes from low to high, the experimenter can feel the apparent change of vibration tactile sensation. The experiment proves the feasibility and accuracy of teleoperation tactile sensing.

7 Conclusion

This paper has designed a multi-modal sensory interactive glove system for teleoperation in VR/AR. The system is small and light and integrates two functions to facilitate the operator to wear perception. At the same time, we realize the multiple-tactile feedback following the skin perception characteristics of the action area. In this way, the proposed system improves the sense of reality and immersion in the tactile feedback. Based on the traditional haptic feedback method, it is enhanced and extended and has specific progressive nature. Six integrated actuators indicate that the system can realize multiple tactile feedback. According to the recognition accuracy, the system overcomes the shortcomings of the traditional tactile feedback research, such as the simple action mode of actuators, which do not conform to the skin perception characteristics.

The field experience of the user's test of the glove system shows that the temperature and vibration sensors have specific stability and exhibit the sensory characteristics of human hand skin. With low cost and high performance, the device can not only be used as a teleoperation tactile control device but also as a VR/AR application tactile experience device. Our system will play an essential role in virtual medical operation, telemedicine work, virtual training, and other fields by adding tactile information based on traditional audio-visual experience and enhancing multi-human-machine integration.

References

1. Wang, D., Guo, Y., Liu, S., Zhang, Y., Xiao, J.: Haptic display for virtual reality: progress and challenges. Virtual Real. Intell. Hardware 1(2), 136–162 (2019)
2. Niedenthal, S., P Lundén, Ehrndal, M., Olofsson, J.: A handheld olfactory display for smell-enabled VR games. In: IEEE International Symposium on Olfaction and Electronic Nose, pp. 1–4 (2019)
3. Narumi, T., Kajinami, T., Nishizaka, S., Tanikawa, T., Hirose, M.: Pseudo-gustatory display system based on cross-modal integration of vision, olfaction and gustation. In: 2011 IEEE Virtual Reality Conference (VR), pp. 127–130 (2011)
4. Cheng-jun, D., Ping, D., Ming-lu, Z., Yan-fang, Z.: Design of mobile robot teleoperation system based on virtual reality. In: 2009 IEEE International Conference on Automation and Logistics, pp. 2024–2029 (2009)
5. Verna, D.: Virtual reality and tele-operation: a common framework. In: World Multiconference on Systemics, Cybernetics and Informatics (SCI 2001) v.3: Emergent Computing and Virtual Engineering, pp. 499–504 (2001)

6. Tamura, Y., Fujiwara, S., Umetani, T., Nakamura, H.: Bracelet-shaped thermal display for representing numerical data. J. Electron. Mater. **40**(5), 823–829 (2011)
7. Ho, H. N., Jones, L. A.: Thermal model for hand-object interactions. Haptic interfaces for virtual environment and teleoperator systems, pp. 461–467(2006)
8. Simon, G., Giulio, R., Laura, S. C., Tristan, V., Olaf, B., Hannes, B.: Encoded and crossmodal thermal stimulation through a fingertip-sized haptic display. Front. Robot. AI **2**(25) (2015)
9. Kato, F., Inoue, Y., Tachi, S.: Haptic display glove capable of force/vibration/temperature. In: 2019 IEEE International Symposium on Measurement and Control in Robotics (ISMCR), D2–2 (2019)
10. Tachi, S., Mlnamlzawa, K., Furukawa, M., Fernando, C.L.: Haptic media construction and utilization of human-harmonized "tangible" information environment. In: International Conference on Artificial Reality & Telexistence, pp. 145–150 (2013)
11. Gabardi, M., Leonardis, D., Solazzi, M., Frisoli, A.: Development of a miniaturized thermal module designed for integration in a wearable haptic device. In: 2018 IEEE Haptics Symposium (HAPTICS), pp. 100–105 (2018)
12. Murakami, T., Person, T., Fernando, C.L., Minamizawa, K.: Altered touch: miniature haptic display with force, thermal and tactile feedback for augmented haptics. In: ACM SIGGRAPH 2017 Emerging Technologies, pp. 1–2 (2017)
13. Watanabe, T., Fukui, S.: A method for controlling tactile sensation of surface roughness using ultrasonic vibration. In: Proceedings of 1995 IEEE International Conference on Robotics and Automation, pp. 1134–1139 (1995)
14. Elhajj, I., et al.: Haptic information in internet-based teleoperation. Trans. Mechatron. IEEE/ASME **6**(3), 295–304 (2001)

Haptic Guidance for Robot Arm Teleoperation Using Ray-Based Holistic Collision Avoidance

Hyunsoo Kim⬛, Wonjung Park⬛, Taeyun Woo⬛, and Jinah Park(✉)⬛

Korea Advanced Institute of Science and Technology, Daejeon, Korea
{khskhs,fabiola,taeyun.woo,jinahpark}@kaist.ac.kr

Abstract. We present a haptic guidance system for teleoperating a robot arm controlled by inverse kinematics. Unlike drones or vehicles, a robot arm occupies 3D space dynamically changing with its various configurations. With limited information on the remote environment and its current configuration, the remotely controlled robot arm has a higher chance of colliding with the surroundings. Consequently, users need to maintain a high level of attention, which results in fatigue during operation. In this paper, we propose a system of haptic force guidance that is robust to both the robot arm configuration and its surroundings. Our system first computes the guiding forces at multiple points in the robot arm using ray-based depth sampling. Then, haptic force feedback is generated by aggregating guiding forces using a motion-based approximate Jacobian. Our system requires minimal prior information about the environment and the robot arm. Moreover, the proposed ray-based depth sampling method is more efficient in computation time than the widely used potential field-based approach. User studies show that our system reduces the risk of collisions, as well as the mental workload during teleoperation in a virtual environment.

Keywords: haptic force guidance · teleoperation · robot arm

1 Introduction

Controlling a robot arm in teleoperation is not a trivial task. The challenge comes from the lack of operators' understanding of the surrounding environment. With the most basic setup, the operator receives limited information about the remote environment through a 2D display. Insufficient surrounding information causes fatigue due to high attention levels and hazards of collisions between the robot arm and the objects/structures in a remote environment.

H. Kim, W. Park and T. Woo—These authors contributed equally.

© The Author(s), under exclusive license to Springer Nature Switzerland AG 2023
D. Wang et al. (Eds.): AsiaHaptics 2022, LNCS 14063, pp. 208–225, 2023.
https://doi.org/10.1007/978-3-031-46839-1_16

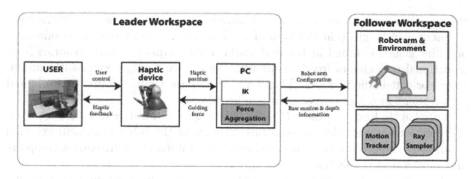

Fig. 1. System overview. Our haptic guidance system assists robot arm teleoperation. Motion and depth information from pre-defined sampling points (green dots) are computed in the follower workspace. The PC in the leader workspace generates haptic force by aggregating the information to prevent potential collisions on any part of the robot arm. (Color figure online)

Previous studies have shown that additional information helps the user better understand the remote environment, and reduces worker fatigue and potential hazards. For example, several studies [1, 7, 21, 22] show that visual cues enhance situational awareness in virtual and augmented reality. In addition, auditory or tactile feedback [16, 19] is proposed to alert workers in dangerous situations. Moreover, among these modalities, some research [2, 5, 13, 14] shows that haptic force feedback can provide richer information by providing direct and active guidance to the user.

To allow the benefits of force feedback in wide use cases, we focus on the robustness of the haptic force feedback system with respect to both the environment and the robot arm configurations. (See Fig. 1 for our system overview.) Here, a robust system means that the haptic guidance system is easy to incorporate into various teleoperation situations regardless of the representation of

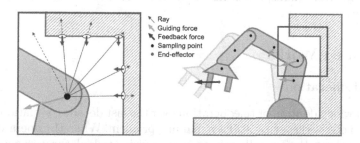

Fig. 2. Overview of our method. *Left.* Distance and normal information about the environment near a sampling point is gathered via multiple rays cast from the point. Distances and normals are then processed into a guiding force. *Right.* Haptic feedback to a user-controlled end-effector is generated by combining the guiding forces from multiple points on the robot arm.

the environment and robot arm. For example, the 3D representation of the environment may be given in the form of meshes in simulated virtual environments, or point clouds scanned in the real world. Robot arms can vary in forms from traditional 6 degree-of-freedom manipulators to emerging redundant manipulators or soft-bodied robots. Therefore, we designed our system with minimal assumptions in mind to accommodate broad cases.

Our haptic force feedback (Fig. 2), which guides the user away from potential collisions at the selected positions throughout the robot arm, achieves high robustness using these two proposed methods: ray-based environment sampling and motion-based Jacobian approximation.

The ray-based environment sampling method, depicted in Fig. 2 (*Left*), acquires information about the surroundings by casting rays. Then, a guiding force(green) is generated that directs away from the collisions.

With our motion-based Jacobian approximation method, guiding forces from multiple sampling points can be correctly combined into single haptic force feedback(purple), as illustrated in Fig. 2 (*Right*). It estimates the Jacobian of the robot arm of unknown configuration by the relative motion of the joints. Our method ensures that the haptic force feedback at the end-effector makes the sampled points move along the desired direction (guiding force) of each point.

To validate our haptic guidance, user study was conducted in multiple virtual environments and robot arm configurations. The user study shows that our system helps reduce mental workload and collisions during a robot arm teleoperation task. Also, our Jacobian approximation is more comfortable than the exact Jacobian method without degrading the accuracy.

The main contributions of our work are as follows.

- A novel haptic force feedback guidance system for teleoperation of a robot arm,
- A ray-based environment sampling algorithm for robustly collecting information from the surrounding environment with minimal interface, and
- A motion-based Jacobian approximation method to transform the guiding directions from multiple points on the robot arm to the user-controlled end-effector.

2   Related Works

2.1   Teleoperation

Despite a wide adoption of teleoperation over the last decades, situational awareness of remote workspace is still a remaining problem. When the operator manipulates the robots, they usually rely on camera vision to look through a workspace. However, the camera offers insufficient views due to constraints from the robot and the environment [4].

Some studies on teleoperation have incorporated auxiliary visual feedback to compensate for the lack of representation of the remote workspace [1,7,21,22]. For example, Walker et al. [21] reduce task completion time using an augmented reality interface that shows the predicted robot movement. Furthermore, Yew et al. [22] show that visual aids using augmented reality enhance situational awareness and reduce cognitive load during the teleoperation of robot manipulators.

Tactile feedback is also utilized as an additional modality in teleoperation. Hikaru et al. [16] improve the maneuverability of construction robots by delivering vibrations of remote robots through a vibrotactile display. In addition, two-dimensional haptic guidance using a fingertip tactile display is suggested for robot manipulator teleoperation [19].

Although visual and tactile feedback augments the information of a remote workspace, they are not suitable for active guidance or direct intervention. To be more specific, haptic tactile feedback can only convey coarse and low-dimensional information. Therefore, we focus on 3 degrees-of-freedom haptic force feedback, which not only augments remote workspace information, but also provides 3-dimensional direct guidance.

2.2   Haptic Force Feedback in the Teleoperation

Some studies have shown that haptic force feedback increases telepresence for mobile robots [2,5,13,14] and robot manipulators [3,8,9,20,23]. For example, haptic force feedback helps surgeons improve their performance and safety [11,15,17,18] in teleoperated surgery. Haptic force feedback usually expresses the surroundings of the end-effector in previous studies. However, the system needs to regard collision-free maneuvering of the entire robot body for stable multi-joint robot manipulator teleoperation.

The potential field-based method is presented as a real-time obstacle avoidance approach for manipulators and mobile robots by Khatib [10]. Further studies have adopted the potential field-based approach to prevent collisions between robot manipulators and obstacles [6,12]. However, their use in dynamic remote workspaces is limited as prior knowledge of the environment is required to define the potential fields of each obstacle.

To overcome these issues, we suggest haptic force feedback that guides the user away from potential collisions of the entire robot body with minimal prior knowledge of the environment.

3   Ray-Based Holistic Collision Avoidance Haptic Feedback

The proposed system provides haptic guidance to users to better understand the remote environment during the teleoperation of the robot manipulator controlled by inverse kinematics (IK).

We designed the system with the following in mind. First, the system should produce a force feedback that guides a user away from potential collisions between the environment and the entire manipulator. Second, the system should be less restrictive, and robust to the configurations of the environment and the

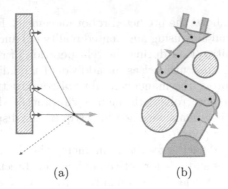

(a)   (b)

Fig. 3. (a) Weighted-averaging normals (green) produce the better guiding force than directions (red). (b) A case when the simple addition of guiding forces fails. Forces from symmetric obstacles cancel each other, failing to guide the end-effector moving further upward. (Color figure online)

robot arm. Finally, the system should be easily implemented on common hardware.

The system computes the haptic force feedback by generating and aggregating forces from sampling points on the manipulator. Sampling points are set by the operator prior to use. At each sampling point, information about the surrounding environment, such as distances and normals, is collected by ray casting. Given the information, the force is generated to guide the point further from the closest surface, a potential collision. Because users control the manipulator via IK, forces from sampling points need to be aggregated in such a manner that the most sampling points move along their desired direction as the user moves the end-effector.

In this section, we first discuss the detailed algorithm to generate forces from sampling points on the manipulator (Sect. 3.1). We then discuss the algorithm for aggregating forces into haptic force feedback to be output by the haptic device (Sect. 3.2). Finally, we explain how we implement and optimize algorithms for our hardware and software platform configuration (Sect. 3.3).

3.1   Ray-Based Environment Sampling

We consider the following two conditions to generate the force at a given point. One is that the force should be collision preventing, that is, repulsive. This means that the force must guide the point further away from the closest surface. The other is that the force generation algorithm must be robust to the environment, which means that it handles various forms and changes in environments.

To comply with the robustness condition, we choose ray-based sampling to gather information about the surroundings. Ray-based sampling provides an abstract interface to the environment, regardless of its representation. It can also be easily optimized with graphics hardware. Moreover, ray-based sampling can be performed in the real world by using depth cameras or LiDAR sensors.

With a ray-based sampling scheme, the force generation algorithm from a sampling point is defined as follows. First, the rays are cast starting from the point to the surrounding environment. These rays produce the closest distances from the point to the environment and the surface normals at the closest point. Then, the guiding forces are determined by distances and normals of each ray casting result. Finally, the guiding forces of each ray are aggregated to generate the final haptic force feedback for the point, as depicted in Fig. 2 (left).

For the guiding direction of a single ray, we choose the surface normal direction at the hit point. The opposite of the ray direction is also a possible choice, and in this case, the resulting force will behave similarly to the Coulomb force. However, as shown in Fig. 3a, this force (red) tends to guide the point farther away from the masses rather than collisions. Surface normal direction guides the point correctly away from the potential collision, as previous potential field approaches do.

The guiding magnitude from a single ray is determined solely by the distance from the ray origin (which is the sampling point) to the ray hit point. To provide effective guidance, this distance-to-magnitude function must be positive, decreasing and vanishing. For example, $1/d^2$ is used, which gives the Coulomb force. However, it explodes as $d \to 0$ and does not vanish for finite values. Thus, for ease of computation, the function is also enforced to be finite and vanish after a certain threshold. In practice, a configurable curve is used for the magnitude function. Combining direction and magnitude, the guiding force F_k of a ray r_k from a sampling point p_i is calculated as

$$F_k = W\left(|q_k - p_i|\right) \hat{n}_{q_k}, \tag{1}$$

where $W : \mathbb{R}^+ \to \mathbb{R}^+$ is the magnitude function, q_k is the hit point of r_k in the environment and $\hat{n}_{q_k}$ is the surface normal at q_k of length 1. We use a simple quadratic decreasing function $W(d) = W_{max}\left[1 - \left(\frac{d}{d_0}\right)^2\right]$ for $0 \le d \le d_0$ as a magnitude function.

The aggregation combines the guiding directions and magnitudes of all rays into a single guiding force for the point. Simply averaging all guiding vectors performs poorly, as many near-zero vectors may dilute a few but significantly important vectors. The resulting force has to emphasize significant vectors rather than insignificant ones. Thus, the guiding force F_i at a sampling point p_i is computed with the following weighted average equation:

$$F_i = \frac{\sum_{k=0}^{M} w_k F_k}{\sum_{k=0}^{M} w_k}, \tag{2}$$

where M denotes the number of rays per sampling point and w_k is the weight, which weighs significant forces even more. We used $w_k = |F_k|$ as the weight function.

3.2   Motion-Based Jacobian Approximation

After generating the guiding forces from multiple sampling points using the above algorithm, the forces are aggregated again into the final haptic feedback guiding the end-effector that the user controls.

We considered the following two constraints for the force aggregation algorithm. One is that the feedback should guide the end-effector so that the near-collision part of a robot arm gets farther from the collision as the IK controls the robot arm. The other is that the algorithm should be robust to the various robot arm manipulators, regardless of their configurations or IK methods.

A simple addition of force vectors from sampling points is an option. More precisely,

$$F = \sum_{i=0}^{N} F_i,$$

where F is the haptic feedback to guide the end-effector, N is the number of total sampling points and F_i is the feedback from the sampling point p_i. However, the simple addition fails to prevent collisions. This is because the manipulator is controlled from a single end-effector using IK. When the end-effector moves along a guiding force at one sampling point, the sampling point is not guaranteed to move to the collision-avoiding direction unless the movement relationship between the end-effector and the sampling point is considered. In specific cases, such as the one depicted in Fig. 3b, the simple addition may cancel forces from multiple sampling points, resulting in no guidance to the end-effector.

Therefore, the forces generated at the sampling points are transformed accordingly considering the movement relationship between the corresponding sampling points and the end-effector, or

$$F = \sum_{i=0}^{N} T_{p_i \to e} (F_i),$$

where $T_{p_i \to e}$ is a vector transformation from the sampling point p_i to the end-effector e.

The movement relation between two points p_i, p_j can be expressed via Jacobian matrix

$$J_{ij} = \frac{dp_j}{dp_i}.$$

Because p_i and p_j are on a robotic manipulator, their positions are functions of the configuration $q \in \mathbb{R}^M$, which is denoted as $p_i = C_i(q)$. If C is known, J_{ij} can be calculated using the chain rule as follows:

$$J_{ij} = \frac{dp_j}{dp_i} \tag{3}$$

$$= \frac{dp_j}{dq} \frac{dq}{dp_i} \tag{4}$$

$$= \frac{dp_j}{dq} \left(\frac{dp_i}{dq}\right)^{-1}. \tag{5}$$

However, $\frac{dp_i}{dq} \in \mathbb{R}^{3 \times M}$ is, in most cases, not invertible. Therefore, instead the right pseudoinverse of the matrix is used, which is defined as

$$A^+ = A^T (AA^T)^{-1}$$

for a matrix $A \in \mathbb{R}^{m \times n}$.

Using an exact Jacobian for aggregation has a few issues. Computing Jacobian requires complete knowledge of the configuration $C_i(q)$. In addition, Jacobian matrices are sometimes numerically unstable or even explode to infinity. For the haptic perception, Jacobian matrices do not need to be as precise as those for the IK method. Therefore, we used the approximate Jacobian from the velocities of the points.

An exact Jacobian matrix transforms the velocity from one point to another point, which means

$$v_j = J_{ij} v_i,$$

where $v_i, v_j \in \mathbb{R}^3$ are the velocity of points in the robot arms, $p_i, p_j \in \mathbb{R}^3$, respectively. We make our approximate Jacobian to comply with this property while reducing the degrees of freedom. An exact Jacobian has 9 degrees of freedom (DoF). By approximating Jacobian using an orthonormal matrix (or a rotation matrix), the DoF decreases to 3. Velocities from two points can determine 2 DoF, which leaves ambiguity of 1 DoF to fully determine orthonormal Jacobian. Assuming that no twist with respect to the velocity vectors can remove the ambiguity and gives the Jacobian matrix, which is a rotation matrix of which the axis is parallel to the cross-product of v_i and v_j and the angle is equal to the angle between v_i and v_j.

The velocities of points are often too noisy, resulting rapidly changing Jacobian matrix. To solve this, the Jacobian matrix can be approximated using an exponential moving average (EMA) of the velocity, or

$$\tilde{v}_i \leftarrow \alpha \tilde{v}_i + (1 - \alpha) v_i,$$

where $\tilde{v}_i$ is the EMA of the velocity v_i and $\alpha \in (0, 1)$ is the decaying parameter. α closer to 1 gives a smoother but slower update of $\tilde{v}_i$.

However, EMA does not resolve the issues that arise when the velocity becomes zero for a while, where the rotation matrix is not well defined. Therefore, we change the EMA coefficient so that $\tilde{v}_i$ remains when $|v_i|$ is nearly zero. Specifically, we let $\alpha = \exp(-\beta |v_i|)$, where $\beta \in (0, \infty)$ is a coefficient that determines the volatility of $\tilde{v}_i$. Higher β gives fast-varying and possibly noisy $\tilde{v}_i$. Given the smoothed velocities, the Jacobian matrix becomes

$$J_{ij} = \texttt{RotationMatrix} \left(\tilde{v}_i \times \tilde{v}_j, \cos^{-1} \left(\frac{\tilde{v}_i \cdot \tilde{v}_j}{|\tilde{v}_i||\tilde{v}_j|} \right) \right). \tag{6}$$

Similar to the aggregating guiding forces from rays for a sampling point, the aggregated result must preserve significant forces and not be diluted by near-zero forces from sampling points. Thus, the weighted average is also used to combine forces from the sampling points. More precisely,

$$F = \sum_{i=0}^{N} w_i J_{ij} F_i,$$

where $w_i = W(|F_i|)$ is a weight determined by an increasing curve W and the magnitude of the feedback $|F_i|$.

3.3 Implementation

The system is implemented on the Unity platform, using Geomagic Touch for the IK input and haptic output. We optimize the force generation algorithm using the rasterization graphics pipeline, similar to the shadow mapping technique. At each sampling point, ray sampling is done by a set of cameras that render the depth and normal of the surrounding environment using a special shader. These camera sets are mainly located at the joints of the robot arm, where most collisions occur.

4 Technical Evaluation

We performed a technical evaluation of the computation time. In Subsect. 4.1, the computation time of the single-point potential field and our multi-point ray-based haptic feedback system is measured. The quantitative comparison between the exact Jacobian matrix and our approximate Jacobian matrix is elaborated in Subsect. 4.2.

4.1 Single-Point Potential Field vs Multi-point Ray-Based Haptic Feedback

A potential field of an object at a certain point is inversely proportional to the distance between the object and the point. The magnitude of collision avoidance feedback generally increases as the robotic manipulator approaches the obstacle. Thus, many studies [12, 14, 15] compute the potential field of each obstacle, and the sum of the potential fields at the end-effector of the robotic manipulator is converted into haptic force.

The haptic feedback based on a single-point potential field (SP) [10] is also calculated using the potential field between the endpoint of the manipulator and the environment. To be more specific, SP searches for the nearest points of all obstacles from the endpoint. Points within the collision risk area are filtered and then summed to haptic feedback. Therefore, the computation time of SP is proportional to the number of obstacles. Also, if the obstacles are different and complex in shape, it will take more time to derive the closest point on the object from the robot manipulator.

However, the computation time of the multi-point ray-based (MR) method is not dependent on the size and the complexity of the environment. MR first captures distances and normals using ray-based sampling from the perspective of the pre-configured multi-point on the robot arm. Since only the local geometry near the endpoint is utilized to generate feedback, the complexity of time does not depend on the number of obstacles.

To compare the time complexity of SP and MR according to the number of obstacles, the average frame time is measured in a virtual environment. The environment for this evaluation consists of n^3 cubes in the uniform arrangement. For $n = 2, 4, 6, 8, 10$, and 12, the computation time of SP and MR methods is measured as depicted in Fig. 4. As the number of objects in the scene increases, the computation time of our MR method takes a constant time, while the computation time of SP increases.

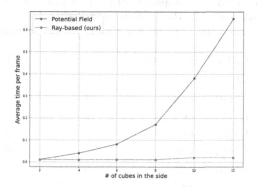

Fig. 4. Computation time comparison between single-point potential field (SP) method and our multi-point ray-based (MR) methods. As the number of obstacles increases, the computation time of SP increases, while our MR is constant.

4.2   Exact Jacobian vs Approximate Jacobian

In this section, the computation time of our motion-based approximate Jacobian (denoted at Eq. 6) is compared with the exact Jacobian computation (denoted at Eq. 5).

We set robot arms with various degrees of freedom (DoF) from 2 to 20 in a static scene with one obstacle near the arm. In our method, more sampling points are needed to represent collision avoidance feedback for complex robot arms with higher DoF. In this sense, the number of sampling points indicated in the fourth column of Table 1 increases as the DoF increases. In each setup, we measure the median time of exact and approximate Jacobian calculations among 300 consecutive frames. Table 1 shows the measurement and speedup of our approximate method compared to the exact computation. The exact Jacobian is up to 400 times slower in complex arms due to the linear solver stage. Our method, which consists only of the rotation matrix, is much more efficient than the exact Jacobian method in terms of computation. Furthermore, we discuss the usability of our approximate algorithm in Subsect. 5.2.

5   User Study

Our multi-point ray-based haptic feedback method is computationally efficient compared to the potential field-based method as elaborated in Sect. 4. Moreover, our method could be applied to arbitrary robot manipulators without prior information on robot configurations using an approximate Jacobian with much better computation cost.

Table 1. The computation time of the exact Jacobian (EJ) and the approximate Jacobian (AJ) methods by the complexity of the robot arm in terms of its degrees of freedom (DoF). #SPs indicates the number of sampling points used in AJ for each configuration of the robot arm. The median time among 300 frames is used.

DoF	Median time per frame (ms)		#SPs (AJ)	Speedup
	EJ	AJ		
2	1.3116	0.0058	2	×226
3	1.3435	0.0054	2	×249
4	1.2702	0.0060	2	×212
6	1.7115	0.0068	2	×252
8	2.1600	0.0077	3	×281
12	2.8661	0.0091	4	×315
16	3.7463	0.0123	5	×305
20	9.9369	0.0244	6	×407

In this section, we evaluate the quality of our haptic feedback through two user studies. The first user study is to analyze whether our haptic feedback is useful for traversing a three-dimensional virtual space. The second user study aims to compare the quality of the haptic feedback generated by the exact Jacobian with our approximate Jacobian.

5.1   User Study 1: Single-Point Potential Field-Based Vs Multi-point Ray-Based Haptic Feedback

Preliminary Study. We conducted a preliminary study to select participants who are proficient in controlling a virtual robot arm with a haptic device out of 18 participants (9 males, 9 females; 18–29 years old, average age: 23.1). The reason for selecting participants is that operators who remotely operate the robot arm are experts or trained people in real-world scenarios. Each participant manipulates the endpoints of the robot arm by touching ten sequentially appearing targets using the Geomagic Touch device. Finally, six people with the least number of collisions were selected for user study 1.

Settings. We evaluate the collision avoidance effect of our haptic feedback compared to the widely used single-point potential field-based approach in five virtual scenes. Participants manipulate the end-effector of the robot arm using a haptic device as depicted in Fig. 5a.

The endpoint of the haptic device corresponds to the end-effector of the virtual robot arm, and the arm configuration is automatically controlled by inverse kinematics. To the scene 1–4 (Fig. 5b-5f), participants control the robot arm to manipulate the robot's end-effector on nine consecutive target positions, *consciously aiming not to collide with obstacles*. In the scene 5 Fig. 5f, participants also manipulate the robot arm like in the other four scenes, however, they have to repeat until they finish the task without any collisions.

We organized five scenes to cover various situations in the user study: scene 1 (Fig. 5b) with two vertical obstacles at different depths that make the user navigate to the left and right of the obstacle; scene 2 (Fig. 5c) with vertical and horizontal obstacles that make the user additionally explore the above and below the obstacle; scene 3 (Fig. 5d) with one vertical obstacle and sphere obstacle that let the user explore the obstacle with a smooth surface; scene 4 (Fig. 5e) with two vertical and one horizontal obstacles that make user explore occluded areas. Finally, scene 5 (Fig. 5f) for the collision-free path design task is configured to make users explore all sides (left, right, top, bottom) of obstacles, smooth surfaces, and occluded areas.

Participants control the virtual robot arm with three conditions of force feedback: without haptic force feedback, the single-point potential field method, and our multi-point ray-based method. These three conditions are given in random order for each scene. The participants then answer the three questions below immediately after each scene.

- **Q1:** Did the feedback help avoiding collisions?
- **Q2:** Did the feedback help designing the path?
- **Q3:** How much mental workload was required to complete the task?

Survey Results. The survey results for our multi-point ray-based (MR), single-point potential field-based (SP), and no haptic feedback conditions are illustrated in Fig. 6. Our MR haptic feedback shows the highest mean for all three questions. In particular, our method exceeds SP in Q3 in terms of mental workload ($p = 0.1019$ in paired t- test). This means that when MR haptic force feedback is applied, operators were less stressed while consciously aiming for a collision-free operation.

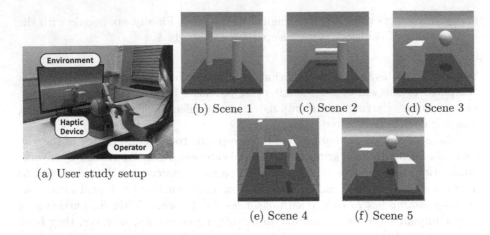

(a) User study setup

(b) Scene 1   (c) Scene 2   (d) Scene 3

(e) Scene 4   (f) Scene 5

Fig. 5. User study environment setup (a) Represents the user study setup. (b)–(f) are five virtual scenes used in user study 1.

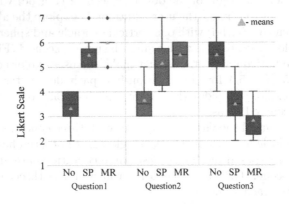

Fig. 6. User study 1 survey results. Participants answered three questions on a 1–7 Likert scale for no haptic feedback, single-point potential field-based (SP), and multi-point ray-based (MR) conditions.

Trajectory Design Results. In the final task with the scene of Fig. 5f, participants designed a collision-free trajectory in which the end-effector moves to nine sequential target positions. The number of trials, the operating time, and the length of the designed path were measured as shown in Table 2. All participants completed a collision-free trajectory design on their first attempt using our multi-point ray-based haptic feedback. Furthermore, our haptic feedback shows the shortest navigation time and the length of the designed path. Experimental results show that our haptic feedback effectively assists in trajectory design in terms of time and distance.

Table 2. Collision-free trajectory design with no haptic feedback, single-point potential field-based (SP), and multi-point ray-based (MR) haptic feedback conditions. Mean ± SD of the number of attempts to complete the collision-free trajectory design, the time to steer the robot arm on the collision-free path, and the distance of the designed path are measured.

Feedback	#Attempts	Time (s)	Path length
no	2.33	86.4 ± 8.71	9.34 ± 1.53
SP	1.67	114 ± 11.78	10.84 ± 1.29
MR (ours)	1	$\mathbf{78 \pm 5.90}$	$\mathbf{8.60 \pm 0.55}$

5.2   User Study 2: Exact Jacobian VS Approximate Jacobian

Settings. We conducted a user study to compare two kinds of haptic force feedback generated by the exact Jacobian and our approximate Jacobian with 18 participants (9 males, 9 females; 18–29 years old, mean age: 23.1). Although exact Jacobian transforms guiding force vectors to the coordinate of the end-effector, it has a limitation that information on the robot arm configuration is necessary in advance, and Jacobian sometimes cannot be derived due to a singularity problem. Thus, we suggest a motion-based approximate Jacobian which can be applied to any arbitrary robot manipulator without prior information. The participants answered the questions below after experiencing exact and approximate Jacobian in two virtual scenes (Fig. 7).

– **Q1:** Did the feedback help you operate the robot arm?
– **Q2:** Did the feedback reflect the environment faithfully?
– **Q3:** How difficult was it to move the robot arm without colliding with nearby objects?
– **Q4:** Did the feedback help reducing the mental workload to avoid collisions?
– **Q5:** Indicate your overall satisfaction with this feedback.

Results. The survey result on the comparison between exact Jacobian(EJ) and approximate Jacobian (AJ) is shown in Fig. 8. Our motion-based approximate Jacobian had better or equal scores on all questions. In interviews, participants reported that AJ is more comfortable because the EJ generates occasionally too strong force that even causes additional collisions.

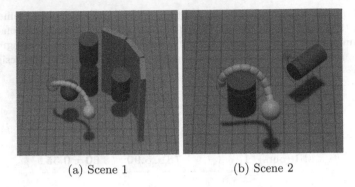

(a) Scene 1   (b) Scene 2

Fig. 7. Scenes in the user study 2 (a) A scene with three points where the haptic feedback is generated differently (b) A scene with rotational movement through cylinder obstacles

6   Discussion

In this section, we discuss each user study in detail and examine some limitations of our study.

6.1   Analysis on User Study 1

Five out of the six participants (except P5) reported that our haptic feedback was helpful to reduce mental workload (Q3). Based on their individual interviews, the participants interpreted the meaning of mental workload as how much feedback helped them care less about the possibility of collisions. In addition, in the difficult scenes (Scene 3, 4 5), four participants (P1, P2, P3, P6) reported that our method is more effective to avoid collisions compared to the single-point potential field-based (SP) feedback. They could not identify that SP avoids collisions at the

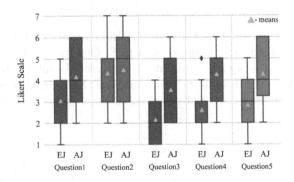

Fig. 8. Survey result for exact Jacobian (EJ) and approximate Jacobian (AJ). Particularly, Q3-A5 have a significant difference between EJ and AJ ($p < 0.05$ in paired t-test).

endpoints, whereas our method avoids collisions at multiple points on the robot arm. However, they mentioned that our haptic feedback gives more information about the entire robot arm and areas not visible to the camera view.

Above all, for the collision-free trajectory design task, all six participants completed at their first trial with our haptic feedback. On the other hand, they needed one to three trials (mean:1.67 and var: 0.67) when using SP. We also quantitatively show that our feedback helps to design an efficient trajectory in terms of the time and length of the path as illustrated in Table 2.

6.2   Analysis on User Study 2

14 out of 18 participants preferred our approximate Jacobian (AJ) method over the exact Jacobian (EJ) method. Based on the survey result, the participants gave similar scores to AJ and EJ to the question about how well the feedback reflects the environment (Q2). This means that AJ is not perceived as less accurate than EJ in terms of reflecting the environment.

Furthermore, participants scored higher to our method on the questions of difficulty, mental workload and overall satisfaction (Q3-Q5). In the individual interview, they answered AJ is more understandable and generates a comfortable magnitude of the haptic force. Moreover, participants sometimes felt uncomfortable with EJ since its excessive force causes other unexpected collisions. This is because AJ transforms the guiding force with a consistent scale across the entire body, whereas EJ amplifies the guiding force created at sampling points close to the base.

In summary, user study 2 verifies that our motion-based Jacobian approximation method is more comfortable than the exact Jacobian without degrading the accuracy.

6.3   Limitations

We show our multi-point ray-based system could decrease mental workload while manipulating the robot arm. Additionally, our haptic feedback also helps users design collision-free trajectories. However, our study still has some limitations that were not tested for various real-world scenarios.

We have yet to apply our system to real-world manipulators. Instead, we designed user studies with both simple (user study 1) and complex robot arm configurations (user study 2). This shows that our system can be applied even to the robot arm with extreme configurations.

In addition, we simulated our teleoperation system only in a virtual workspace. We expect our haptic feedback could be applied to real-world workspaces by attaching depth cameras or LiDAR sensors to real robot arms.

7   Conclusion

In this paper, we introduce a novel haptic force feedback system that helps operators better understand the remote environment during robot arm teleoperation.

By providing a guiding force to the user-controlled end-effector, the user can avoid collisions effectively with less mental workload.

Our system achieves it by generating guiding forces at multiple points on the robot arm and merging the forces by transforming them into end-effector coordinates. We improve the robustness of the environment by ray-based environment sampling. Also, our system can be applied to any robot arm by motion-based approximate Jacobian.

In quantitative evaluation, we show that our robustness-focused design also benefits computational performance compared to previous methods. The ray-based environment sampling method runs faster than the potential-field-based method, as it can be easily optimized using the graphics pipeline. The motion-based Jacobian approximation method also helps in performance by eliminating the linear solver used in exact Jacobian computation.

The results of user studies show the advantages of our method in designing a collision-free trajectory. Our system is better at reducing collisions and mental workload, and preferred over the potential field-based method. We also demonstrate that our approximate Jacobian produces more stable feedback without reducing accuracy compared to the exact Jacobian.

We believe that our haptic feedback facilitates various robotic control tasks in a virtual environment, such as teleoperation or simulation. We expect our system can be applied in real-world scenarios utilizing depth sensors for environment sampling, but we leave this to future work.

Acknowledgement. This work was supported by Korea Institute of Energy Technology Evaluation and Planning (KETEP) grant funded by the Korea government (MOTIE) (20201510300280, Development of a REMOTE DISMANTLING TRAINING SYSTEM with force-torque responding virtual nuclear power plant)

References

1. Arevalo Arboleda, S., Rücker, F., Dierks, T., Gerken, J.: Assisting manipulation and grasping in robot teleoperation with augmented reality visual cues. In: Proceedings of the 2021 CHI Conference on Human Factors in Computing Systems, pp. 1–14 (2021)
2. Brandt, A.M., Colton, M.B.: Haptic collision avoidance for a remotely operated quadrotor uav in indoor environments. In: 2010 IEEE International Conference on Systems, Man and Cybernetics, pp. 2724–2731. IEEE (2010)
3. Clark, J.P., Lentini, G., Barontini, F., Catalano, M.G., Bianchi, M., O'Malley, M.K.: On the role of wearable haptics for force feedback in teleimpedance control for dual-arm robotic teleoperation. In: 2019 International Conference on Robotics and Automation (ICRA), pp. 5187–5193. IEEE (2019)
4. Desbats, P., Geffard, F., Piolain, G., Coudray, A.: Force-feedback teleoperation of an industrial robot in a nuclear spent fuel reprocessing plant. Industrial Robot: An International Journal (2006)
5. Diolaiti, N., Melchiorri, C.: Teleoperation of a mobile robot through haptic feedback. In: IEEE International Workshop HAVE Haptic Virtual Environments and Their, pp. 67–72. IEEE (2002)

6. Garcia-Hernandez, N., Parra-Vega, V.: Haptic teleoperated robotic system for an effective obstacle avoidance. In: 2009 Second International Conferences on Advances in Computer-Human Interactions, pp. 255–260. IEEE (2009)

7. González, C., Solanes, J.E., Munoz, A., Gracia, L., Girbés-Juan, V., Tornero, J.: Advanced teleoperation and control system for industrial robots based on augmented virtuality and haptic feedback. J. Manuf. Syst. **59**, 283–298 (2021)

8. Guanyang, L., Xuda, G., Lingzhi, L., Yan, W.: Haptic based teleoperation with master-slave motion mapping and haptic rendering for space exploration. Chin. J. Aeronaut. **32**(3), 723–736 (2019)

9. Ishikawa, S., Ishibashi, Y., Huang, P., Tateiwa, Y.: Robot position control using force information for cooperative work in remote robot systems with force feedback. Int. J. Commun. Netw. Syst. Sci. **14**(1), 1–13 (2021)

10. Khatib, O.: Real-time obstacle avoidance for manipulators and mobile robots. In: Autonomous robot vehicles, pp. 396–404. Springer (1986)

11. Kitagawa, M., Okamura, A.M., Bethea, B.T., Gott, V.L., Baumgartner, W.A.: Analysis of suture manipulation forces for teleoperation with force feedback. In: International Conference on Medical Image Computing and Computer-Assisted Intervention, pp. 155–162. Springer (2002)

12. Kuiper, R.J., Heck, D.J., Kuling, I.A., Abbink, D.A.: Evaluation of haptic and visual cues for repulsive or attractive guidance in nonholonomic steering tasks. IEEE Trans. Hum.-Mach. Syst. **46**(5), 672–683 (2016)

13. Lam, T.M., Mulder, M., Van Paassen, M.: Haptic interface for uav collision avoidance. Int. J. Aviat. Psychol. **17**(2), 167–195 (2007)

14. Lam, T.M., Boschloo, H.W., Mulder, M., Van Paassen, M.M.: Artificial force field for haptic feedback in uav teleoperation. IEEE Trans. Syst. Man Cybern.-Part A Syst. Hum. **39**(6), 1316–1330 (2009)

15. Molinero, M.B., et al.: Haptic guidance for robot-assisted endovascular procedures: implementation and evaluation on surgical simulator. In: 2019 IEEE/RSJ International Conference on Intelligent Robots and Systems (IROS), pp. 5398–5403. IEEE (2019)

16. Nagano, H., Takenouchi, H., Cao, N., Konyo, M., Tadokoro, S.: Tactile feedback system of high-frequency vibration signals for supporting delicate teleoperation of construction robots. Adv. Robot. **34**(11), 730–743 (2020)

17. Oh, J.S., Choi, S.H., Choi, S.B.: Control of repulsive force in a virtual environment using an electrorheological haptic master for a surgical robot application. Smart Mater. Struct. **23**(1), 015010 (2013)

18. Okamura, A.M.: Methods for haptic feedback in teleoperated robot-assisted surgery. Ind. Robot Int. J. **31**(6), 499–508 (2004)

19. Sarakoglou, I., Garcia-Hernandez, N., Tsagarakis, N.G., Caldwell, D.G.: A high performance tactile feedback display and its integration in teleoperation. IEEE Trans. Haptics **5**(3), 252–263 (2012)

20. Song, G., Guo, S., Wang, Q.: A tele-operation system based on haptic feedback. In: 2006 IEEE International Conference on Information Acquisition, pp. 1127–1131 (2006). https://doi.org/10.1109/ICIA.2006.305903

21. Walker, M.E., Hedayati, H., Szafir, D.: Robot teleoperation with augmented reality virtual surrogates. In: 2019 14th ACM/IEEE International Conference on Human-Robot Interaction (HRI), pp. 202–210. IEEE (2019)

22. Yew, A., Ong, S., Nee, A.: Immersive augmented reality environment for the teleoperation of maintenance robots. Procedia Cirp **61**, 305–310 (2017)

23. Zhao, Z., Huang, P., Lu, Z., Liu, Z.: Augmented reality for enhancing tele-robotic system with force feedback. Robot. Auton. Syst. **96**, 93–101 (2017)

QoE-Driven Scheduling for Haptic Communications with Reinforcement learning

Junru Chen[⊠], Zhuoru Yu, and Qian Liu

Department of Computer Science and Technology, Dalian University of Technology, Dalian, China
{junruchen,yuzhuoru}@mail.dlut.edu.cn, qianliu@dlut.edu.cn

Abstract. With the rise of the Tactile Internet (TI) over 5G networks, haptic teleoperation systems have attracted extensive attentions as one of the key use cases of the TI. For a typical teleoperation setup, a human operator (i.e. the leader) interacts with a robot (i.e. the follower) in the remote environment with haptic input/output devices, where haptic information is bilaterally exchanged between them. Because of the human-in-the-loop nature of haptic teleoperation systems, the quality of experience (QoE) becomes an important performance indicator of the system. It is well known that the performance of a teleoperation system degrades when there exists communication latencies between the leader and the follower. As a result, how to gain the maximum overall QoE for teleoperation sessions sharing the same communication network becomes a huge challenge. In the presence of different communication latencies, different control schemes are applied to stabilize the teleoperation system. Since different control schemes have different sensitivities to the communication delay, most recently a QoE-delay model was developed to reveal the QoE performance of control schemes with respect to round-trip delays. In this paper, we take full advantage of the QoE-delay model, and propose a novel reinforcement learning based scheduling algorithm for haptic communications aiming at maximizing the overall QoE of all active sessions sharing the communication network. Simulation results confirm the efficiency of the proposed scheduling algorithm.

Keywords: Haptic teleoperation systems · QoE-Delay model · scheduling · reinforcement learning

1 Introduction

The 5G technology [1] enables the Tactile Internet (TI) [2–4] with ultra-low latency communication supports. As one of the key use cases of the TI, haptic teleoperation systems [5] have attracted various attentions in both academia and industry in the past few years. A typical setup of multi-session teleoperation is shown in Fig. 1. Each session consists of a leader, a follower, and the shared communication network between them. The human operators at the leader side can directly interact with the local haptic device to manipulate the follower in the remote environment. The communication network transmits the position and velocity information of the leader to the remote device in the real

D. Wang et al. (Eds.): AsiaHaptics 2022, LNCS 14063, pp. 226–238, 2023.
https://doi.org/10.1007/978-3-031-46839-1_17

time. After receiving the information, the follower interacts with the remote environment, and transmits back the haptic information (e.g. force and torque information) and video captured in the remote side to the leader side through the communication network. The human operator integrates the visual and haptic information to make a real-time experience of interaction with the remote environment, and adjusts his/her next action accordingly. Since the global control loop is closed by the communication network, the teleoperation system is very sensitive to the communication delay.

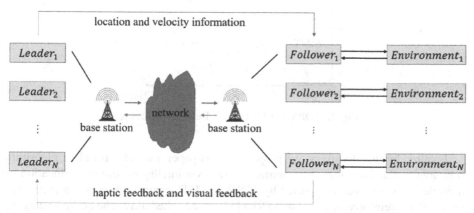

Fig. 1. A typical multi-session teleoperation system sharing the same communication network.

As shown above, QoE [6] is closely related to communication delay. Therefore, the communication delay must be limited within a maximum tolerant level. In addition, the communication delay may cause the instability of the entire system since the globe control loop is closed by the communication network. As a result, a control scheme should be adopted in order to maintain the system stability [7, 8]. Furthermore, different control schemes have different sensitivity to the communication delay. In the paper, two control schemes are studied: Time-Domain Passivity Approach (TDPA) and Model-Mediated Teleoperation (MMT) [9]. In contrast to the MMT, the TDPA is more sensitive to the communication delay, but can achieve better QoE when there is none/negligible delay. This way, the TDPA is suitable for the low-delay leader-follower interaction. On the other hand, the QoE performance of the MMT is determined by the accuracy of the generative model at the leader side. Therefore, it is tolerable to a relatively large delay.

The relationship among different control schemes, communication latencies and QoE was firstly revealed in [10], which built a QoE-Delay model for TDPA and MMT schemes based on the subjective evaluation of a one-dimensional spring damper environment. The developed model can be expressed as

$$F(T, S_k) = D_{S_k} + \frac{A_{S_k} - D_{S_k}}{1 + (\frac{T}{C_{S_k}})^{B_{S_k}}} \tag{1}$$

where F represents functional equation, T represents the communication delay. The value of k is 1 or 2, S_1 and S_2 represent the TDPA and MMT control schemes, respectively.

$A_{S_1} = 2.088$, $A_{S_2} = 0$, $B_{S_1} = -1.82$, $B_{S_2} = -1.187$, $C_{S_1} = 58.48$, $C_{S_2} = 793.7$, $D_{S_1} = 4.585$, $D_{S_2} = 3.64$.

Based on Eq. (1), we can obtain the Fig. 2 which illustrates an optimal solution of TDPA and MMT to achieve the best QoE by adaptively selecting MMT or TDPA teleoperation sessions based on their current end-to-end delay.

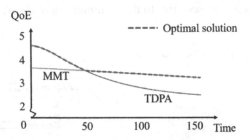

Fig. 2. TDPA and MMT QoE-Delay model curve.

Inspired by this discovery, we propose in this paper a novel scheduling algorithm to guarantee the QoE of haptic communications via intelligent resource allocation of multiple haptic sessions (supported by TDPA or MMT control schemes). In particular, we develop a reinforcement learning (RL) [11] based scheduling scheme by leveraging the above mentioned QoE-Delay model. Experimental results confirm the efficiency of the proposed scheduler.

The rest of the paper is organized as follows. We present the background knowledge of scheduling algorithms widely used in the current 5G networks (which are also selected as comparison algorithms in this paper), and the scheme of reinforcement learning in Sect. 2. The proposed RL-based scheduler is illustrated in Sect. 3. Experimental results are presented in Sect. 4, and finally Sect. 5 concludes the paper with a summary.

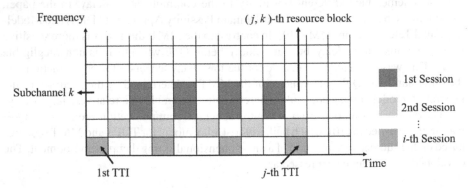

Fig. 3. LTE/5G radio resource structure.

2   Background Knowledge

In this section, we first introduce two popular schedulers utilized in the LTE/5G wireless networks, i.e. the proportional fair (PF) scheduler and the exponential proportional fairness (EXP) scheduler. We also present the basic structure of the reinforcement learning and explain a bit how to use it for resource allocation in communication networks.

Based on the radio resource structure shown in Fig. 3, we compute the value of a scheduling metric m_{ij} at the beginning of the j-th transmission time interval (TTI) for a particular resource block at the k-th subchannel. This resource block (j, k) will be assigned to the $\hat{i}$-th session by a scheduler if

$$\hat{i} = \underset{i}{\operatorname{argmax}} m_{ij} \tag{2}$$

For the PF scheduler, the scheduling metric m_{ij} is defined as

$$m_{ij} = \frac{r_{ij}}{\overline{R}_i} \tag{3}$$

where $r_{i,j}$ indicates the instantaneous achievable throughput of a particular resource block at the j-th TTI once allocated to the i-th session. $\overline{R}_i$ presents the average transmission data rate of the i-th session/flow, which can be obtained via

$$\overline{R}_i(j) = 0.8\overline{R}_i(j-1) + 0.2R_i(j) \tag{4}$$

where $\overline{R}_i(j)$ is the data rate achieved by the i-th session/flow in the j-th TTI, and $\overline{R}_i(j-1)$ is that of the previous TTI.

The EXP scheduler was designed to increase the priority of real-time flows with a scheduling metric m_{ij} defined as

$$m_{i,j} = \exp(\frac{\alpha_i D_{HOL,i} - \chi}{1 + \sqrt{\chi}})\frac{r_{i,j}}{\overline{R}_i} \tag{5}$$

$$\alpha_i = -\frac{log\delta_i}{\tau_i} \tag{6}$$

$$\chi = \frac{1}{N_{rt}} \sum_{k=1}^{N_{rt}} \alpha_i D_{HOL,i} \tag{7}$$

where τ_i is the packet delay threshold; the probability δ_i is defined as the maximum probability that the delay of the head-of-line packet (i.e., the first packet to be transmitted in the queue) $D_{HOL,i}$ exceeds the delay threshold. N_{rt} presents the number of active real-time sessions/flows.

Reinforcement Learning (RL) is a popular approach in machine learning research area where an agent discovers a mapping from situations to actions so as to maximize the value of a scalar reward or reinforcement signal. In contrast to other forms of learning, such as classification tasks, the agent is not told what the target actions should be but instead must rely on trial and error to find which actions produce the highest reward. The basic scheme of reinforcement learning is shown in Fig. 4.

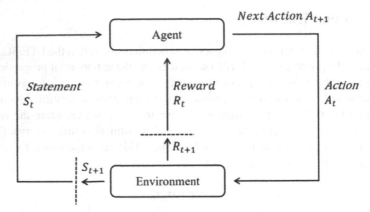

Fig. 4. Basic scheme of reinforcement learning.

We can observe from Fig. 4 that at the current state S_t, after making an action A_t, it has some impact on the environment. It first feeds back a reward signal R_t to the agent, then the agent can enter a new state S_{t+1}, and make a new action A_{t+1} to form a cycle.

In [12–15], the authors combined the reinforcement learning (RL) to the scheduler design. Especially in [15], the author utilizes the Deep Deterministic Policy Gradient (DDPG) algorithm to minimize the queuing delay experienced by the users.

3   Proposed RL-Based Scheduling Algorithm

In this section, we introduce the proposed RL-based scheduling algorithm in detail. As introduced in Sect. 1, a haptic teleoperation session consists of a leader device, a follower device and the communication network between them. In this paper, we focus on the teleoperation session with the TDPA (or MMT) control scheme, where the exchanged haptic information includes the location/velocity information from the leader to the follower, the haptic and the video feedback from the follower to the leader. In addition, we include non-real-time (NRT) streams to compete the network resources with teleoperation sessions. The implementation of the proposed RL-based scheduling algorithm (as shown in Fig. 5(a)) includes two steps: (1) RL model training; (2) Scheduling with the trained RL model and the QoE-Delay model.

For the RL model training step, the setup of RL scheme is shown in the lower block of Fig. 5(b). The inputs are metadata collected in the scheduling process, including the maximal time delay (MTD) of a packet, the time stamp of a packet arrival at the base station (i.e. Create_time), whether a packet dropped at the base station (i.e. Drop), the time stamp of a packet successfully received or dropped (i.e. Finish_time), the current delay, throughput and QoE (calculated via the QoE-Delay model). According to the above inputs, we formulate the state space, the action space and the reward function of the RL model, as shown in Tables 1 and 2 and Eqs. (5)–(6).

For the state space, $Throughput_{instant}$ is used to improve the network resource utilization; $AverageDelay_{total}$ and $Delay_{instant}$ are adopted to calculate the QoE based on

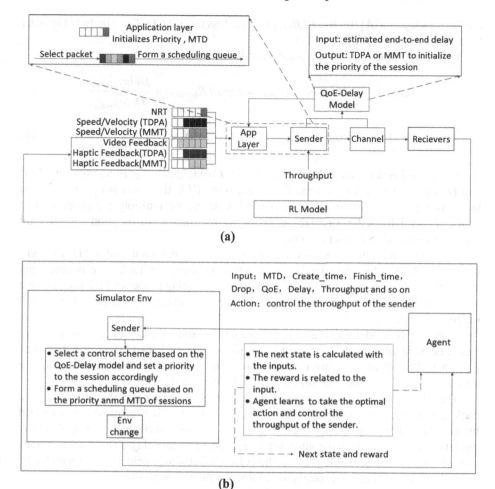

Fig. 5. (a). Implementation scheme of the proposed RL based scheduling algorithm. (b) RL model training.

Table 1. State space.

State space
$Throughput_{instant}$
$AverageDelay_{total}$
$Delay_{instant}$
PLR_{total}
QoE

the QoE-Delay model [10]; the PLR_{total} (packet loss rate) and QoE are included in order to improve the total QoE.

The reward functions are desgined as follows.

$$\text{reward}- = Throughput_{instant} * exp(PLR_{instant}) * \frac{Delay_{instant}}{Delay_{total}} \tag{8}$$

$$\text{reward}+ = Throughput_{instant} * exp(1 - PLR_{instant}) * \frac{\overline{Delay_{total}}}{Delay_{instant}} \tag{9}$$

The reward is set to directly correlate to the $Throughput_{instant}$. In addition, the PLR and $Delay$ are also impact factors. The larger is the PLR, the lower is the $reward$. The larger is the $Delay$, the lower is the $reward$. Besides, we multiply the proportion of PLR exponentially and normalize the $Delay$ so that the reward function can take full consideration of QoS impact factors.

The action space includes three actions, i.e. increase, maintain, and reduce throughput, respectively. The corresponding conditions are shown in Table 2. It is noted that the "action" is the output of the RL model after the training process which provides the amount of data, i.e. throughput, to be pushed out the scheduling queue at the current scheduling cycle.

After the RL model training step, we reach to the second step of the proposed algorithm, i.e. scheduling with the trained RL model and the QoE-Delay model. Combining Figs. 5 and 6, we first present the skeleton of the proposed scheduling process. The detailed flow chart of the proposed scheduler is illustrated in Fig. 6.

The ultimate goal of the proposed scheduler is to form a scheduling queue with packets to be pushed into the channel. The order of packets in this queue is determined by the assigned priority of a particular teleoperation session according to the QoE-Delay model (based on the adopted control scheme and the current delay). The amount of data to push out of the scheduling queue at the current scheduling cycle is determined by the trained RL model (i.e. the throughput obtained in the action module).

As to Fig. 6, when the base station receives data streams/sessions, different sessions are assigned with different priorities. The range of priority is set as 1 to 5, where 1 indicates the highest priority. At the current j-th TTI, a number of packets arrive at the base station. Thus we can initialize $Create\_time_j$, MTD_j, $Priority_j$, respectively. The sender sorts packets according to $Priority_j$. As for the same $Priority$, packets are sorted according to the formula in Fig. 6. After sorting, the sender forms a scheduling queue. The receiver sends back an ACK if the $Packet_j$ is received. If no ACK is feedback to the sender, the sender (base station) decides whether to retransmitted or dropped the $Packet_j$ according to the formula $Cur\_time > MTD_j + Create\_time_j$. The packet will be dropped once exceeds the MTD. After that, when no data packets are in the queue or no free subchannel exists, the scheduling process in j-th TTI finishes.

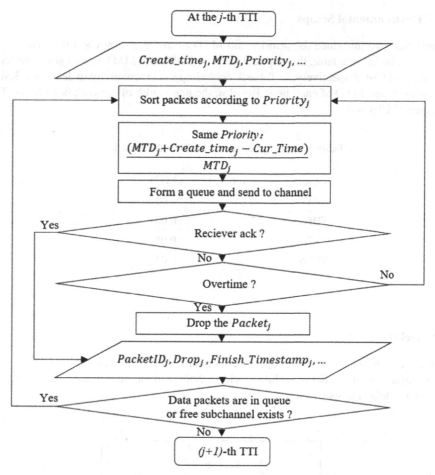

Fig. 6. Flow chart of the proposed scheduling algorithm.

Table 2. Action space.

Action space	Conditions
Increase throughput	Below the lowest throughput setting
Maintain throughput	Appropriate throughput
Reduce throughput	Exceed the network bandwidth

4 Experimental Results

In this section, we evaluate the performance of the proposed scheduler and compare it with the PF and EXP schedulers.

4.1 Environmental Setups

In this part, we introduce the priority and MTD of different flows and the structure of flow trace in the simulator. For haptic flows, the TDPA and MMT packet sizes are set to 12 bit and 24 bit, respectively. In Table 3, according to the sensitivity to delay, we design the priority and MTD of each flow. Besides, the bandwidth of network is 10 MHz. The number of UEs is 4.

Table 3. Initial priority and MTD of different flows.

Type	Priority	MTD/s
MMT	2	0.02
TDPA	2	0.02
NRT	4	0.05
Video	3	0.04

4.2 Delay

In this section, we compare the delay performance of the three algorithms. Figure 7 is the comparison of the delay including video, NRT and haptic information. Figure 8 is the haptic delay comparison.

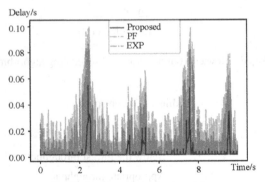

Fig. 7. Total communication delay.

We can see that the proposed algorithm outperforms EXP and PF on the delay including video, NRT and haptic information. EXP and PF is more affected by the scheduling of video streams. When a large number of video streams are scheduled, haptic streams of EXP and PF will be seriously influenced. Proposed algorithm guarantees the haptic delay better, meanwhile, its total delay is also better than EXP and PF.

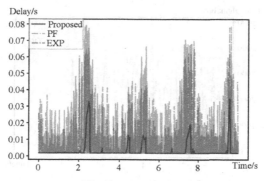

Fig. 8. Haptic delay.

4.3 Throughput

We compare the throughput performance of the three algorithms. Figure 9 is the comparison of the throughput including video, NRT and haptic information. Figure 10 is the haptic throughput comparison.

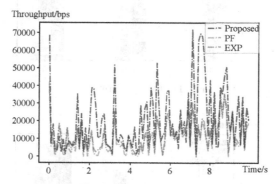

Fig. 9. Total throughput.

From Fig. 9 and Fig. 10, the proposed algorithm not only guarantees the delay, but also increases the utilization of limited resource. The two traditional algorithms are greatly affected by video and NRT streams, can not guarantee the throughput of haptic information.

4.4 QoE and Loss Rate

TDPA, MMT and total average QoE are calculated using the QoE-Delay model presented in [10]. As is shown in the Fig. 12. We also calculated the packet loss rate of TDPA, MMT, video stream, and NRT stream, respectively.

As is shown in Fig. 11, the proposed algorithm guarantees the QoE of TDPA and MMT respectively. Whether in the case of large or small delay, the proposed algorithm can improve the haptic QoE compared with the two traditional algorithms.

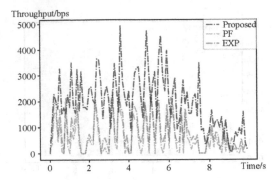

Fig. 10. Haptic throughput.

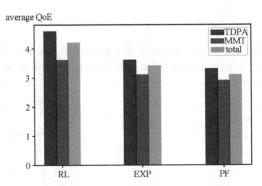

Fig. 11. QoE performance.

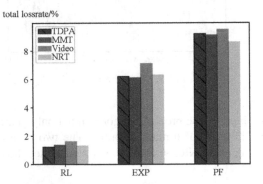

Fig. 12. Comparison on the packet loss rate.

The two existing algorithms have obvious packet loss in the large scheduling of information flows, fail to guarantee the haptic QoE. The packet loss rate seriously affects the QoE of the system. Our proposed algorithm not only decreases the packet loss rate of haptic information, but also is much better than the two traditional algorithms on the delay and throughput performance, which effectively guarantees the stability of the whole system. As a result, the proposed algorithm outperforms EXP and PF.

5 Conclusion

We presented in this paper a novel RL-based scheduling algorithm to guarantee the total QoE of multiple haptic sessions sharing the same communication network. We took full advantage of the QoE-Delay model [10] and the RL schema, and proposed new reward function and state/action spaces for the RL model so as to achieve satisfactory network resource utilization and the QoE performance. Simulation results show that the proposed algorithm outperformed the popular PF and EXP schedulers in various compared scenarios. Besides, the performance of video and NRT flows is also increased. Simulation results confirm the efficiency of the proposed scheduler.

Acknowledgements. This work was supported in part by the National Key Research and Development Program of China (No. 2021ZD0112400), in part by the National Science Foundation of China (Grant No. 62071083 and U1808206), and in part by the Fundamental Research Funds for the Central Universities (No. DUT21GJ208).

References

1. Johansson, N.A., Wang, Y.P.E., Eriksson, E.: Radio access for ultra reliable and low-latency 5G communications. In: IEEE International Conference on Communication Workshop, pp. 1184–1189 (2015)
2. Holland, O., Steinbach, E., Prasad, R.V.: The IEEE 1918.1 tactile internet standards working group and its standards. Proc. IEEE **107**(2), 256–279 (2019)
3. Antonakoglou, K., Xu, X., Steinbach, E.: Toward haptic communications over the 5G tactile internet. IEEE Commun. Surv. Tutor. **1**(4), 1 (2018)
4. Sharma, S.K., Woungang, I., Anpalagan, A.: Toward tactile internet in Beyond 5G Era: recent advances, current issues, and future directions. IEEE Access **8**, 56948–56991 (2020)
5. Aijaz. A.: Toward human-in-the-loop mobile networks: a radio resource allocation perspective on haptic communications. IEEE Trans. Wirel. Commun. 1 (2018)
6. Abe, T., Komatsu, Y., Ohnishi, H.: QoE assessment of adaptive viscoelasticity control in remote control system with haptic and visual senses. IN: IEEE International Conference on Consumer Electronics-Taiwan (ICCE-TW), Taichung, Taiwan, China, pp. 1–2 (2018)
7. Ryu, J.-H., Artigas, J., Preusche, C.: A passive bilateral control scheme for a teleoperator with time-varying communication delay. Mechatronics **20**(7), 812–823 (2010)
8. Hannaford, B.: A design framework for teleoperators with kinesthetic feedback. IEEE Trans. Robot. Autom.Autom. **5**(4), 426–434 (1989)
9. Mitra, P., Niemeyer, G.: Model-mediated Telemanipulation. Int. J. Robot. Res. **27**(2), 253–262 (2008)
10. Xu, X., Liu, Q., Steinbach, E.: Toward QoE-driven dynamic control scheme switching for time-delayed teleoperation systems: a dedicated case study, pp. 1–6. IEEE (2017)
11. Sutton, R., Barto, A.: Reinforcement Learning: An Introduction, 2nd edn. MITPress, Cambridge (2018)

12. Ortiz, A., Al-Shatri, H., Li, X.: Reinforcement learning for energy harvesting point-to-point communications. In: IEEE International Conference on Communications, pp. 1–6. IEEE (2016)
13. Luong, N.C., et al.: Applications of deep reinforcement learning in communications and networking: a survey. IEEE Commun. Surv. Tutor. **21**(4), 3133–3174 (2019)
14. Elsayed, M., Erol-Kantarci, M.: Deep reinforcement learning for reducing latency in mission critical services. In: Proceedings of Global Communications Conference (GLOBECOM), pp. 1–6. IEEE (2018)
15. Sharma, N., et al.: Deep reinforcement learning for delay-sensitive LTE downlink scheduling. In: 2020 IEEE 31st Annual International Symposium on Personal,Indoor and Mobile Radio Communications. IEEE (2020)
16. Piro, G., Grieco, L.A., Boggia, G.: Simulating LTE cellular systems: an open-source framework. IEEE Trans. Veh. Technol.Veh. Technol. **60**(2), 498–513 (2011)

Author Index

D. Wang et al. (Eds.): AsiaHaptics 2022, LNCS 14063, pp. 239–240, 2023.
https://doi.org/10.1007/978-3-031-46839-1

Printed in the United States
by Baker & Taylor Publisher Services